Multidisciplinary Approach to Luxury Consumption and AI

Vera Teixeira Vale
University of Aveiro, Portugal

IGI Global
Scientific Publishing
Publishing Tomorrow's Research Today

Vice President of Editorial Melissa Wagner
Director of Acquisitions Mikaela Felty
Director of Book Development Jocelynn Hessler
Production Manager Mike Brehm
Cover Design Jose Rosado

Published in the United States of America by
IGI Global Scientific Publishing
701 East Chocolate Avenue
Hershey, PA, 17033, USA
Tel: 717-533-8845 | Fax: 717-533-7115
Website: https://www.igi-global.com E-mail: cust@igi-global.com

Library of Congress Cataloging-in-Publication Data

Names: Vale, Vera, 1975- editor.
Title: Multidisciplinary approach to luxury consumption and AI / edited by Vera Cristina Fontes Teixeira Vale.
Description: Hershey, PA : IGI Global Scientific Publishing, [2026] | Includes bibliographical references and index. | Summary: "This book aims to provide relevant theoretical frameworks and the latest empirical research in the field"-- Provided by publisher.
Identifiers: LCCN 2025011499 (print) | LCCN 2025011500 (ebook) | ISBN 9798369384220 (hardcover) | ISBN 9798369384237 (paperback) | ISBN 9798369384244 (ebook)
Subjects: LCSH: Luxury goods industry. | Artificial intelligence. | Consumption (Economics)
Classification: LCC HD9999.L852 M85 2025 (print) | LCC HD9999.L852 (ebook) | DDC 339.4/7--dc23/eng/20250819
LC record available at https://lccn.loc.gov/2025011499
LC ebook record available at https://lccn.loc.gov/2025011500

British Cataloguing in Publication Data
A Cataloguing in Publication record for this book is available from the British Library.

Table of Contents

Detailed Table of Contents

Artificial Intelligence (AI) is revolutionizing the luxury market by improving personalization, marketing, product design, supply chain, customer experience, fraud prevention, sustainability, and customer loyalty. AI algorithms create personalized recommendations, using customer information to ensure a tailored shopping experience. Chatbots and virtual assistants provide timely customer attention, while AI-based customer segmentation targets customers based on preferences and age. AI aids in product development, design, and sustainable practices, while also ensuring timely supply chain and inventory management. AI prevents infringement of luxury brands and fraudulent practices, and contributes to customer retention and loyalty programs. The advancement of AI could lead to revolutions in the luxury industry.

Households in Kano metropolis, like in other developing parts of the world, made decision under poverty condition, poor information and a society wide low-education level. The ramification of poor economic development is felt in all sectors of the society. Unlike the rich, the living condition of the poor is constraint; his low purchasing power has restricted him to the fringe of society. Just like the rich of the advanced economies of the world who want to enjoy their mammoth wealth through extravagant expenditures, the rich of the less developed countries are also keen to imitate their rich world counterparts through conspicuous consumption. Households' inherent characteristics may have played a role in influencing how they perceived information. This study tries to find out the influence of information on households' consumption visa-vis other factors in Kano metropolis. Kano metropolis is a multi cultural environment that has in its mid people of all races, income groups and cultures.

Preface

Luxury consumption has long been associated with status, exclusivity, and indulgence, transcending mere necessity to embody cultural, emotional, and psychological value. In recent years, however, luxury markets have entered a period of profound transformation. The rise of artificial intelligence (AI), along with digitalization, shifting consumer values, and evolving global dynamics, is reshaping how luxury goods are produced, marketed, and consumed.

This volume brings together diverse perspectives on the intersection of luxury consumption, AI, and broader societal contexts. It highlights the ways in which advanced technologies are influencing design, personalization, sustainability, and customer experiences, while also acknowledging the socioeconomic conditions, cultural patterns, and behavioral biases that shape consumption practices around the world.

By combining insights from management, technology, consumer psychology, and economics, the book provides a multidisciplinary lens to understand luxury consumption in an era increasingly driven by AI and digital innovation.

CHAPTER OVERVIEW

Chapter 1 explores the role of AI in shaping the future of luxury consumption, highlighting its emotional, psychological, and symbolic dimensions.

Chapter 2 examines shifting consumer trends, the growing influence of younger, digitally savvy buyers, and the strategic challenges luxury brands face in adapting to sustainability demands, e-commerce expansion, and market uncertainties.

Chapter 3 analyzes how AI is transforming the luxury fashion industry, particularly in areas such as design innovation, personalization, sustainability, and brand competitiveness.

Chapter 4 investigates the impact of AI on the luxury market in India, with particular attention to its role in economic development, job creation, digital consumerism, and immersive customer experiences.

Chapter 5 looks at how AI is revolutionizing the luxury sector through enhanced personalization, marketing strategies, supply chain management, fraud prevention, and sustainable practices.

Chapter 6 addresses the tension between poverty and conspicuous consumption in household decision-making, showing how socioeconomic conditions, information access, and cultural contexts influence luxury-related behaviors.

Chapter 7 considers the influence of cognitive biases on consumer decision-making in logistics services, applying nudge theory to explore strategies that guide individuals toward better choices without restricting freedom.

This book underscores that luxury consumption cannot be understood in isolation—it is shaped by technological innovation, cultural aspirations, economic realities, and human psychology. AI serves as both a catalyst and a disruptor, enabling unprecedented personalization, efficiency, and creativity while challenging traditional notions of exclusivity and heritage.

By adopting a multidisciplinary approach, the volume reveals how luxury consumption in the digital age reflects broader societal transformations, offering insights not only for researchers and practitioners in luxury markets but also for those studying consumer behavior, digital innovation, and economic development.

Vera Teixeira Vale

University of Aveiro, Portugal

Chapter 1

AI and Its Importance in the Development of Luxury Consumption

Priyanka Pawar
https://orcid.org/0009-0005-1043-419X
Indira College of Engineering and Management, India

Gaganpreet Kaur Ahluwalia
https://orcid.org/0000-0001-7955-6551
Indira School of Business Studies, PGDM, India

Nilesh Anute
https://orcid.org/0000-0001-6599-813X
Sri Balaji University, India

Prashant Kalshetti
https://orcid.org/0000-0003-3553-2093
Global Business School and Research Centre, Dr. D.Y. Patil Vidyapeeth, India

Shailesh Tripathi
Sri Balaji University, India

P. Selvakumar
https://orcid.org/0000-0002-3650-4548
Department of Science and Humanities, Nehru Institute of Technology, Coimbatore, India

ABSTRACT

Luxury consumption refers to the purchase and use of high-end goods and services that go beyond mere necessity and serve as a symbol of status, exclusivity, and personal indulgence. Luxury goods often possess superior

DOI: 10.4018/979-8-3693-8422-0.ch001

craftsmanship, heritage, innovation, and brand prestige, distinguishing them from mass-market products. These goods range across various industries, including fashion, automobiles, jewelry, travel, hospitality, and fine dining. Unlike essential products, luxury items are not driven by practical necessity but rather by emotional, psychological, and social motivations.

INTRODUCTION TO LUXURY CONSUMPTION

Luxury consumption refers to the purchase and use of high-end goods and services that go beyond mere necessity and serve as a symbol of status, exclusivity, and personal indulgence. Luxury goods often possess superior craftsmanship, heritage, innovation, and brand prestige, distinguishing them from mass-market products. These goods range across various industries, including fashion, automobiles, jewelry, travel, hospitality, and fine dining. Unlike essential products, luxury items are not driven by practical necessity but rather by emotional, psychological, and social motivations. Consumers of luxury goods seek exclusivity, superior quality, rarity, and an enhanced overall experience.Luxury consumption is often associated with wealth and social status, as acquiring luxury products signals a certain level of financial success and cultural refinement. However, with the changing economic landscape and shifting consumer preferences, luxury consumption is no longer limited to the ultra-wealthy. The concept of "accessible luxury" has emerged, allowing a broader audience to partake in luxury experiences through premium product lines, brand collaborations, and the rise of second-hand luxury markets.During the Middle Ages, luxury goods remained confined to nobility, and sumptuary laws restricted their use among commoners. However, with the onset of the Renaissance, the expansion of trade routes, and the rise of mercantile wealth, luxury consumption began to spread beyond the royal courts. The Industrial Revolution further transformed the landscape of luxury by enabling mass production, creating new markets, and allowing the emerging middle class to access luxury goods that were previously exclusive to the elite.The 20th century saw the rise of iconic luxury brands such as Louis Vuitton, Chanel, Gucci, and Rolex. The concept of owning luxury is evolving beyond physical goods, as digital assets gain prominence in the luxury space.While accessibility to luxury has expanded, ultra-high-net-worth individuals (UHNWIs) continue to drive demand for bespoke, hyper-personalized luxury services. This includes exclusive travel experiences, private art collections, limited-edition automobiles, and rare watch auctions. The growing desire for privacy, discretion, and unique offerings has led to the rise of invitation-only experiences and private memberships in luxury hospitality, real estate, and fine dining The luxury market is experiencing rapid growth in emerging economies, particularly in Asia, the Middle East, and Africa.

The Role of Technology in Shaping Luxury Consumption

Technology has played a transformative role in the evolution of luxury consumption, shaping the way high-end brands interact with consumers, design products, and deliver experiences. From the earliest advancements in craftsmanship to the digital revolution and the rise of artificial intelligence, technological progress has continuously redefined what luxury means(Aguirre et al., 2015). Today, digital innovations, artificial intelligence, blockchain, and the metaverse are influencing how luxury brands operate, engage with their audience, and expand their offerings beyond physical goods. This discussion explores the impact of technology on luxury consumption across three key periods: the past, present, and future. Historically, luxury has been synonymous with superior craftsmanship, exclusivity, and artistry. While luxury consumption was initially defined by handcrafted goods made by skilled artisans, technological advancements have played a crucial role in refining and expanding the luxury industry. Before the Industrial Revolution, luxury items were produced by hand, requiring meticulous craftsmanship and long production times. Luxury brands adapted by designing bespoke travel accessories, such as Louis Vuitton's iconic(André et al., 2018) luggage collection. This era marked the intersection of technology and luxury, where engineering advancements enhanced consumer experience.The COVID-19 pandemic accelerated this shift, with luxury brands investing heavily in virtual shopping experiences, augmented reality (AR) fitting rooms, and AI-driven recommendations to replicate in-store experiences online(Andrews, 2016). Technologies such as virtual try-ons, 360-degree product views, and AI-powered personal shopping assistants have become standard in digital luxury retail.AI is transforming luxury consumption by enabling hyper-personalized experiences. AI-driven algorithms analyze consumer preferences, browsing behavior, and purchase history to provide tailored recommendations. Brands like Burberry and Louis Vuitton use AI-powered chatbots and virtual stylists to offer concierge-level service to online shoppers. Brands such as LVMH and Cartier have adopted blockchain-based platforms like AURA to track product origins and ensure transparency in the supply chain.Blockchain is also facilitating the rise of luxury resale markets. Digital certificates of authenticity make it easier for consumers to buy and sell pre-owned luxury goods with confidence.Luxury brands are venturing into the metaverse, where digital fashion, NFTs (non-fungible tokens), and virtual experiences are redefining ownership and exclusivity. Brands like Balenciaga and Dolce & Gabbana have launched digital fashion collections, allowing consumers to purchase virtual outfits for their online avatars. While luxury brands once relied on heritage and exclusivity, they now embrace technological innovation to remain relevant to modern consumers(Baum et al., 2011). The future of luxury consumption will be driven by AI, blockchain, sustainability, and immersive digital experiences, creating a new era where personalization, authenticity, and digital ownership redefine what it means to be luxurious. As luxury brands continue to innovate, technology will remain the driving force behind the next generation of high-end experiences.

Artificial Intelligence (AI) and its Relevance to Luxury Consumption: An Overview"_: Introduction to AI and its relevance to luxury consumption, including its potential applications and benefits.

Artificial Intelligence (AI) has become a transformative force across industries, and luxury consumption is no exception. As AI continues to evolve, it is reshaping how luxury brands engage with consumers, personalize experiences, optimize supply chains, and innovate products. AI's ability to analyze vast amounts of data, recognize patterns, and make intelligent decisions enables luxury brands to maintain exclusivity while meeting the demands of modern consumers. However, AI is now being integrated into multiple facets of the luxury industry(Bettman, 2013), from marketing and customer service to product development and supply chain management. AI-driven technologies enable luxury brands to enhance customer experiences, drive innovation, and streamline operations while preserving their prestige. Luxury brands face challenges in managing inventory due to the exclusivity and limited production of their products. Machine learning algorithms analyze consumer behavior, sentiment, and social media interactions to develop precise marketing strategiesThe luxury industry faces significant challenges with counterfeit products(Biswas et al., 2013). AI-powered authentication solutions help combat fake luxury goods by verifying product authenticity through advanced image recognition and blockchain integration. As AI continues to evolve, luxury brands will leverage its capabilities to create seamless, data-driven, and immersive consumer experiences.

AI-Powered Personalization in Luxury Retail

Personalization has always been a cornerstone of the luxury retail experience, where exclusivity, tailor-made services, and deep customer relationships set high-end brands apart. With the advent of Artificial Intelligence (AI), luxury retailers now have the ability to elevate personalization to unprecedented levels. AI-powered personalization enhances every stage of the customer journey, from product recommendations and virtual styling to hyper-personalized services and post-purchase engagement.Luxury consumers expect brands to not only understand their preferences but to anticipate their needs, offering seamless and intuitive experiences across multiple channels. As a result, AI-driven personalization is transforming luxury retail, increasing customer satisfaction, deepening brand loyalty, and redefining the meaning of exclusivity.(Boyd & Holton, 2018)This discussion explores how AI is reshaping personalization in luxury retail, its impact on customer experience, and the future of AI-driven personalization in the high-end market. These technologies enable brands to analyze customer data, predict preferences,(Carpenter, 2015) and tailor experiences accordingly. By leveraging AI, luxury brands can offer hyper-personalized recommendations, provide bespoke customer service, and create immersive digital experiences that resonate with affluent consumers. AI-Powered AI-powered smart mirrors and interactive kiosks enhance in-store personalization by recognizing customers and displaying tailored product suggestions based on their past purchases. Predictive Shopping and Anticipatory Personalization(Castelo, 2019): AI algorithms analyze purchasing patterns to predict what customers may want next. High-net-worth individuals receive exclusive invitations to limited-edition collections or early access to upcoming products based on their buying history. AI-powered personalization is transforming luxury retail by offering customers a seamless, customized, and immersive shopping experience. By leveraging AI technologies, luxury brands can anticipate customer needs, enhance engagement, and reinforce exclusivity—ensuring long-term loyalty and satisfaction. As AI continues to evolve, its role in luxury retail will expand, creating even more refined, hyper-personalized experiences that redefine the luxury shopping experience.

AI-Driven Luxury Product Design: Creating Unique and Exclusive Products

Luxury brands have long been defined by their commitment to exclusivity, craftsmanship, and artistic innovation. From haute couture fashion and bespoke jewelry to high-end automobiles and luxury watches, every element of design in the luxury sector is carefully curated to embody uniqueness and sophistication. Today, Artificial Intelligence (AI) is emerging as a transformative force in luxury product design, redefining the creative process and pushing the boundaries of exclusivity.AI's ability to analyze vast datasets, recognize design trends, generate unique patterns, and optimize materials is revolutionizing how luxury products are conceptualized, designed, and produced. By leveraging AI-powered design tools, generative algorithms, and machine learning, luxury brands are creating truly one-of-a-kind products that cater to the evolving preferences of their elite clientele. AI is not replacing human creativity but rather augmenting it—offering new possibilities in design innovation, personalization, and production efficiency. AI acts as a creative assistant, providing insights, generating design variations, and refining concepts in real-time.Luxury fashion houses are leveraging AI to create exclusive, (Castelo & Ward, 2016)AI-generated haute couture collections that blend human creativity with machine intelligence. Some luxury brands offer AI-driven bespoke tailoring services where customers receive uniquely designed outfits tailored to their exact specifications. AI-Enhanced Digital Fashion: AI is playing a key role in creating digital fashion collections for the metaverse. Brands like Balenciaga and Dolce & Gabbana have launched AI-generated digital garments that exist exclusively in virtual spaces, catering to the rising demand for luxury in the digital world.

AI-Powered Customization Platforms: Luxury jewelry brands are incorporating AI-powered customization tools that allow customers to design their own bespoke rings, necklaces, and watches. By selecting materials, gemstones, and engravings, customers can create one-of-a-kind pieces tailored to their preferences.AI-Assisted Craftsmanship:(Castelo et al., 2018) AI is being used to optimize gemstone selection, ensuring that each stone is of the highest quality and perfectly suited for its setting. High-end watchmakers, such as Patek Philippe and Rolex, use AI-driven precision engineering tools to refine intricate watch mechanisms.Luxury car manufacturers are integrating AI into their design processes to create custom, high-performance vehicles that cater to the unique preferences of their elite clientele. AI assists in designing ultra-efficient, high-performance vehicles by analyzing aerodynamics, fuel efficiency, and structural integrity. Luxury brands like Bugatti and Ferrari use AI-driven simulations to optimize the speed and handling of their vehicles.

AI-Enabled Luxury Supply Chain Management: Optimizing Efficiency and Sustainability

AI-powered blockchain solutions ensure ethical sourcing of luxury materials, such as diamonds, rare leathers, and exotic woods, by tracking supply chains for authenticity and sustainability. Smart Manufacturing and Production Planning: AI-driven automation enhances the efficiency of high-end craftsmanship by optimizing production schedules, improving quality control, and reducing material waste.AI-Powered Logistics and Last-Mile Delivery Optimization: AI helps luxury brands streamline global distribution, ensuring that high-end products reach consumers faster while minimizing carbon footprints.Luxury brands must maintain a delicate balance between scarcity and availability, ensuring that their products remain exclusive while meeting customer demand. AI-powered demand forecasting helps optimize inventory by:Analyzing Real-Time Market Data(Davenport & Ronanki, 2018): AI tracks consumer preferences, economic trends, and social media sentiment to predict demand shifts and adjust production accordingly. Reducing Carbon Footprint in Material Sourcing: AI optimizes global sourcing strategies, minimizing transportation emissions and selecting suppliers based on environmental impact.Luxury watchmakers like Rolex and Patek Philippe use AI-driven material tracking systems to verify the ethical origins of precious metals and gemstones, ensuring sustainable craftsmanship.

Luxury brands like Cartier and Dior partner with AI-driven logistics companies to ensure secure, carbon-neutral, and on-time delivery of their high-end products.As AI technology evolves, the future of luxury supply chain management will become even more sophisticated By integrating AI-driven demand forecasting, sustainable sourcing, smart manufacturing, and optimized logistics, luxury brands can uphold their heritage of exclusivity while embracing innovation and sustainability.As AI technology continues to evolve, its role in luxury supply chains will become even more essential, paving the way for a future where high-end brands can maintain their legacy of excellence while championing responsible and ethical business practices.

AI-Driven Market Research and Analytics in Luxury Consumption

The luxury industry thrives on exclusivity, craftsmanship, and a deep understanding of consumer desires. Unlike mass-market retail, where trends are dictated by widespread consumption, luxury brands must anticipate the evolving preferences of a highly discerning clientele. Understanding customer behavior in this sector is not just about identifying purchasing trends—it's about predicting aspirations, emotional drivers, and cultural shifts that influence high-net-worth individuals (HNWIs) and ultra-high-net-worth individuals (UHNWIs).Artificial Intelligence (AI) is revolutionizing market research and analytics in the luxury industry, providing brands with unprecedented insights into customer behavior.(Leung et al., 2018) AI-powered tools analyze vast amounts of data, including social media trends, online searches, purchase history, and even biometric feedback, to uncover patterns that help brands tailor their marketing strategies, refine product offerings, and enhance customer engagement. AI categorizes consumers based on demographics, purchasing patterns, and psychological profiles, enabling hyper-personalized marketing. Sentiment Analysis and Social Listening: AI scans social media, forums, and reviews to gauge public perception and brand sentiment in real time. Luxury brands rely on exclusivity and trend-setting rather than following mainstream fashion cycles(Longoni et al., 2019). Monitoring Emerging Market Trends: AI tracks social media conversations, luxury forums, and digital publications to detect rising luxury trends, such as sustainable fashion or digital couture. Luxury consumers demand bespoke experiences.

Wealth Level and Spending Behavior: AI distinguishes between aspirational buyers, HNWIs, and UHNWIs, tailoring product offerings accordingly.Emotional and Psychological Triggers: AI analyzes consumer sentiment to determine what drives luxury purchases—status, craftsmanship, heritage, or exclusivity. Luxury brands are leveraging AI to analyze consumer engagement on a deeper level through visual and biometric data.AI-Based Facial Expression Analysis:(Lowy, 2016) AI examines customer reactions to luxury advertisements, product displays, and digital campaigns to measure emotional engagement. AI provides insights into economic conditions, luxury spending habits, and geopolitical influences on the high-end market. Luxury watchmakers like Rolex and Audemars Piguet use AI-driven competitive intelligence to position their products strategically while maintaining exclusivity.

As AI technology advances, its role in luxury market research will expand further:AI-Powered Virtual Luxury Assistants: AI-driven virtual stylists will provide bespoke shopping recommendations based on real-time consumer insights.AI-Generated Emotional AI Marketing: AI will create marketing campaigns that dynamically adjust based on consumer emotional responses.

AI-Powered Social Media Monitoring and Analysis in Luxury Brands

Luxury brands thrive on exclusivity, prestige, and an emotional connection with their clientele. In an era where social media plays a critical role in shaping consumer perceptions, luxury brands must remain attuned to public sentiment, emerging trends, and customer expectations. Unlike mass-market brands, which focus on broad audience engagement, luxury brands must maintain an aura of desirability while ensuring that their digital presence aligns with their refined image.

By leveraging AI-driven tools, luxury brands can analyze millions of online conversations across platforms like Instagram, Twitter, TikTok, and WeChat to gauge consumer sentiment, identify emerging influencers, and optimize brand positioning(Martin et al., 2017).This discussion explores the transformative role of AI in social media monitoring for luxury brands, its ability to track customer sentiment, and how it enhances brand reputation, customer engagement, and strategic decision-making .Luxury brands must carefully manage their image, as even minor missteps can damage their exclusivity and prestige. AI-powered sentiment analysis enables brands to:Gauge Consumer Emotions in Real Time: AI assesses whether online conversations about the brand are positive, neutral, or negative. AI pinpoints luxury trends that vary across different markets, helping brands tailor their offerings globally.Detecting Shifts in Sustainability Preferences: AI tracks consumer discussions on ethical luxury consumption, guiding brands in their sustainability efforts.Brands like Gucci and Dior use (Parekh, 2018)AI-powered trend detection to adjust their marketing strategies, ensuring they remain trendsetters in the luxury industry.Influencers and celebrities play a crucial role in shaping luxury brand desirability. AI-driven analysis helps brands:Identify High-Value Brand Ambassadors: AI evaluates influencers' audience demographics, engagement rates, and brand alignment. AI enhances content strategies by:Determining Optimal Posting Times: AI identifies when luxury audiences are most active on social media.Personalizing Content for Different Segments: AI tailors content based on consumer demographics and interests.Analyzing Visual Trends in Luxury Marketing: AI assesses which styles of imagery and video content generate the highest engagement.Luxury brands like Cartier and Tiffany & Co(Pedersen et al., 2018). use AI to optimize their digital storytelling, ensuring that their content remains visually captivating and brand-appropriate.AI helps luxury brands maintain their elite status by ensuring that their social media presence aligns with their brand values and exclusivity.

AI-Driven Predictive Analytics in Luxury Consumption: Forecasting Demand and Trends

Luxury brands operate in an environment where exclusivity, craftsmanship, and prestige define success. Unlike mass-market brands that rely on high-volume sales, luxury consumption is driven by exclusivity, cultural influence, and emotional appeal. Accurately forecasting demand and identifying emerging trends are critical for luxury brands to maintain relevance while preserving their aura of exclusivity.Artificial Intelligence (AI) has revolutionized predictive analytics in the luxury industry by providing deep insights into consumer preferences, economic patterns, and evolving market trends. The Role of AI in Predictive Analytics for Luxury Brands I-driven predictive analytics empowers luxury brands to:(Power, 2017) Forecast Demand Accurately: AI predicts demand for luxury products by analyzing consumer behavior, economic indicators, and seasonal trends.Identify Emerging Fashion and Lifestyle Trends: AI detects shifting preferences in high-end fashion, jewelry, automobiles, and luxury travel. Enhance Inventory and Supply Chain Management: AI ensures optimal inventory levels, reducing overproduction and maintaining exclusivity. Improve Personalized Marketing Strategies: AI tailors recommendations and advertising campaigns to high-net-worth individuals (HNWIs) and ultra-high-net-worth individuals (UHNWIs). For instance, AI-driven trend forecasting has helped Gucci and Balenciaga stay ahead of consumer expectations by predicting the rise of gender-fluid fashion and sustainable luxury materials.AI enhances the luxury shopping experience by predicting what customers desire before they even express it. AI predicts when to introduce price increases or limited-edition releases to enhance brand desirability.Prevent Market Saturation:(Rahwan et al., 2019) AI ensures that luxury products remain aspirational by controlling availability and pricing fluctuations.Luxury brands like Chanel and Cartier use AI-driven pricing models to strategically adjust prices, reinforcing their exclusivity and prestige.The Impact of AI-Driven Predictive Analytics on Luxury Brands. Enhancing Brand Exclusivity and PrestigeAI-driven forecasting helps brands maintain exclusivity by ensuring that only the right products are available to the right customers at the right time.

Case Study: How Luxury Brand X Used AI to Enhance Customer Experience and Drive Sales

Artificial Intelligence (AI) is revolutionizing the luxury industry, enabling brands to create hyper-personalized customer experiences, optimize marketing strategies, and drive sales growth. Luxury brands operate in an environment where exclusivity, craftsmanship, and superior customer service are paramount (Reese, 2018) successfully implemented AI-driven solutions to enhance customer experience and boost sales. Through AI-powered personalization, predictive analytics, and immersive digital innovations, the brand transformed its approach to customer engagement, solidifying its position as an industry leader in luxury retail. Evolving Consumer Expectations: The brand implemented an AI-powered virtual stylist that recommended outfits and accessories based on individual preferences, past purchases, and real-time fashion trends.Personalized In-Store Experiences: VIP clients received customized shopping experiences, where AI-powered CRM systems provided sales associates with detailed customer insights, including their preferred styles, sizes, and purchase history.Dynamic Product Recommendations: AI algorithms curated personalized product recommendations on the brand's website and mobile app, leading to higher conversion rates.(Schatsky et al., 2019)As a result, customers experienced a highly curated shopping journey, increasing satisfaction and brand loyalty.Luxury Brand X integrated AI-powered virtual assistants and chatbots to elevate its customer service:24/7 AI Concierge Service: An AI-powered chatbot provided real-time assistance, answering inquiries about product details, store locations, and appointment scheduling.Multilingual AI Assistants: (Schrift et al., 2017)This AI-driven approach significantly reduced response times and improved customer satisfaction.Luxury Brand X leveraged AI-driven predictive analytics to optimize inventory and supply chain management:Real-Time Demand

Forecasting: AI analyzed historical sales data, online searches, and social media trends to predict demand for specific products.Optimized Inventory Management: The brand used AI to balance stock levels, ensuring that best-selling products were always available while maintaining exclusivity. The brand launched an immersive AI-powered virtual showroom, allowing customers to explore new collections in a digital luxury environment. AI in Live Shopping Events: The brand hosted AI-driven live-streamed shopping events, where AI-powered recommendations tailored product suggestions to viewers in real time.These innovations elevated customer engagement and provided an exclusive digital luxury shopping experience. Luxury Brand X experienced remarkable success following its AI-driven transformation: Increased Sales and Conversion Rates(Shankar, 2018): AI-driven demand forecasting reduced inventory waste by 30%, ensuring the right products were available at the right time.(Tucker, 2018)Greater Engagement with Younger Consumers: AI-powered digital experiences attracted millennial and Gen Z luxury shoppers, increasing engagement by 45% on social media.Higher ROI on Marketing Campaigns: AI-driven influencer tracking and sentiment analysis optimized marketing spend, resulting in a 25% increase in marketing ROI.By integrating AI across its operations, Luxury Brand X successfully enhanced customer experience, optimized sales strategies, and solidified its position as a leader in the luxury market.

Example of AI-Driven Luxury Product Design: The Story Behind Luxury Brand Y's AI-Generated Products

Artificial Intelligence (AI) is reshaping the landscape of luxury product design by pushing the boundaries of creativity, craftsmanship, and innovation. Traditionally, luxury product design has been a highly manual, artisan-driven process, where expert designers and skilled artisans work tirelessly to craft products that exude quality, exclusivity, and aesthetic appeal. However, in recent years, a growing number of luxury brands have turned to AI to assist with or entirely drive the product design process.In this case study, we will explore how Luxury Brand Y, a prestigious name in the high-end fashion and accessories market, integrated AI-driven design technology to create a range of innovative, one-of-a-kind luxury products.(van Lente et al., 2013) By blending machine learning, data-driven insights, and cutting-edge generative design algorithms, Luxury Brand Y developed a collection of products that not only exemplified exclusivity and high-quality craftsmanship but also pushed the boundaries of traditional luxury design. This case study delves into the story behind the brand's AI-generated products, shedding light on the creative process, challenges faced, and the impact this innovative approach has had on their design philosophy and market positioning. AI systems examined various materials and fabrics, analyzing which textures, finishes, and combinations were most popular among their target demographic(Verhoef et al., 2017).By analyzing this historical data, AI generated recommendations that allowed designers to create products that aligned with consumer preferences and anticipated future trends.Generative design algorithms are one of the most powerful applications of AI in luxury product design. These algorithms are designed to generate multiple iterations of a design based on specific parameters, such as aesthetics, functionality, and material constraints. For Luxury Brand Y, the introduction of generative design unlocked entirely new creative possibilities.Form Exploration: AI explored an infinite range of design possibilities for each product, generating forms that designers could never have conceived through traditional methods. The algorithms were trained to create highly detailed, intricate designs while adhering to the brand's signature style.Customization and Personalization: While AI-driven designs were innovative, they still reflected the brand's commitment to traditional luxury craftsmanship. For example, some products were hand-finished by artisans to maintain the level of detail and artistry that Luxury Brand Y is known for.This hybrid approach ensured that the AI-driven designs aligned with the brand's heritage while embracing the benefits of modern technology.(Villasenor, 2019)Once the designs were finalized, Luxury Brand Y introduced its AI-driven products to the market. The products were launched in a limited edition, reinforcing the brand's commitment to exclusivity and luxury.

Luxury Brand Y's AI-driven design initiative represents a groundbreaking approach to luxury product creation, blending the precision of artificial intelligence with the artistry of human craftsmanship(Wainer et al., 2006). By using AI-powered generative design, the brand successfully created exclusive, innovative products that maintained its commitment to quality and elegance while embracing the future of design.This case study highlights the significant potential of AI to revolutionize luxury product design, offering brands the opportunity to enhance creativity, improve personalization, and stay ahead of evolving consumer demands. As AI technology continues to advance, it will play an increasingly important role in shaping the future of luxury design, allowing brands to create products that are as innovative and personalized as their clientele.

AI in Luxury Fashion: A Review of Current Applications and Future Directions

AI in luxury fashion, highlighting potential developments and opportunities that brands may leverage to remain at the forefront of the luxury market.(Wang & Kosinski, 2018)AI is making waves in the product development stage of luxury fashion. Traditionally, this has been a highly artistic and manually intensive process, with designers and artisans creating exclusive pieces based on creativity, trends, and craftsmanship. However, AI is now augmenting the design process in several ways:Generative Design: AI-powered generative design tools can create an infinite number of design variations based on input criteria such as material, functionality, and aesthetic preferences. AI has become a critical tool in enabling this level of customization in several ways:AI-Driven Recommendations(Wirtz et al., 2018): AI algorithms track consumer behavior and preferences across various touchpoints, such as online shopping, social media, and in-store interactions. This data allows brands to offer personalized product recommendations that reflect individual tastes, past purchases, and browsing patterns. These AI-powered personalization strategies elevate customer experience by offering individualized interactions and services, which is essential in the luxury sector, where customers expect tailored and unique experiences.(You et al., 2016)---Demand Forecasting: By analyzing past sales data, seasonal trends, and consumer behavior, AI can predict which products will be in high demand and when. This predictive capability enables luxury brands to stock their stores with the right amount of inventory, reducing both overstocking and stockouts. Accurate demand forecasting also helps brands maintain the exclusive nature of their products by ensuring that limited-edition items remain scarce while avoiding unnecessary surplus.Supply Chain Optimization: AI tools can monitor social media platforms to track customer sentiment and measure the impact of marketing campaigns. Brands can use AI to analyze public sentiment regarding their products and brand, allowing them to fine-tune their marketing efforts. Additionally, AI can identify influential social media figures whose endorsements could help elevate a brand's status and drive sales.Chatbots and Virtual Assistants for Engagement: AI will likely become a central tool for luxury fashion brands in creating immersive digital experiences. Virtual showrooms, fashion shows, and try-on experiences could become more sophisticated with AI,(Zhao et al., 2012) allowing consumers to experience products in a fully digital environment. These virtual experiences could be combined with blockchain for digital ownership and exclusivity, creating new ways for consumers to engage with luxury fashion brands in the metaverse.

Challenges and Limitations of AI in Luxury Consumption: Data Quality, Ethics, and Transparency

Artificial Intelligence (AI) has emerged as a transformative force within the luxury consumption industry, offering new opportunities for brands to enhance personalization, optimize supply chains, and revolutionize customer experiences. For example, certain demographic groups may be underrepresented in the data, leading to biased (Lee et al., 2009)AI models that fail to accurately reflect the diversity of luxury consumers. In addition, data from online platforms may not always be an accurate reflection of in-store behavior, potentially creating gaps in how AI interprets consumer preferences. For example, if AI systems are trained on limited or non-representative consumer data, they might make assumptions or recommendations that do not resonate with the brand's target demographic, undermining personalization(Kober et al., 2013) efforts.Luxury brands often use data from a variety of sources—online and offline interactions, point-of-sale systems, social media, loyalty programs, and customer surveys. Integrating and synchronizing this data into a single, cohesive system can be a significant challenge. This process can be resource-intensive, requiring both time and expertise, but it is crucial for ensuring that AI-powered systems produce reliable and relevant results.

The increasing reliance on AI in luxury(Knight, 2017) fashion—from design and production to customer service and marketing—raises concerns about the potential displacement of human labor. However, luxury consumers are often highly discerning and expect a sense of agency and understanding in their purchasing decisions(Kim & Duhachek, 2018). For this reason, luxury brands must offer transparency in how AI-generated recommendations are formed.If customers understand the reasoning behind the suggestions—such as how their past behavior, preferences, and feedback influenced the product recommendations—they are more likely to trust the process and feel empowered in their decision-making.

Future Directions for AI in Luxury Consumption: Emerging Trends and Technologies

The integration of Artificial Intelligence (AI) into luxury consumption has already made a profound impact on the way luxury brands engage with their customers(Kidd & Breazeal, 2008), design products, and streamline operations. As the luxury sector continues to evolve in the face of shifting consumer demands and technological advances, AI is poised to play an even more pivotal role in shaping its future. This transformation is driven by a combination of emerging trends and technologies that promise to redefine customer experiences, enhance brand offerings, and create more sustainable and efficient operational frameworks.In this exploration, we delve into the future directions of AI in luxury consumption, identifying emerging trends and groundbreaking technologies that will shape the luxury industry in the years to come. We focus on how these developments could revolutionize design, marketing, customer engagement, personalization, and sustainability, ensuring that luxury brands remain competitive, innovative, and aligned with the needs of the next generation of luxury consumers.The Metaverse, a collective virtual shared space that combines physical reality with virtual environments, is rapidly gaining attention across various sectors, including luxury consumption.(Ghahramani, 2015) Luxury brands have already begun experimenting with virtual worlds, and AI is expected to play a central role in shaping these experiences. AI's integration with the Metaverse promises to create new avenues for customer engagement, product interaction, and exclusivity in ways that have never been seen before.As luxury brands explore the Metaverse, AI-driven digital fashion will become a key element of their future strategies. Brands like Balenciaga, Gucci, and Prada have already ventured into the virtual realm, releasing digital-only products and virtual collections in online spaces. These AI-generated virtual products may serve as a form of self-expression for consumers in the Metaverse, allowing them to engage with luxury brands in entirely new ways.AI will enable hyper-personalized virtual products by allowing consumers to create customized fashion items in a virtual environment. These virtual products could range from exclusive digital clothing to limited-edition accessories, each designed with AI algorithms that adjust to the virtual environment and the consumer's preferences. AI's ability to create, design, and tailor these products will ensure that they remain unique, rare, and collectible—core tenets of luxury.In the Metaverse, AI-driven virtual showrooms and fashion shows will transform the way luxury brands present their collections. Consumers will be able to explore luxury products in a 3D environment, trying them on virtually through avatars or interacting with them in ways that go beyond the constraints of traditional e-commerce. Luxury brands will leverage AI to optimize the design of these virtual spaces, ensuring that they are not only aesthetically appealing but also functionally intuitive for consumers. AI could also help predict trends in the Metaverse, allowing brands to showcase products in the most relevant and appealing manner to virtual audiences.This move into the Metaverse will further blur the lines between (Giebelhausen et al., 2014)physical and digital luxury consumption, expanding opportunities for innovation, engagement, and exclusivity in the virtual realm.rands can use AI to explore new, sustainable materials, or optimize the use of existing materials to reduce waste. AI systems can analyze the environmental impact of different materials and suggest eco-friendly alternatives that maintain the aesthetic and performance standards expected in luxury fashion. Moreover, AI can track the lifecycle of materials, ensuring that sourcing practices align with ethical and sustainability goals. This process can significantly reduce the carbon footprint of luxury products and increase the use of recycled and sustainable materials.AI is also poised to play a critical role in reducing waste within the luxury fashion industry. By leveraging data and machine learning models, brands can better predict demand, adjust production schedules, and minimize overproduction. Additionally, AI can help facilitate circular fashion initiatives, where luxury items are recycled, repaired, or resold rather than discarded. AI-powered platforms can help track the lifecycle of a product, offering consumers the opportunity to repair or recycle their luxury items rather than dispose of them.Furthermore, AI-driven recommendations can help consumers make more sustainable choices by suggesting products that are made from eco-friendly materials or are designed with longevity in mind. By incorporating (Gans et al., 2017)AI into sustainability efforts, luxury brands can align their operations with the growing consumer demand for responsible consumption.The demand for hyper-personalized luxury experiences is on the rise, and AI is enabling brands to deliver increasingly tailored offerings to their customers. As AI technology continues to evolve, the future of personalized luxury consumption will be driven by greater customization, real-time engagement, and seamless cross-channel experiences.One of the most important future applications of AI in luxury consumption is the development of more sophisticated recommendation systems. These AI-powered systems will not only suggest products based on past purchases or browsing habits but will also factor in a customer's broader lifestyle, preferences, and social influences. Machine learning models will continuously refine product suggestions in real time, ensuring that consumers are presented with the most relevant luxury items at any given moment. Moreover, these recommendation systems will become highly interactive, learning from consumer feedback and preferences over time. As a result, the personalized experience will continuously improve, offering consumers an intuitive, seamless shopping journey that feels unique to them. (Haslam et al., 2005)AI-powered chatbots are already a valuable tool in luxury retail, but their capabilities will continue to expand in the future. Future AI chatbots will offer more dynamic and sophisticated customer service, providing personalized recommendations, assisting with after-sales service, and even answering complex questions about a brand's heritage or craftsmanship.These AI systems will be able to provide real-time, human-like interactions, allowing customers to access personalized assistance 24/7. With advanced natural language processing and emotional recognition capabilities, these AI chatbots will become more empathetic and responsive, enhancing the overall customer experience while maintaining the luxury brand's commitment to excellence.The future of luxury fashion may see the rise of AI-powered virtual stylists that work with consumers to create custom looks based on their preferences, body types, and personal style. These virtual stylists can generate personalized clothing recommendations, offer advice on how to wear items, and even predict which pieces would complement a consumer's existing wardrobe.Luxury brands may also incorporate AI-generated avatars that consumers can use to virtually try on clothing and accessories. These avatars, which could be modeled after the customer's appearance, will allow consumers to visualize products on themselves without ever stepping into a store(Goldfarb & Tucker, 2013). AI-driven virtual fitting rooms will simulate fabric textures, lighting conditions, and movement, providing an accurate representation of how luxury products will fit and feel in real life.As AI technology continues to improve, luxury brands will increasingly turn to AI-driven analytics to gain deeper insights into customer behavior, market trends, and brand performance. The future of AI in luxury consumption will see advanced analytics used not only for personalization and demand forecasting but also for more strategic decision-making across the entire business.AI-powered predictive analytics will become more advanced, enabling luxury brands to more accurately forecast demand, inventory levels, and seasonal trends. By analyzing large datasets, including consumer behavior, economic factors, and market conditions, AI can predict with greater precision which products will be in demand at specific times of the year, allowing brands to optimize production, reduce waste, and avoid stockouts.Consumer sentiment analysis, powered by AI, will become an invaluable tool for luxury brands in understanding their customer base. AI will be able to track online discussions, reviews, and social media conversations to gauge consumer opinions about products, marketing campaigns, and overall brand perception. By analyzing this data, luxury brands can fine-tune their strategies, improve customer service, and proactively address potential issues before they escalate. Moreover, AI-driven sentiment analysis will help brands identify trends and shifts in consumer behavior, providing real-time feedback on how their products and messaging are resonating with their target audience. Brands that provide clear explanations about how their AI systems work will be better positioned to build trust and foster (Gaudin, 2016)long-term relationships with their consumers The development of ethical AI systems will be a key challenge for luxury brands in the future. AI models must be designed to avoid biases, respect consumer privacy, and ensure fairness

The Role of Human-AI Collaboration in Luxury Consumption: Balancing Technology and Human Touch

In the luxury consumption landscape, the fusion of advanced technology with human expertise has become a defining factor in creating exceptional experiences for customers. For instance, AI systems can process consumer data to uncover trends and preferences that humans may overlook, providing insights that can guide the creative process.(French, 2018) This information can be used by designers to create products that resonate with consumers on a deeper level, blending data-driven insights with artistic and cultural sensibilities.In customer service, AI chatbots and virtual assistants can provide customers with immediate responses to inquiries, helping to streamline communication and ensure that basic information is readily available. While AI can enhance efficiency, optimize production processes, and offer insights into market demand, it is the human touch that imbues luxury products with their unique value.(Davenport et al., 2011)For example, in high-end fashion, the role of a skilled artisan is paramount in creating intricate, one-of-a-kind designs. They can understand the nuances of a customer's preferences, provide thoughtful recommendations, and offer a level of empathy and understanding that AI cannot replicate.In this way, AI acts as a tool that enhances human interaction, allowing luxury brands to deliver a more refined and tailored experience to each consumer.In the realm of luxury retail, the human experience is often as important as the product itself. AI offers a powerful tool for enhancing human interaction in retail settings, both online and offline. Virtual assistants, for example, can provide customers with immediate answers to common questions and help them navigate through digital catalogs. One of the key challenges is ensuring that AI systems are designed to respect consumer privacy and data security. (Dedehayir & Steinert, 2016)Customers must feel confident that their personal information is being used ethically and in a way that benefits them without infringing on their rights.Furthermore, AI should never overshadow the human aspect of luxury. While AI can enhance the efficiency of luxury brand operations, it is essential that the personal, bespoke nature of luxury consumption remains at the forefront.

Conclusion: The Impact of AI on Luxury Consumption and Future Directions

The impact of artificial intelligence (AI) on luxury consumption has been profound and multifaceted, reshaping how brands design, produce, market, and deliver their products. As luxury consumption continues to evolve(Fowler, 2019), it is essential to assess the key findings regarding the impact of AI and explore the future directions that will define the next phase of the luxury industry.AI's ability to deliver highly personalized experiences has been one of its most significant contributions to the luxury sector. By analyzing vast amounts of customer data—ranging from purchase history and browsing behavior to social media activity and preferences—AI allows brands to tailor their offerings in ways that were previously unimaginable. Personalized product recommendations, customized marketing campaigns, and bespoke services have become central to the luxury consumer experience, ensuring that brands can cater to the unique desires of each individual client.Furthermore, AI's ability to predict consumer trends and preferences has led to more intuitive, data-driven designs. In retail, AI-powered virtual assistants and chatbots offer real-time assistance, ensuring that customers receive relevant information quickly.

Luxury brands have long relied on complex, global supply chains to source materials, manufacture products, and deliver them to customers. AI has enabled brands to optimize these supply chains by predicting demand, managing inventory, reducing waste, and ensuring that products are delivered efficiently and sustainably. In addition to understanding consumer sentiment, AI also provides invaluable insights into market trends. By analyzing large datasets across multiple platforms, AI systems can forecast future trends, enabling brands to make more informed decisions about product launches, pricing strategies, and marketing efforts. This predictive capability helps luxury brands stay ahead of the curve, ensuring that they remain at the forefront of an ever-evolving industry. While the integration of AI in luxury consumption offers numerous advantages(Hassler, 2018), it also brings with it ethical challenges that brands must address. One of the most significant concerns revolves around data privacy. As luxury brands gather more personal data from customers to create personalized experiences, they must ensure that this data is handled responsibly and transparently. From personalized customer experiences to optimized product design, AI has transformed how luxury brands engage with their consumers and create exceptional products. However, the key to successfully navigating this transformation lies in striking the right balance between technology and human expertise. While AI can provide efficiency, innovation, and data-driven insights, the human touch remains essential in creating the emotional connections, craftsmanship, and exclusivity that define luxury. .

Recommendations for Luxury Brands: Leveraging AI to Enhance Customer Experience and Drive Business Growth

The luxury industry, historically characterized by exclusivity, craftsmanship, and personalized experiences, is undergoing a profound transformation driven by technological innovations, particularly artificial intelligence (AI). In this rapidly evolving environment, luxury brands must leverage AI strategically to enhance the customer experience, streamline operations, and drive long-term business growth. By incorporating AI in a thoughtful and integrated manner, luxury brands can provide unparalleled personalized experiences, create more efficient business processes, optimize customer engagement, and stay competitive in an increasingly digital world. This section provides practical recommendations for luxury brands on how to effectively harness AI to achieve these goals while preserving the essence of luxury and exclusivity.One of the most powerful applications of AI in luxury consumption is personalization. Luxury consumers expect tailored experiences that cater to their unique tastes, preferences, and lifestyles. By leveraging AI-driven insights, luxury brands can create highly personalized interactions across various touchpoints, from online and in-store experiences to post-purchase services. Here are a few key recommendations:Personalized Product Recommendations: Use AI to analyze customer data, including past purchases, browsing behavior, and social media activity, to deliver personalized product recommendations.

This level of personalization not only enhances the shopping experience but also drives higher conversion rates and fosters long-term customer loyalty. Tailored Marketing Campaigns: AI can help brands deliver hyper-targeted marketing messages based on consumer data, such as demographics, behavior, and preferences. By using machine learning algorithms to segment customers, brands can send personalized email campaigns, social media ads, and exclusive offers that resonate with each customer, making them feel valued and understood.Customized Shopping Experience: Implement AI-powered tools such as virtual assistants, chatbots, and personalized shopping experiences on e-commerce platforms. These tools can guide customers through their shopping journey, suggesting products based on their preferences and providing real-time support. For instance, a customer browsing luxury handbags may receive tailored recommendations for bags that match their personal style or previous purchases. AI can help luxury brands streamline supply chains, reduce waste, and optimize product distribution, all while meeting the growing demand for sustainable practices.Supply Chain Optimization: AI-powered predictive analytics can help luxury brands forecast demand more accurately, enabling them to adjust production schedules and manage inventory more effectively. This minimizes overproduction, reduces the risk of unsold stock, and optimizes the allocation of resources, leading to cost savings and a reduced environmental impact.Sustainable Sourcing: AI can play a crucial role in helping luxury brands trace the provenance of raw materials and ensure they are sourced sustainably. By leveraging AI for real-time monitoring and transparency, brands can verify the ethical sourcing of materials, from leather and gemstones to textiles, ensuring that they meet sustainability standards and appeal to the increasingly eco-conscious consumer.

CONCLUSION

Automation of Repetitive Tasks: Luxury brands can use AI to automate repetitive tasks such as inventory management, pricing updates, and customer service queries. Automation can reduce the burden on staff, increase operational efficiency, and allow employees to focus on more strategic, customer-facing activities, ultimately driving business growth.Building strong, lasting relationships with luxury consumers requires more than just offering premium products—it involves creating memorable, high-touch experiences that resonate with customers on an emotional level. AI can assist in providing this personalized engagement, which in turn drives customer satisfaction and loyalty.AI-Powered Customer Support: Implement AI chatbots and virtual assistants that provide immediate, around-the-clock customer service, responding to queries regarding product details, order tracking, and return policies. By using natural language processing (NLP), AI can provide a human-like interaction, ensuring a seamless customer experience. However, when the inquiry requires a higher level of expertise or emotional intelligence, AI should seamlessly escalate the issue to a human representative.Loyalty Programs: Use AI to optimize loyalty programs(Harding, 2017) by analyzing customer behavior and preferences to offer personalized rewards and incentives. For example, AI can suggest custom rewards based on a customer's purchase history or provide access to exclusive events that align with their interests, making the loyalty program feel more valuable and individualizedExclusive Offers and Experiences: AI can identify high-value customers and provide them with personalized offers, exclusive events, or early access to new collections. For example, AI can send targeted invites to VIP customers for private brand events, special shopping sessions, or personalized styling consultations, enhancing their sense of exclusivity and belonging to an elite group.Post-Purchase Engagement: AI can also help brands maintain engagement with customers after the purchase has been made. Personalized follow-ups via email or SMS can offer styling tips, care instructions, and exclusive content, deepening the connection between the consumer and the brand and encouraging repeat purchases.AI's capabilities in product design offer luxury brands the opportunity to push the boundaries of creativity while maintaining the highest levels of craftsmanship and exclusivity. AI-driven tools can aid in the ideation, prototyping, and design phases, enabling brands to create innovative, cutting-edge products that appeal to consumers' evolving tastes.(Fleming, 2019)Data-Driven Design: By using AI to analyze consumer preferences, trends, and social media discussions, luxury brands can generate design ideas that reflect current market desires. This can help brands stay ahead of trends and create products that resonate with their target audience. For instance, an AI-powered tool can scan global fashion trends and generate new collections inspired by the preferences of their most loyal customersVirtual Prototyping: AI can help luxury brands develop and test virtual prototypes of products, such as accessories or garments, before committing to production. This process accelerates the design cycle and enables designers to visualize concepts in 3D, test materials, and explore color schemes—all without the need for physical prototypes. This not only reduces costs but also enhances creativity by allowing rapid iteration.Customization and Personalization: AI can allow consumers to take part in the design process by offering them customization options for their luxury products. For example, AI platforms can allow customers to personalize the color, material, and engraving options for luxury bags, watches, or footwear. This creates unique, one-of-a-kind items, enhancing the feeling of exclusivity.AI-Assisted Craftsmanship: Luxury brands that pride themselves on craftsmanship can combine AI and human artistry in the creation of bespoke products. While AI can assist with identifying consumer preferences, managing designs, and even optimizing production processes, the final touch—the artistry and attention to detail—should remain firmly in human hands. AI and artisans can work collaboratively to bring new ideas to life with the highest level of skill.The shopping experience is rapidly becoming more immersive, personalized, and digital, especially in the luxury industry. Consumers increasingly expect to interact with luxury brands in innovative ways, whether through virtual or augmented reality, advanced e-commerce platforms, or experiential in-store technologies. AI can enhance these experiences and make them more engaging and convenient for consumers.Augmented Reality (AR) and Virtual Reality (VR) Integration: AI can power immersive AR and VR shopping experiences that allow customers to virtually try on products, such as clothing, accessories, or even makeup, from the comfort of their own homes. These technologies enable consumers to see how items will look on them or in their living spaces before making a purchase, creating a more engaging and informed shopping experience.AI-Powered Visual Search: Implement AI-powered visual search tools that allow customers to upload photos and find similar luxury products online. This technology can enhance the digital shopping experience by making it easier for consumers to discover products that match their style or preferences, streamlining the path to purchase.Enhanced In-Store Experience: AI can also enhance physical store visits by integrating virtual assistants and smart mirrors that allow customers to interact with products digitally. For example, AI-driven mirrors can show customers how a garment or accessory looks on them without having to try it on physically, improving convenience while maintaining the luxurious in-store experience.Seamless Omnichannel Shopping: As luxury consumers increasingly engage with brands across multiple platforms—online, in-store, and on mobile—AI can help create a seamless omnichannel experience. By integrating AI into the e-commerce platform, mobile apps, and brick-and-mortar stores, brands can offer consistent, personalized experiences that follow the consumer across various touchpoints.As luxury brands incorporate AI into their operations, protecting customer data and maintaining ethical practices must be top priorities. Consumers are increasingly aware of how their personal data is being used, and luxury brands must ensure that they are handling sensitive information responsibly.Data Privacy and Transparency: Luxury brands must invest in robust data security measures to protect customer information. This includes encrypting sensitive data, ensuring that third-party vendors follow the same security standards, and being transparent with customers about how their data is used. Offering clear privacy policies and ensuring compliance with regulations such as GDPR is essential for building trust.Ethical AI Implementation: AI must be implemented with a focus on ethical considerations, including fairness, transparency, and inclusivity. Luxury brands should ensure that AI systems

REFERENCES

Aguirre, E., Mahr, D., Grewal, D., de Ruyter, K., & Wetzels, M. (2015). Unraveling the personalization paradox: The effect of information collection and trust-building strategies on online advertisement effectiveness. *Journal of Retailing*, *91*(1), 34–49.

André, Q., Carmon, Z., Wertenbroch, K., Crum, A., Frank, D., & Goldstein, W.. (2018). Consumer choice and autonomy in the age of artificial intelligence and big data. *Customer Needs and Solutions*, *5*(1–2), 28–37.

Andrews, T. (2016). Meet the robot monk spreading the teachings of Buddhism around China. Washington Post, April 27. Retrieved February 11, 2019 from https://www.washingtonpost.com/news/morning-mix/wp/2016/04/27/meet-the-robot-monk-spreading-the-teachings-of-buddhism-around-china/?utm_term=.fed52d90bff3. Accessed 11 Feb 2019

Baum, S. D., Goertzel, B., & Goertzel, T. G. (2011). How long until human-level AI? Results from an expert assessment. *Technological Forecasting and Social Change*, *78*(1), 185–195.

Bettman, J. (2013). Perceived risk and its components: A model and empirical test. *Journal of Marketing*, *10*(2), 184–190.

Biswas, A., Bhowmick, S., Guha, A., & Grewal, D. (2013). Consumer evaluations of sale prices: Role of the subtraction principle. *Journal of Marketing*, *77*(4), 49–66.

Boyd, R., & Holton, R. J. (2018). Technology, innovation, employment and power: Does robotics and artificial intelligence really mean social transformation? *Journal of Sociology (Melbourne, Vic.)*, *54*(3), 331–345.

Carpenter, J. (2015). IBM's Virginia Rometty tells NU grads: Technology will enhance us. Retrieved February 11, 2019 from https://www.chicagotribune.com/bluesky/originals/ct-northwestern-virginia-rometty-ibm-bsi-20150619-story.html

Castelo, N. (2019). Blurring the line between human and machine: Marketing artificial intelligence (doctoral dissertation). Retrieved from Columbia University Academic Commons. https://doi.org/DOI: 10.7916/d8-k7vk-0s40

Castelo, N., Bos, M., & Lehman, D. (2018). Consumer adoption of algorithms that blur the line between human and machine. Graduate School of Business: Columbia University Working Paper.

Castelo, N., & Ward, A. (2016). Political affiliation moderates attitudes towards artificial intelligence. In Moreau, P., & Puntoni, S. (Eds.), *NA - advances in consumer research* (pp. 723–723). Association for Consumer Research.

Davenport, T. H., Dalle Mule, L., & Lucker, J. (2011). Know what your customers want before they do. *Harvard Business Review*, *89*(12), 84–92.

Davenport, T. H., & Ronanki, R. (2018). Artificial intelligence for the real world. *Harvard Business Review*, *96*(1), 108–116.

Dedehayir, O., & Steinert, M. (2016). The hype cycle model: A review and future directions. *Technological Forecasting and Social Change*, *108*, 28–41.

Fleming, P. (2019). Robots and organization studies: Why robots might not want to steal your job. *Organization Studies*, *40*(1), 23–38.

Fowler, G. (2019). The doorbells have eyes: The privacy battles brewing over home security cameras. Retrieved February 11, 2019 from https://www.sltrib.com/news/business/2019/02/01/doorbells-have-eyes/

French, K. (2018). Your new best friend: AI chatbot. Retrieved February 13, 2019 from https://futurism.com/ai-chatbot-meaningful-conversation

Gans, J., Agrawal, A., & Goldfarb, A. (2017). How AI will change strategy: A thought experiment. Harvard business review online. Retrieved February 11, 2019 from https://hbr.org/product/how-ai-will-change-strategy-a-thought-experiment/H03XDI-PDF-ENG

Gaudin, S. (2016). At stitch fix, data scientists and a.I. become personal stylists. Retrieved February 11, 2019 from https://www.computerworld.com/article/3067264/artificial-intelligence/at-stitch-fix-data-scientists-and-ai-become-personal-stylists.html

Ghahramani, Z. (2015). Probabilistic machine learning and artificial intelligence. *Nature*, *521*(7553), 452–459.

Giebelhausen, M., Robinson, S. G., Sirianni, N. J., & Brady, M. K. (2014). Touch versus tech: When technology functions as a barrier or a benefit to service encounters. *Journal of Marketing*, *78*(4), 113–124.

Goldfarb, A., & Tucker, C. (2013). Why managing consumer privacy can be an opportunity. *MIT Sloan Management Review*, *54*(3), 10–12.

Harding, K. (2017). AI and machine learning for predictive data scoring. Retrieved February 11, 2019 from https://www.objectiveit.com/blog/use-ai-and-machine-learning-for-predictive-lead-scoring on 13 February 2019.

Haslam, N., Bain, P., Douge, L., Lee, M., & Bastian, B. (2005). More human than you: Attributing humanness to self and others. *Journal of Personality and Social Psychology*, *89*(6), 937–950.

Hassler, C. A. (2018). Meet Replika, the AI Bot that wants to be your best friend. Retrieved February 11, 2019 from https://www.popsugar.com/news/Replika-Bot-AI-App-Review-Interview-Eugenia-Kuyda-44216396

Kidd, C. D., & Breazeal, C. (2008, September). Robots at home: Understanding long-term human-robot interaction. In *Proceedings of the IEEE International Conference of Intelligent Robot Systems* (pp. 3230–3235).

Kim, T., & Duhachek, A. (2018). *The impact of artificial agents on persuasion: A construal level account*. ACR Asia-Pacific Advances.

Knight, W. (2017). Forget killer robots – bias is the real AI danger. Retrieved February 11, 2019 from https://www.technologyreview.com/s/608986/forget-killer-robotsbias-is-the-real-ai-danger/

Kober, J., Bagnell, J. A., & Peters, J. (2013). Reinforcement learning in robotics: A survey. *The International Journal of Robotics Research*, *32*(11), 1238–1274.

Lee, A. Y., Keller, P. A., & Sternthal, B. (2009). Value from regulatory construal fit: The persuasive impact of fit between consumer goals and message concreteness. *The Journal of Consumer Research, 36*(5), 735–747.

Leung, E., Paolacci, G., & Puntoni, S. (2018). Man versus machine: Resisting automation in identity-based consumer behavior. *JMR, Journal of Marketing Research, 55*(6), 818–831.

Longoni, C., Bonezzi, A., & Morewedge, C. K. (2019). (forthcoming). Resistance to Medical Artificial Intelligence. *The Journal of Consumer Research.*

Lowy, J. (2016). Self-driving cars are 'absolutely not' ready for deployment. Retrieved February 11, 2019 from https://www.pbs.org/newshour/science/self-driving-cars-are-absolutely-not-ready-for-deployment

Martin, K. D., Borah, A., & Palmatier, R. W. (2017). Data privacy: Effects on customer and firm performance. *Journal of Marketing, 81*(1), 36–58.

Parekh, J. (2018). Why Programmatic provides a better digital marketing landscape. Retrieved February 13, 2019 from https://www.adweek.com/programmatic/why-programmatic-provides-a-better-digital-marketing-landscape/

Pedersen, I., Reid, S., & Aspevig, K. (2018). Developing social robots for aging populations: A literature review of recent academic sources. *Sociology Compass, 12*(6).

Power, B. (2017). How AI is streamlining marketing and sales. Harvard Business Review, June 12. Retrieved February 11, 2019 from https://hbr.org/2017/06/how-ai-is-streamlining-marketing-and-sales

Rahwan, I., Cebrian, M., Obradovich, N., Bongard, J., Bonnefon, J. F., & Breazeal, C.. (2019). Machine behavior. *Nature, 568*(7753), 477–486.

Reese, B. (2018). *The fourth age: Smart robots, conscious computers and the future of humanity*. Atria Books.

Schatsky, D., Katyal, V., Iyengar, S., & Chauhan, R. (2019). Why enterprises shouldn't wait for AI regulation. Retrieved July 11, 2019 from https://www2.deloitte.com/insights/us/en/focus/signals-for-strategists/ethical-artificial-intelligence.html

Schrift, R. Y., Wertenbroch, K., André, Q., & Frank, D. H. (2017). Threatening free will. Presentation at the *Symposium on Alienation and Meaning in Production and Consumption, Technische Universität München.*

Shankar, V. (2018). How artificial intelligence (AI) is reshaping retailing. *Journal of Retailing*, *94*(4), vi–xi.

Tucker, C. (2018). Privacy, algorithms, and artificial intelligence. In *The Economics of Artificial Intelligence: An Agenda.* University of Chicago Press.

van Lente, H., Spitters, C., & Peine, A. (2013). Comparing technological hype cycles: Towards a theory. *Technological Forecasting and Social Change*, *80*(8), 1615–1628.

Verhoef, P. C., Stephen, A. T., Kannan, P. K., Luo, X., Abhishek, V., & Andrews, M.. (2017). Consumer connectivity in a complex, technology-enabled, and mobile-oriented world with smart products. *Journal of Interactive Marketing*, *40*, 1–8.

Villasenor, J. (2019). Artificial intelligence and bias: Four key challenges. Retrieved February 11, 2019 from https://www.brookings.edu/blog/techtank/2019/01/03/artificial-intelligence-and-bias-four-key-challenges/

Wainer, J., Feil-Seifer, D. J., Shell, D. A., & Mataric, M. J. (2006, September). The role of physical embodiment in human-robot interaction. In *Proceedings of the IEEE International Symposium of Robot Human Interaction Communication* (pp.6-8).

Wang, Y., & Kosinski, M. (2018). Deep neural networks are more accurate than humans at detecting sexual orientation from facial images. *Journal of Personality and Social Psychology*, *114*(2), 246–257.

Wirtz, J., Patterson, P. G., Kunz, W. H., Gruber, T., Lu, V. N., Paluch, S., & Martins, A. (2018). Brave new world: Service robots in the frontline. *Journal of Service Management*, *29*(5), 907–931.

You, Q., Jin, H., Wang, Z., Fang, C., & Luo, J. (2016). Image captioning with semantic attention. In *Proceedings of the IEEE conference on computer vision and pattern recognition* (pp. 4651-4659).

Zhao, M., Hoeffler, S., & Dahl, D. W. (2012). Imagination difficulty and new product evaluation. *Journal of Product Innovation Management, 29*(S1), 76–90.

Chapter 2
Luxury in Transition: Embracing New Consumer Trends and Market Dynamics

Albérico Travassos Rosário
https://orcid.org/0000-0003-4793-4110
GOVCOPP, Escola Superior de Ciências Empresariais, Instituto Politécnico de Setúbal, Portugal

Aihoor Aleem
https://orcid.org/0000-0002-3707-5511
BRU, ISCTE, University Institute of Lisbon, Portugal & IADE, Universidade Europeia, Portugal

ABSTRACT

The luxury goods market has grown significantly in recent years, driven by rising disposable incomes, global travel, and the aspirational buying behaviours of emerging markets. However, this growth presents challenges and opportunities for luxury brands. The evolving consumer base is younger, more diverse, and digitally savvy, demanding personalized experiences and valuing sustainability. This shift forces brands to adapt quickly. Counterfeiting and brand dilution also threaten the exclusivity of luxury goods, while economic uncertainties and political tensions impact consumer spending. Still, there are opportunities: e-commerce and digital marketing provide new ways to reach global audiences, and innovation in tech and sustainability can help brands stand out. Those that navigate

DOI: 10.4018/979-8-3693-8422-0.ch002

these challenges and embrace new trends will thrive. A systematic review of 48 academic documents on luxury brands and their consumption from the Scopus database is planned.

INTRODUCTION

The consumption of luxury brands has significantly grown in recent years. This is evidenced in Statista Market Insights report (2024), which found that sales from luxury products are projected to reach US$ 473.90 billion in 2024. This revenue will grow at a CAGR of 4.04% between 2024-2029, reaching US $577.79 billion by 2029. Luxury brands combine prestige with high prices, often only accessible to upper-class and middle-class consumers. This creates a sense of exclusivity, making luxury brands appealing to consumers who value ownership of such items. However, Seo and Buchanan-Oliver (2019) found that contemporary consumers are reinterpreting the meaning of luxury, resulting in changes in consumption behaviors. Given these changes and their impacts, the concept of luxury brand consumption has been examined in multiple disciplines, including economics, sociology, anthropology, and evolutionary psychology. This is because luxury consumption intersects with fundamental human behaviors and societal structures, influencing economic trends, cultural norms, social status hierarchies, and even evolutionary drives for status and resource acquisition.

Historically, the consumption of luxury goods was a privilege reserved for the affluent, signifying wealth and high social status. Wang (2022) explain that the possession of luxury products signifies wealth, success, and achievement due to their exclusivity and high price points. As a result, luxury brands have always been used as an indicator of one's social status. However, with the rise of globalization, digital commerce, and shifting cultural dynamics, the concept of luxury brand consumption has evolved significantly. Today, luxury is not merely a reflection of financial capability but is also tied to personal expression, lifestyle choices, and experiential value. Seo and Buchanan-Oliver (2019) capture this change, arguing that today's definition of luxury is “disputed, subjective, and personalized.” As a result, brands must navigate a complex and increasingly competitive market where consumers' motivations vary, ranging from the desire for social recognition to the pursuit of individual identity. The democratization of luxury through accessible digital platforms has broadened its appeal, making it a subject of interest for economists, marketers, and sociologists who examine the cultural implications of such consumption patterns.

The changes in global markets and consumer demands significantly shape the global luxury markets. This has created new opportunities for innovation and challenges that luxury brands must address to ensure continuous, long-term growth. For instance, the emergence of trends like luxury resale, digital fashion, and collaborations with influencers reflect the changing dynamics of the luxury market. Brands must now balance the need to uphold their traditional values of exclusivity and craftsmanship while embracing modern demands for inclusivity and digital engagement. This study aims to critically analyze the contemporary consumption of luxury brands, identifying emerging challenges and opportunities, based on a systematic review of international scientific literature. Research paper will explore the contemporary consumption of luxury brands, including the challenges and opportunities that arise in this evolving luxury market. It focuses on the strategic adaptations brands must make to remain relevant and desirable in a rapidly shifting global marketplace.

METHODOLOGICAL APPROACH

This study employs a systematic bibliometric literature review (LRSB) to analyze and synthesize the academic discourse surrounding luxury brands and their consumption. A structured search process was followed to ensure a comprehensive examination of relevant literature. The PRISMA 2020 framework, designed for systematic reviews, guided the search and selection process. This model ensured transparency and rigor in identifying, screening, and reporting sources (Haddaway et al., 2022). The initial search was conducted using Scopus, a multidisciplinary database known for its extensive coverage of peer-reviewed literature.

To gather and select relevant materials, the Scopus database was utilized, following the recommendations of Rosário & Casaca (2023); Rosário et al. (2023, 2021). They describe Scopus as one of the largest and most comprehensive curated abstract and citation databases available, offering a wide range of sources, including conference proceedings, books, and journal articles that cover global and regional research areas. Scopus also ensures high data quality through an independent Content Selection and Advisory Board, which enforces a rigorous content selection and re-evaluation process.

Unlike traditional literature reviews, the LRSB (Systematic Bibliometric Literature Review) method adopts a thorough approach to analyzing published research on the chosen topic, as highlighted by Rosário & Casaca (2023); Rosário et al. (2023, 2021). This method aims to refine the selection of articles to those most relevant to the research. It also establishes a transparent audit trail, allowing readers to evaluate the methodologies, findings, and overall quality of the selected studies.

The LRSB method follows a detailed process for screening and selecting sources to ensure the reliability and relevance of the data. This process is organized into a three-phase, six-step procedure, as illustrated in Table 1, according to Rosário & Casaca (2023); Rosário et al. (2023, 2021)

Table 1. Process of systematic LRSB.

Fase	Step	Description
Exploration	Step 1	formulating the research problem
	Step 2	searching for appropriate literature
	Step 3	critical appraisal of the selected studies
	Step 4	data synthesis from individual sources
Interpretation	Step 5	reporting findings and recommendations
Communication	Step 6	Presentation of the LRSB report

Source: adapted *Rosário & Casaca (2023); Rosário et al. (2023, 2021).*

The researchers utilized the Scopus database to identify and select reliable sources that scholars and scientists widely recognize. It is important to acknowledge that this study had a limitation, as it focused solely on the Scopus database and excluded other academic and scientific databases, with the search covering publications up to September 2024. The literature search emphasized peer-reviewed scientific and academic publications.

The search strategy focused on capturing various documents related to luxury brands and their consumption. The initial search term used was "Luxury," which yielded 18,390 sources. To narrow the focus to the specific subject matter of interest, the search was refined to include the keywords "luxury brands" in combination with "luxury." This adjustment reduced the results to 1,761 documents, offering a more targeted perspective. In the final step, the search was further limited to the exact keywords "luxury consumption" to ensure that the documents selected were relevant to the study topic. This resulted in 48 relevant documents that formed the basis of the subsequent literature review.

The search process is summarized in Table 2 below.

Table 2. Screening Methodology.

<table>
<tr><th>Database Scopus</th><th>Screening</th><th>Publications</th></tr>
<tr><td>Meta-search</td><td>Keyword: Luxury</td><td>18,390</td></tr>
<tr><td>First Inclusion Criterion</td><td>Keyword: Luxury, Luxury Brands</td><td>1,761</td></tr>
<tr><td>First Inclusion Criterion</td><td>Keyword: Luxury, Luxury Brands
Exact keywords: Luxury Consumption</td><td rowspan="2">48</td></tr>
<tr><td>Screening</td><td>Keyword: Luxury, Luxury Brands
Exact keywords: Luxury Consumption
Published until September 2024</td></tr>
</table>

Source: own elaboration

We used content and thematic analysis methods to identify, examine and present the different documents described by Rosário & Casaca (2023); Rosário et al. (2023, 2021).

The selection criteria were meticulously applied to include relevant and high-quality academic sources. Studies were considered if they focused on luxury brands and their consumption. The eligibility of the documents was assessed based on relevance to the research topic, methodological rigor, and publication in peer-reviewed outlets (Figure 1).

Figure 1. PRISMA 2020 flow diagram for the systematic literature search.

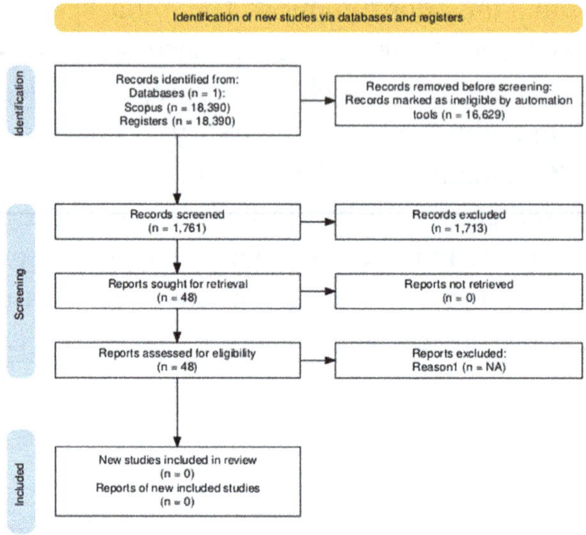

Subsequently, the 48 scientific and academic documents indexed in Scopus were analyzed through both narrative and bibliometric approaches, following the guidelines of Rosário & Casaca (2023); Rosário et al. (2023, 2021), to explore their content and uncover recurring themes that directly addressed the research questions. Of A análise dos 48 documentos foi realizada com auxílio do software VOSviewer para mapeamento de palavras-chave e co-citações, complementada por leitura temática narrativa selected, 47 articles, and 1 book.

PUBLICATION DISTRIBUTION

Peer-reviewed articles on luxury brands and their consumption. September 2024. The years 2020 and 2024 presented the highest number of peer-reviewed publications on the topic, reaching 7. The concentration of publications in the years 2020–2024 demonstrates a growing interest in the topic, driven by changes in consumer behavior and pressures for sustainability. Figure 2 summarizes the peer-reviewed literature published up to September 2024.

Figure 2. Documents by year

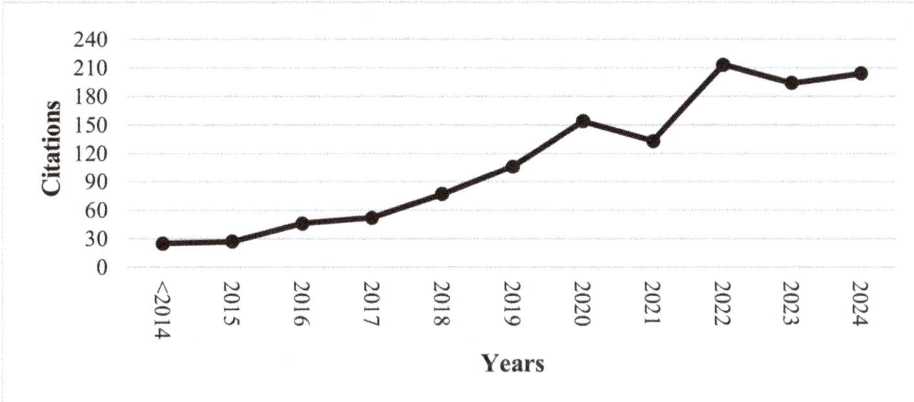

Source: own elaboration

Figure 3 displays the countries exhibiting the highest levels of scientific output in specific research areas, with particular emphasis on ITALY, USA, and Germany, which boast the greatest number of publications.

Figure 3. Scientific production by country.

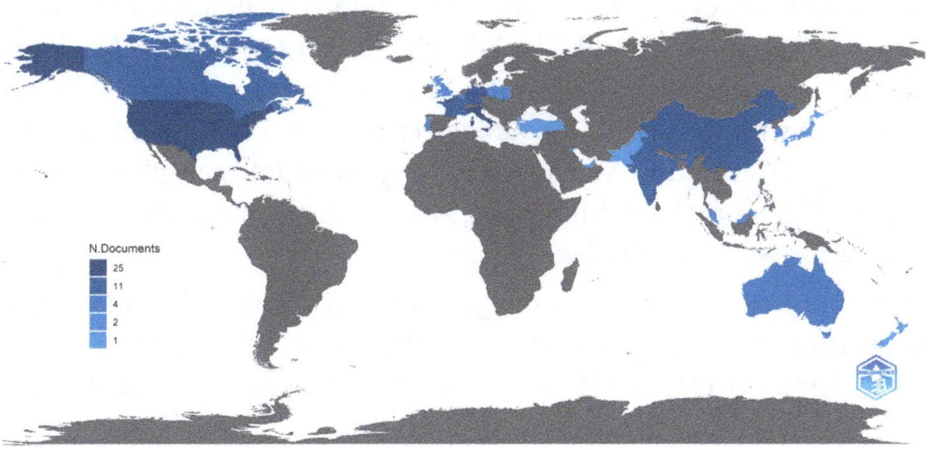

Table 3, along with Figure 3, visually illustrates the top 10 nations making notable scientific contributions in the examined domains. The objective of this investigation is to identify countries that prioritize studying luxury brands and their consumption.

Table 3. Top 10 countries by number of publications.

Country	Number of Publications
ITALY	25
USA	25
GERMANY	15
CHINA	13
FRANCE	12
INDIA	11
CANADA	10
AUSTRALIA	5
BELGIUM	4
PORTUGAL	4

Source: own elaboration

The publications were sorted out as follows: Journal Of Business Research (7); Developments In Marketing Science Proceedings Of The Academy Of Marketing Science (6); Psychology And Marketing (3); Journal Of Retailing And Consumer Services (3); with 2 documents (Palgrave Advances In Luxury; Journal Of Global Scholars Of Marketing Science Bridging Asia And The World; Journal Of Fashion Marketing And Management; Journal Of Brand Management; International Review Of Retail Distribution And Consumer Research; International Journal Of Retail And Distribution Management; European Journal Of Marketing; Asia Pacific Journal Of Marketing And Logistics; and the remaining publications with 1 document.

In Table 4 we analyze the Scimago Journal & Country Rank (SJR), the best quartile, and the H index by Journal Of Consumer Research publication with 5,430 (SJR), Q1, and H index 220. There is a total of 16 publications in Q1, 3 publications in Q2, and 2 publications in Q3 and Q4.

Publications from the best quartile Q1 represent 64% of the titles of the 25 publications; the best quartile Q2 represents 12%, the best Q3 represents 8%, and the best Q4 represents 8%of each of the titles of 93 publications. Finally, 2 publications without indexing data represent 8% of publications. As shown in Table 3, the significant majority of publications do not have SJR.

Table 4. Scimago journal & country rank impact factor.

Title	SJR	Best Quartile	H index
Journal Of Consumer Research	5,430	Q1	220
Journal Of Consumer Psychology	3,530	Q1	139
Journal Of Business Research	3,130	Q1	265
Journal Of Retailing And Consumer Services	2,990	Q1	143
Psychology And Marketing	2,760	Q1	143
Journal Of International Marketing	2,180	Q1	107
Journal Of Product And Brand Management	1,690	Q1	104
Journal Of Marketing Management	1,450	Q1	90
European Journal Of Marketing	1,270	Q1	154
Journal Of Brand Management	1,170	Q1	68
International Journal Of Retail And Distribution Management	1,170	Q1	101
Journal Of Consumer Culture	1,090	Q1	65
Asia Pacific Journal Of Marketing And Logistics	0,960	Q1	63
Journal Of Fashion Marketing And Management	0,910	Q1	67
Spanish Journal Of Marketing Esic	0,910	Q2	30
Journal Of Global Fashion Marketing	0,890	Q1	30
Journal Of International Consumer Marketing	0,770	Q2	56
International Review Of Retail Distribution And Consumer Research	0,660	Q2	49
Journal Of Global Scholars Of Marketing Science Bridging Asia And The World	0,540	Q1	24
Evolutionary Psychology	0,400	Q3	48
Journal Of Developmental Entrepreneurship	0,340	Q3	32
African Journal Of Business And Economic Research	0,170	Q4	10
Micro And Macro Marketing	0,130	Q4	4
Developments In Marketing Science Proceedings Of The Academy Of Marketing Science	-*	-*	-*
Palgrave Advances In Luxury	-*	-*	-*

Note: *data not available.
Source: own elaboration

The subject areas covered by the 48 scientific and/or academic documents were: Business, Management and Accounting (47); Psychology

(8); Social Sciences (7); Economics, Econometrics and Finance (6); Arts and Humanities (4); and Neuroscience (1).

The most quoted article was "Understanding luxury consumption in China: Consumer perceptions of best-known brands" by Lingjing & Yanqun (2012), with 275 quotes published in Journal of Business Research 1,530 (SJR), the best quartile (Q1) and with H index (195), this article investigates the "underlying motivations for luxury consumption among Chinese middle-class consumers by testing the relationships between psychological traits and attitudes toward the best-known luxury brands".

In Figure 4 we can analyze citation changes for documents published up to September 2024. The period ≤2014-2024 shows a positive net growth in citations with an R2 of 93%, reaching 213 citations in 2023.

Figure 4. Evolution of citations between ≤2014 and 2024.

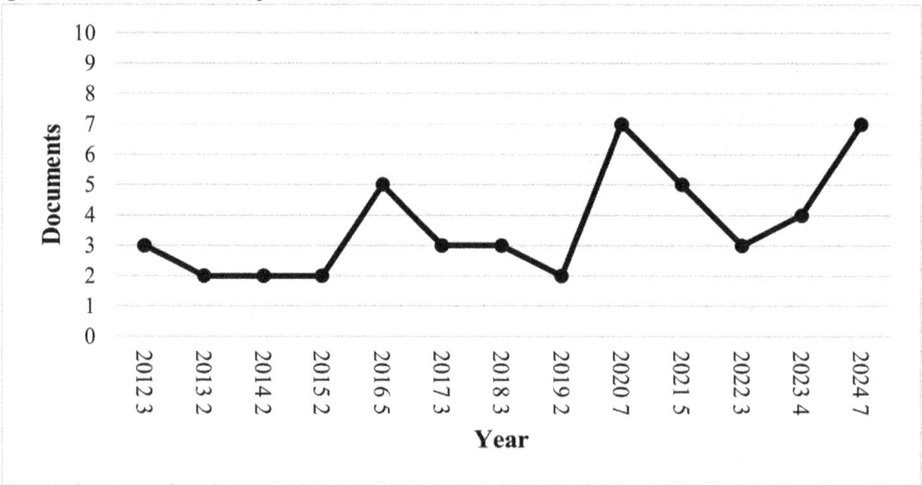

Source: own elaboration

The h-index evaluates the productivity and influence of published works by determining the maximum number of articles that have each garnered at least the same number of citations. From the total articles selected for the h-index, 17 were cited at least 17 times. Citations from all scientific and academic documents from the period up to 2014 through September 2024 totalled 1,232 across 48 documents, with 9 of those documents not being cited. Self-citations during the period up to 2013 through September 2023 amounted to 1,174.

The bibliometric analysis, using the main keywords "Luxury brands and their consumption: challenges and opportunities," revealed important indicators of the evolving landscape of scientific and academic information, as shown in Figure 5. These findings were generated using VOSviewer scientific software, focusing on the key search terms "Luxury," "Luxury Brands," and "Luxury Consumption."

Figure 5. network of all keywords

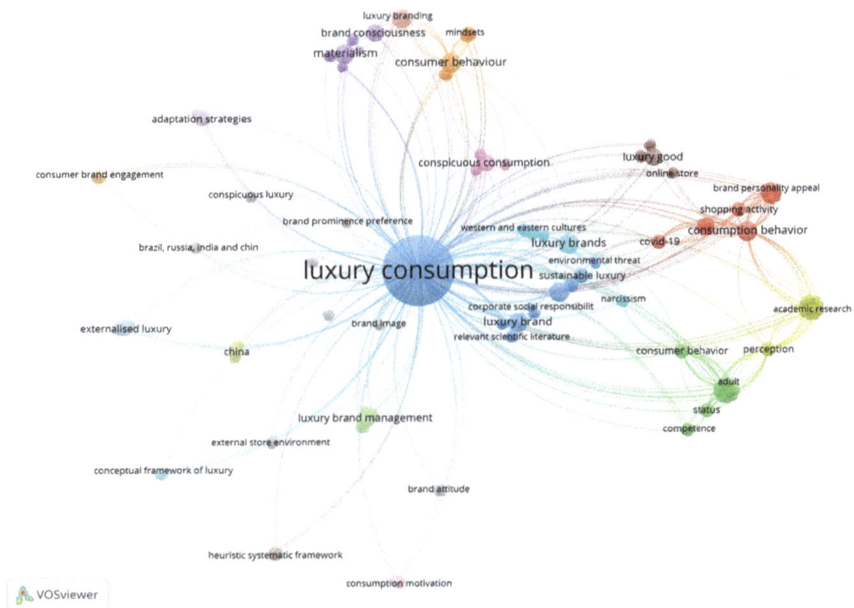

This study is based on scientific and academic literature exploring luxury brands and their consumption. Figure 6 provides a detailed view of the interconnected keywords, helping to highlight the relationships between keywords in each academic article. This approach helps identify the themes discussed in these studies and offers valuable insights into potential future research directions. Furthermore, Figure 7 showcases a substantial number of co-citations and clusters, strengthening the analysis of cited references.

Figure 6. network of Linked Keywords

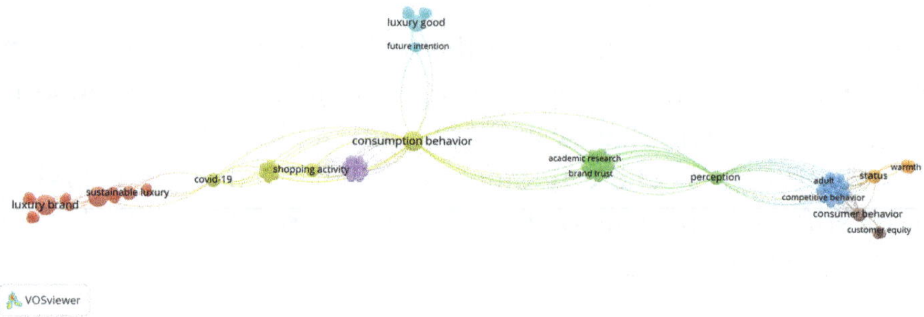

Figure 7. network of co-citation

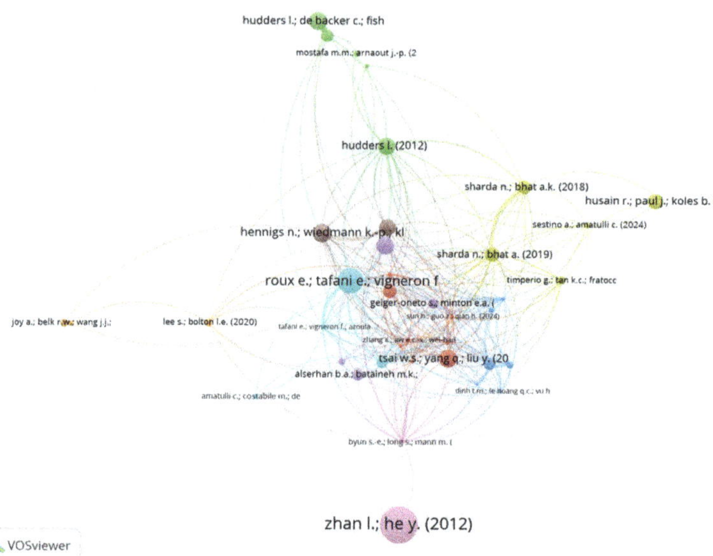

THEORETICAL PERSPECTIVES

Luxury products are often perceived as status symbols. They offer material value and emotional and social rewards. Consumers of luxury brands frequently engage in aspirational purchasing, where the desire to signal wealth, success, or personal identity becomes a key motivator (Alserhan et al., 2014). In addition, the evolving dynamics of the luxury market, influenced by shifts in generational values and technological advancements, have transformed how luxury brands are consumed and perceived. For instance, Wang (2022) indicates that contemporary luxury consumption is no longer primarily defined by the status-centric, wealth-related perspective due to the diluted definition of wealth and status. Traditionally, people acquired wealth and status by birth. However, these can be earned today. In addition, luxury brands have globalized and democratized their products, making them more affordable to larger populations worldwide (Zhang et al., 2024). This has significantly changed the exclusivity and high status previously associated with luxury. However, it has also created more opportunities for luxury brands to serve a larger consumer base and accommodate global cultural and economic aspects. Understanding consumption behaviors provides crucial insights into the challenges and opportunities luxury brands face in today's marketplace.

Conceptualizing Brand Luxury

Brand luxury is a multifaceted concept that transcends the functional aspects of a product and taps into the emotional, social, and psychological dimensions of consumer behavior. Unlike standard consumer goods, luxury brands symbolize more than quality; they represent a lifestyle, embody exclusivity, and convey status. Ma and Coelho (2024) describe luxurious products as unique, non-essential, high-priced items. They are purchased for their high levels of symbolic or emotional value to customers rather than necessity. The notion of luxury has evolved, shifting from its traditional association with the upper echelons of society to a broader, more accessible form of consumption (Timperio et al., 2016; Ma & Coelho, 2024). However, even as luxury becomes more democratized through digital platforms and global access, its core attributes of prestige, rarity, and superior craftsmanship remain intact. Luxury brands, therefore, must strike a delicate balance between maintaining an air of exclusivity while adapting to modern consumer expectations of inclusivity, transparency, and social responsibility.

Luxury consumption is driven by both external and internal motivations. Externally, luxury goods serve as status symbols, offering consumers a way to signal their wealth, success, or membership in a privileged social group (Soni & Kumar, 2024). Internally, luxury consumption satisfies emotional desires, fulfilling a need for self-expression, personal indulgence, and identity formation (Amatulli & Guido, 2012). The conceptualization of brand luxury is thus a dynamic interplay between the tangible attributes of the product, such as quality and craftsmanship, and the intangible, symbolic value it holds for consumers (Ma & Coelho, 2024). This complex relationship indicates the importance of understanding brand luxury from both a product-centric and consumer-centric perspective, as it effectively positions brands within an increasingly competitive and fragmented marketplace.

Product-Centric Brand Luxury

Product-centric brand luxury focuses on the intrinsic attributes of the product itself, emphasizing quality, craftsmanship, and attention to detail. In this perspective, the luxury of a brand is primarily defined by the physical characteristics of its offerings, such as the materials used, the precision of manufacturing, and the exclusivity of the design (Amatulli & Guido, 2012). Luxury products are often handmade or crafted using traditional techniques, which contribute to their uniqueness and justify their premium pricing (Ma & Coelho, 2024). The rarity of these products further improves their desirability. Consumers are willing to pay a higher price for something not mass-produced or widely available. In addition, the heritage and legacy of a brand can enhance the product's luxury appeal. Many luxury consumers are drawn to brands with a long-standing history of excellence and innovation.

A product-centric approach is essential in maintaining the perceived value of luxury brands in an era of increased competition and market saturation. While luxury brands must innovate and adapt to modern consumer preferences, they must also preserve the craftsmanship and quality that differentiate them from mainstream or fast-fashion products. This perspective is reflected in Aleem et al. (2024, p.145) perspective that luxury products are recognized for "high quality, offer authentic value, have a prestigious image, be worthy of a premium price and be capable of inspiring a deep connection with the consumer." In this sense, the product becomes a key touchpoint in the brand's luxury narrative, conveying its commitment to excellence and its position at the pinnacle of the market (Ma & Coelho, 2024). This focus on the product is especially important in industries like fashion, automobiles, and jewelry, where the physical attributes of luxury items are integral to their identity. However, as the luxury market evolves, the product-centric view must be complemented by a deeper understanding of the consumer's experience and emotional connection to the brand.

Consumer-Centric Brand Luxury

Consumer-centric brand luxury shifts the focus from the product's intrinsic qualities to the consumer's perceptions, experiences, and emotional engagement with the brand. This approach emphasizes the symbolic value that luxury products hold for consumers, where the consumption of luxury goods is often tied to self-expression, social identity, and personal fulfillment. Ma and Coelho (2024) categorize luxury consumption into three major categories: how consumers perceive luxury brands, their attitudes and emotions toward luxury, and the motivations behind and impacts of purchasing luxury goods. This context shows that luxury is not just about owning a high-quality product but about the emotional journey and experiential elements that come with it (Amatulli et al., 2022). For example, consumers may associate luxury brands with a sense of accomplishment, reward, or aspiration. This makes purchasing and owning such goods an important part of their self-concept (Chen et al., 2023). This perspective also highlights how luxury brands must align with the values and lifestyles of their consumers, particularly in a market increasingly driven by younger generations who prioritize experiences, authenticity, and sustainability.

In a consumer-centric model, the luxury brand's value lies in its relationship with its audience. The personalization of the customer experience, the exclusivity of services, and the brand's ability to create meaningful connections with its consumers all contribute to the perception of luxury

(Ma & Coelho, 2024). This has become even more critical in the digital age, where brands can no longer rely solely on product attributes to differentiate themselves. Social media, influencer collaborations, and direct engagement with consumers through digital platforms have created new opportunities for luxury brands to build emotional loyalty and deepen consumer connections (Amatulli et al., 2022). The consumer-centric approach also recognizes that luxury consumption is not homogeneous since consumers vary widely in their motivations and values. Understanding and responding to these diverse consumer needs allows luxury brands to stay relevant and thrive in an increasingly competitive and fragmented market.

Factors that Influence Luxury Consumption Behaviors

A complex interplay of external and internal factors shapes the decision to purchase luxury goods. Consumers are motivated by cultural values, social dynamics, personal desires, and the perceived attributes of luxury brands. Understanding these factors provides insights into the psychology of luxury consumption and helps brands align their strategies to resonate with their target audience.

Culture Dimensions

Cultural dimensions are crucial in shaping how consumers engage with luxury brands. Different cultures have varying values, norms, and expectations regarding luxury, influencing the meaning and appeal of luxury consumption (Joy et al., 2020). For instance, in some societies, luxury is strongly associated with status, wealth, and power, while in others, it may be more closely tied to self-expression or personal fulfillment (Amatulli & Guido, 2012). Individualistic cultures often emphasize luxury consumption to showcase personal success and uniqueness. In contrast, Tafani et al. (2024) explain that collectivist cultures may view it as a way to reflect group affiliation and social harmony. These cultural nuances help brands tailor their offerings and marketing strategies to align with the cultural context of their target markets.

Quality and Craftmanship

One of the defining features of luxury brands is the superior quality and craftsmanship associated with their products. Unlike mass-market goods, luxury items are often handmade or produced using high-quality materials and meticulous techniques, which justify their premium pricing (Nazarani & Suparna, 2021; König et al., 2016). Consumers who value quality and attention to detail are drawn to luxury products because they offer a sense of durability, uniqueness, and refinement. Lee and Bolton (2020) explain that the association of luxury with exceptional craftsmanship is a matter of physical product attributes and a key part of the brand's identity. Consumers are willing to invest in luxury goods because they perceive them as timeless pieces that reflect skill, artistry, and heritage, elevating the product beyond mere functionality.

Social Influence

Social influence is a powerful factor in luxury consumption. Individuals often make purchasing decisions based on the behaviors and preferences of their peers, social groups, or cultural elites. According to Ma and Coelho (2024), the desire to fit in or stand out within certain social circles can drive consumers to buy high-end products that signal their status and alignment with particular lifestyles. In addition, social media and influencers amplify this dynamic by showcasing luxury products as symbols of success, beauty, or sophistication (Donvito et al., 2016). This encourages consumers to emulate those they admire. The validation and admiration gained from owning luxury items, whether in-person or online, significantly impact consumer decisions, making social influence a key driver in luxury consumption.

Conspicuous Consumption

Conspicuous consumption refers to the practice of purchasing luxury goods to display wealth, status, and success publicly. For some consumers, owning luxury products is less about personal satisfaction and more about projecting a desired image to others (Jiang et al., 2021). This behavior is rooted in the idea that the visibility of one's possessions can enhance social standing and earn admiration or envy from peers (Zhang et al., 2024). The symbolic power of luxury brands as status symbols makes them particularly appealing to consumers who are motivated by social comparison and competition (Correia & Kozak, 2023). Conspicuous consumption is especially prevalent in societies where material wealth is a dominant indicator of success, and it drives demand for luxury brands that are highly visible and instantly recognizable.

Urge to Purchase

The urge to purchase luxury goods is often driven by emotional and psychological factors beyond rational decision-making. Ma and Coelho (2024) indicate that this impulse can be triggered by various stimuli, such as advertisements, social media influence, or limited-time offers that create a sense of urgency. The emotional allure of luxury, often associated with indulgence, reward, and pleasure, can lead consumers to make spontaneous or impulsive purchases (Joy et al., 2020). This urge is particularly strong when luxury brands are positioned as symbols of aspiration or personal achievement, tapping into consumers' desires for self-gratification (Mostafa & Arnaout, 2020). In addition, the fear of missing out (FOMO) on exclusive or limited-edition items can further fuel the urge to buy luxury products.

Life Satisfaction

Life satisfaction and luxury consumption are closely related. Consumers who feel content and fulfilled in their lives may seek luxury goods as a way to enhance their well-being or reflect their success (Hudders, 2012). For some consumers, purchasing luxury items is a reward for personal achievements, contributing to their overall sense of happiness and life satisfaction. On the other hand, Lim and Kim (2015) found that individuals who feel a lack of fulfillment or satisfaction in other areas of their lives may turn to luxury consumption to compensate for these emotional gaps. The relationship between life satisfaction and luxury consumption highlights the role of material goods in fulfilling psychological needs, whether through self-reward or symbolic validation.

Luxury Spending

Both external economic factors and individual psychological drivers influence luxury spending patterns. On a macroeconomic level, luxury consumption tends to rise in periods of economic stability and growth, where disposable income is higher, and consumers feel more confident in spending on non-essential items (Ma & Coelho, 2024). However, personal factors such as income, wealth, and financial security also dictate luxury spending behavior. Consumers with higher disposable incomes are more likely to consume luxury, viewing it as a normal part of their lifestyle (Kim et al., 2022). Conversely, Madinga et al. (2021) found that luxury spending can also occur among consumers with limited financial means who prioritize these purchases as a form of self-expression or status enhancement, even if it involves significant financial sacrifice. Understanding luxury spending habits helps brands develop pricing strategies and product lines that cater to different market segments.

Opportunities for Luxury Brand Consumption

The luxury market continues to evolve, with brands and consumers adapting to significant shifts in technology, cultural values, and economic trends. As luxury brands expand their reach and reimagine their offerings, several key opportunities have emerged that allow them to stay competitive, relevant, and aligned with consumer demands (Amatulli et al., 2016). From leveraging digital platforms and embracing sustainability to tapping into personal and emotional needs, luxury brands can explore various avenues to enhance their appeal and customer engagement. This section explores some of the most promising opportunities in luxury brand consumption.

Digital Transformation and E-Commerce

The digital transformation of the luxury market allows brands to reach and engage with a broader audience through e-commerce. Historically, luxury brands were cautious about moving online, fearing that the digital environment might undermine the exclusivity and personalized experience they were known for (Liu, 2023). However, the rise of sophisticated digital platforms and the growing preference for online shopping have shifted this paradigm. E-commerce allows luxury brands to offer an immersive shopping experience, from high-definition product images to virtual try-ons and personalized recommendations (Wang, 2022). This digital presence expands a brand's reach and provides an opportunity to connect with tech-savvy consumers who value convenience and innovation. Integrating advanced technologies such as augmented reality (AR) and artificial intelligence (AI) enables luxury brands to enhance the online shopping experience, making it as engaging and exclusive as in-store visits (Sestino & Amatulli, 2024). Moreover, digital channels enable brands to gather valuable consumer preferences and behavior data for more targeted and effective marketing strategies. Embracing e-commerce thus represents a significant opportunity for luxury brands to modernize their approach, attract new customers, and enhance their overall market presence.

Sustainability and Ethical Consumption

Sustainability and ethical consumption have emerged as critical factors influencing modern consumer behavior, particularly in the luxury sector. Consumers increasingly seek brands that align with their values as they become more environmentally and socially conscious (Amatulli et al., 2017). This shift presents a substantial opportunity for luxury brands to lead in sustainable practices and ethical sourcing. They can adopt eco-friendly materials, reduce carbon footprints, and ensure fair labor practices to differentiate themselves (Donato et al., 2020). This approach meets consumer demand for responsible consumption and enhances brand loyalty among those prioritizing sustainability. Dinh et al. (2024) explain that luxury brands can also leverage their commitment to sustainability as a key part of their brand narrative, promoting their efforts through transparent communication and certifications. This focus on ethical consumption can lead to long-term benefits, including improved brand reputation, increased customer trust, and a stronger competitive edge (Amatulli et al., 2021).

Embracing sustainability is a strategic opportunity to align with evolving consumer expectations and contribute to a more sustainable future.

Self-Gifting and Materialism

Self-gifting has become a notable trend in luxury consumption, allowing brands to tap into consumers' psychological motivations and personal rewards. Purchasing luxury goods as a form of self-reward or personal indulgence reflects deeper emotional and psychological needs (Aouina-Mejri et al., 2020). Consumers often engage in self-gifting to celebrate achievements, mark milestones, or simply as a form of self-care. This behavior is closely linked to materialism, where luxury items symbolize success, self-worth, and personal gratification (Kang & Park, 2016). Luxury brands can capitalize on this trend by positioning their products as ideal choices for self-gifting, emphasizing the emotional and psychological benefits of owning such items. Marketing strategies highlighting the personal satisfaction and self-affirmation associated with luxury purchases can resonate deeply with consumers seeking to enhance their well-being through material indulgence (Sun et al., 2024; Aouina-Mejri et al., 2020). In addition, creating personalized shopping experiences or offering exclusive limited-edition items can further appeal to consumers looking to reward themselves. Luxury brands that align with the self-gifting trend can foster stronger emotional connections with their customers and encourage repeat purchases driven by personal satisfaction.

Personalization and Customization

Personalization and customization represent a significant opportunity for luxury brands to enhance customer engagement and satisfaction. In a market where exclusivity and individuality are highly valued, offering bespoke products and personalized experiences can set a brand apart from competitors (Razmus et al., 2023). Consumers are increasingly seeking products that reflect their unique tastes, preferences, and identities, and luxury brands are well-positioned to meet this demand through customization options. Whether through tailored designs, personalized services, or exclusive experiences, customization allows consumers to engage more deeply with a brand and create products that hold personal significance (Sestino & Amatulli, 2024). This approach enhances the perceived value of luxury items and strengthens customer loyalty by providing a sense of ownership and exclusivity. According to Roux et al. (2017), luxury brands can leverage data-driven insights to offer personalized recommendations and experiences, further enhancing the customer journey. They can embrace personalization and customization to cater to evolving customer preferences and provide products and services that are unique and deeply aligned with individual desires and aspirations.

Brand Trust and Resonance

Building and maintaining brand trust is crucial for luxury brands, as consumers increasingly prioritize authenticity and transparency. Technological advancements have made information readily accessible. Consumer scrutiny has also increased. As a result, luxury brands must ensure that they uphold their promises of quality, exclusivity, and ethical practices (Husain et al., 2022). Trust is established through consistent product quality, transparent business practices, and alignment with consumer values. When luxury brands build trust, they develop long-term loyalty and emotional resonance with their audience (Jain & Schultz, 2017). This trust enhances the brand's reputation and encourages repeat purchases and customer advocacy. Furthermore, a strong brand resonance connects deeply with consumers emotionally, making them more likely to choose the brand over competitors (Kim & Chang, 2023). Luxury brands should focus on authenticity, transparency, and reliability to create lasting customer relationships and strengthen their position in a competitive market. In this context, brand trust becomes a valuable asset, differentiating luxury brands and driving sustained success.

Expansion into Emerging Markets

Emerging markets offer a promising opportunity for luxury brands to tap into new sources of growth and revenue. As economic development continues in regions such as Asia, Africa, and Latin America, the number of affluent consumers is rising, creating new demand for luxury goods (Tsai et al., 2013). Emerging markets often feature a growing middle class with increasing disposable income and a desire for premium products. Luxury brands can capitalize on this trend by tailoring their strategies to these regions' cultural preferences and values (Jiang et al., 2021; Ganesh et al., 2018). Localizing marketing efforts, establishing a retail presence, and partnering with regional influencers can help brands effectively connect with new consumers. Moreover, emerging markets often have younger, aspirational consumers who view luxury products as symbols of success and status (Zhan & He, 2012). Luxury brands that expand to these markets can diversify their customer base, increase their global footprint, and drive growth. Adapting to the unique characteristics of emerging markets and addressing local preferences are key to successfully capturing this new segment of consumers and sustaining long-term success.

Experiential Luxury

Experiential luxury represents a growing trend where consumers seek more than high-end products. They desire immersive and memorable experiences that enhance their overall lifestyle. This shift towards experiential luxury allows brands to create unique and engaging experiences beyond material goods (Sharda & Bhat, 2018). Consumers, particularly younger ones, increasingly value experiences such as exclusive events, luxury travel, and personalized services that provide emotional fulfillment and social value. Luxury brands can capitalize on this trend by offering bespoke experiences that align with their brand identity and resonate with consumers' aspirations (Husain et al., 2022). These experiences can range from private shopping events and customized travel itineraries to exclusive access to art exhibitions or cultural events. According to Lee et al. (2018), this opportunity allows luxury brands to create deeper emotional connections with their audience and enhance their overall luxury experience. This approach adds intangible value and promotes long-term customer loyalty and advocacy.

Resale and Circular Economy

The rise of the resale market and circular economy presents a unique opportunity for luxury brands to align with sustainability and extend the lifecycle of their products. As consumers become more environmentally conscious, they are increasingly interested in purchasing second-hand luxury items as a sustainable alternative to new products (Gasulla Tortajada et al., 2024). The luxury resale market is growing, with many consumers viewing pre-owned luxury goods as a way to access high-quality items at a more affordable price while contributing to a circular economy. Luxury brands can leverage this trend by embracing resale and offering official channels for pre-owned products, either through branded resale platforms or partnerships with third-party resellers (Alim et al., 2022). Participating in the circular economy can enhance their reputation for sustainability, appeal to eco-conscious consumers, and create new revenue streams (Byun et al., 2020). Promoting the durability and timelessness of luxury products is a key selling point in the resale market. This further reinforces the value of these items and aligns with broader trends towards responsible consumption.

Influencer and Celebrity Collaborations

Influencer and celebrity collaborations are an opportunity for luxury brands seeking to enhance their market presence and engage with consumers in a meaningful way. This trend capitalizes on the influence and reach of prominent figures to drive brand visibility, credibility, and desirability (Creevey et al., 2022). Influencers and celebrities often have substantial followings on social media platforms, and their endorsement can significantly impact consumer perceptions and purchasing decisions. Luxury brands can partner with well-known personalities to tap into their established networks and leverage their influence to promote products in an authentic and aspirational way (Moraes et al., 2019). These collaborations can take various forms, including exclusive product lines, co-branded collections, and promotional campaigns. For instance, a luxury brand might work with a high-profile fashion influencer to design a limited-edition collection or engage a renowned celebrity as the face of a new advertising campaign (Firouznia et al., 2024). Such partnerships generate buzz and media coverage and align the brand with the celebrity's or influencer's personal brand, enhancing the luxury brand's appeal among their fanbase.

Challenges of Luxury Brand Consumption

Consumer preferences and market dynamics are changing rapidly. As a result, luxury brands must navigate a range of obstacles to maintain their status and relevance. These challenges stem from internal brand considerations and external pressures in a rapidly changing marketplace. This section explores some of the key challenges faced by luxury brands today.

Meeting Consumer Expectations

One of the major challenges luxury brands face is consistently meeting their consumers' high expectations. Luxury consumers often demand high-quality products and an exceptional experience throughout their engagement with the brand (Liu, 2023). This includes everything from product design and craftsmanship to customer service, packaging, and after-sales support. The exclusivity and prestige associated with luxury brands increase consumer expectations to a point where even minor lapses can lead to dissatisfaction or loss of brand loyalty (Kang & Park, 2016). Consumers' instant access to online reviews and social media today means a single negative experience can significantly tarnish a brand's reputation (Firouznia et al., 2024). Besides, brands must maintain consistent quality and service across different regions and cultures. Balancing global presence with the localized, personalized experience expected by luxury consumers remains a critical challenge for luxury brands.

Complexity of Value in Luxury

Luxury brands face the challenge of defining and communicating the value of their products, which is more complex than mass-market goods. The value of luxury items often goes beyond the tangible aspects, such as quality and craftsmanship (Hennigs et al., 2015). It includes intangible elements like heritage, exclusivity, status, and emotional satisfaction.

These abstract qualities make it difficult for luxury brands to justify their high price points to consumers (Lee et al., 2018; Roux et al., 2017). For instance, a luxury item may be appreciated for its craftsmanship and the brand's history, limited availability, or the prestige it conveys to the owner. Lim and Kim (2015) explain that balancing traditional luxury elements with new consumer priorities can be challenging, as brands risk alienating their loyal customer base while trying to appeal to new audiences. The complexity of this value proposition requires luxury brands to maintain an intricate balance in their marketing and product offerings.

Exquisite Poverty

The concept of "exquisite poverty" presents a unique challenge in luxury brand consumption. It refers to a situation where consumers invest heavily in luxury products despite the potential for financial strain, often in pursuing status or social validation (Zhang et al., 2022). This phenomenon highlights the potential disconnect between the material benefits of owning luxury items and the emotional or financial toll they can take. Consumers may feel compelled to purchase luxury goods to fit in with a certain social class or to project an image of success (Wang et al., 2022). For luxury brands, this challenge lies in balancing the aspirational appeal of their products with responsible marketing that does not encourage overconsumption or contribute to financial distress among their target audiences (Hennigs et al., 2015). The rising awareness of this issue among consumers could push brands to reconsider how they position their products to ensure that they promote authenticity and long-term value rather than fleeting status symbols.

Changing Definition of Luxury

Traditionally, luxury was defined by attributes such as exclusivity, superior quality, and high price points. However, with shifting consumer preferences, especially among younger generations, the meaning of luxury has expanded. Today, luxury is increasingly associated with sustainability, personalization, and ethical consumption (Gasulla Tortajada et al., 2024). For instance, environmentally conscious consumers may prioritize luxury brands that promote sustainable practices or use eco-friendly materials, while others may seek products that are customizable to reflect their identities (Alim et al., 2022; Husain et al., 2022). This change presents a significant challenge for traditional luxury brands, which must now adapt their offerings and narratives to stay relevant (Wang, 2022). At the same time, brands need to be cautious not to dilute the essence of luxury by compromising on the exclusivity and prestige that originally defined their market. The changing definition of luxury requires brands to innovate continuously while staying true to the core elements that define their heritage and appeal.

CONCLUSION

Luxury consumption is a dynamic and multifaceted concept, influenced by various factors that present opportunities and pose challenges for brands. Luxury brands are uniquely positioned to offer high-quality products and an aspirational lifestyle deeply embedded in society's cultural, social, and economic aspects. However, maintaining this position requires constant innovation and adaptation to meet evolving consumer expectations, technological advancements, and shifting values. For luxury brands, the ability to meet these expectations while preserving their heritage and exclusivity is key to maintaining relevance in an increasingly competitive market.

Opportunities for growth in luxury brand consumption are plentiful. One is the rise of digital transformation and the expansion into e-commerce. These advancements allow luxury brands to reach new, tech-savvy consumers who value both convenience and exclusivity in their shopping experiences. The integration of sustainability and ethical consumption into the luxury market also reflects a broader societal shift toward responsible consumerism. This offers brands an opportunity to appeal to environmentally conscious consumers. Self-gifting, materialism, personalization, and customization present new avenues for brands to connect with consumers on a more intimate, individual level. Expanding into emerging markets further extends the potential for luxury brands to increase their global footprint. Experiential luxury and the rise of the resale and circular economy provide alternative avenues for growth, particularly as consumers seek unique, immersive experiences and more sustainable ways to engage with luxury goods.

Despite these opportunities, luxury brands face a series of challenges that must be navigated carefully. Meeting the ever-increasing consumer expectations is one of the most pressing issues. Today's consumers demand flawless products and an exceptional, personalized experience at every stage of their interaction with the brand. The complexity of value in luxury, where intangible factors such as status, heritage, and emotional fulfillment play a critical role in consumer perceptions, adds further pressure on brands to effectively communicate and justify their high price points. The concept of exquisite poverty places a responsibility on luxury brands to market their products ethically, without contributing to consumer financial strain. Additionally, the complexity of the meaning of luxury in contemporary society presents another challenge. Luxury brands must navigate these shifting values while remaining true to the elements that have historically defined their appeal.

In the field of luxury brands and their consumption, several theories and practical insights contribute to understanding consumer behavior, brand management, and market dynamics. Here are some of the key contributions: (i) Seminal work on conspicuous consumption highlights that consumers purchase luxury goods to signal wealth and status. This desire to showcase one's economic power drives the demand for high-end products. In practice, luxury brands leverage this by emphasizing exclusivity, craftsmanship, and heritage. Products often have limited availability or come with a hefty price tag, ensuring that they remain status symbols; (ii) Maslow's hierarchy places self-actualization at the top, where individuals seek personal fulfillment, including through aesthetics and luxury experiences. Luxury consumption can be seen as part of self-actualization, offering consumers a way to express their identity and individuality. Luxury brands tailor marketing messages that connect their products to personal growth, unique experiences, and lifestyle enhancement. For example, brands like Louis Vuitton or Chanel sell not just products but also narratives of personal empowerment and self-expression; (iii) Pierre Bourdieu introduced the concept of cultural capital, where taste plays a role in defining social status. In luxury consumption, individuals with high cultural capital often buy luxury goods that align with their refined tastes, distinguishing them from others. This is evident in the differentiation within luxury brands between mass luxury (accessible luxury for the broader affluent audience) and haute couture (exclusive luxury for the elite). Brands offer different tiers of products to cater to both the aspirational and the elite; (iv) The "8 Ps" framework of luxury brand management, proposed by Jean-Noël Kapferer and Vincent Bastien, expands on the traditional 4 Ps (Product, Price, Place, Promotion) by adding: a) Performance: The quality of luxury goods must be impeccable; b) Pedigree: Luxury brands often emphasize their heritage and history; c) Paucity: Luxury brands limit production to maintain exclusivity; d) Personalization: Offering customized products or services to clients. Luxury brands like Hermès, Rolex, and Rolls-Royce manage their brand strategy carefully, ensuring a balance between heritage and innovation, scarcity and accessibility; (v) Consumers of luxury products often seek authenticity, looking for brands that offer genuine craftsmanship and a rich history. Storytelling in luxury branding emphasizes narratives that communicate the heritage, craftsmanship, and values of the brand. Gucci, for example, connects its products with its historical origins, while at the same time tapping into modern cultural trends through collaborations with artists and influencers; (vi) Self-congruity theory states that consumers are drawn to brands that align with their self-image or the image they aspire to project. In luxury consumption, this symbolic alignment is crucial. Luxury brands focus on creating a brand image that reflects exclusivity, aspiration, and lifestyle. Consumers, in turn, purchase these products to reinforce or project an ideal self-image; (vii) Beyond the product itself, luxury brands are increasingly focusing on creating an immersive brand experience. Consumers today value the experiences associated with luxury, such as personalized services or exclusive events, as much as the physical products. Luxury brands like Tiffany & Co. or Dior curate exclusive brand experiences, from high-profile events to personalized shopping experiences, reinforcing a sense of exclusivity and prestige; (viii) The rise of digital channels has transformed luxury brand strategies. Brands are now engaging with consumers online while maintaining the exclusivity and high-end image through selective digital presence and limited online product offerings. Luxury brands use digital channels to reach younger, tech-savvy consumers without compromising their premium image. For instance, Chanel and Cartier engage with consumers on social media but offer limited e-commerce options, ensuring exclusivity; (ix) There is an increasing trend toward sustainable and ethical consumption, even in the luxury segment. Consumers are becoming more aware of the environmental and social impact of their purchases, leading to a demand for transparency and sustainability in luxury. Brands like Stella McCartney and LVMH are integrating sustainable practices into their value chain, promoting eco-friendly products and responsible sourcing while maintaining their luxury appeal; (x) In luxury consumption, social influence plays a critical role. Opinion leaders, celebrities, and influencers can drive luxury brand perception and desirability. Luxury brands collaborate with influencers and celebrities to enhance their visibility and desirability. For instance, collaborations with high-profile individuals like Beyoncé for Tiffany & Co. have amplified the brand's appeal.

These theories and practices highlight the intricate dynamics of luxury brand management and consumer behavior, reflecting the importance of exclusivity, heritage, authenticity, and evolving societal values in the luxury market.

The luxury sector is undergoing rapid transformation, driven by evolving consumer preferences, technological advancements, and global societal changes. Here are some of the promising future lines of investigation for luxury brands and their consumption:

(i) Investigating how luxury brands can balance sustainability with exclusivity and desirability. As consumers become more eco-conscious, luxury brands must explore sustainable practices, such as ethical sourcing, circular economy models, and eco-friendly production without losing their high-end appeal.

    Key Questions:

    - How do luxury consumers perceive sustainability in the context of exclusivity?
    - What strategies can luxury brands adopt to align sustainability with luxury?
    - Can sustainable luxury products maintain or even enhance brand desirability?

(ii) The shift to digital platforms for luxury consumption presents a new area for exploration. Luxury brands must innovate while maintaining exclusivity online, including omnichannel experiences, virtual reality (VR) shopping, and blockchain-based product authentication.

Key Questions:

- How can luxury brands create personalized, exclusive experiences online?
- What role will AI and machine learning play in enhancing the luxury consumer journey?
- How can blockchain ensure authenticity and fight counterfeit luxury goods?

(iii) The rise of the metaverse and virtual goods opens new opportunities for luxury brands to explore digital ownership, NFTs, and virtual fashion. Luxury consumption is expanding beyond physical products into digital assets and experiences.

Key Questions:

- What are the implications of virtual luxury goods on consumer behavior and brand loyalty?
- How will NFTs impact luxury brand value, especially in the art, fashion, and collectibles markets?
- Can virtual luxury experiences (VR showrooms, digital fashion) replicate or surpass the allure of physical luxury?

(iv) As luxury brands expand globally, understanding cultural differences in the perception and consumption of luxury is critical. Particularly, how luxury brands can tailor their offerings to diverse markets, such as China, India, Africa, and Latin America.

Key Questions:

- How do cultural factors influence luxury consumption in emerging markets?
- What are the cultural sensitivities luxury brands must consider in global marketing strategies?
- How can luxury brands localize their strategies while maintaining a global brand identity?

(v) The increasing number of cross-industry collaborations between luxury brands and sectors like tech, automotive, and sportswear offers fertile ground for research. These collaborations bring unique value propositions to consumers but also present challenges for brand identity.

Key Questions:

- How do collaborations between luxury and non-luxury brands impact consumer perception?
- What factors make cross-industry collaborations successful for luxury brands?
- How can collaborations maintain the luxury brand's exclusivity and prestige?

These future lines of investigation reflect the growing complexity and evolving nature of luxury consumption. As consumer expectations shift and technology reshapes retail, these research areas will help luxury brands navigate and define their roles in a rapidly changing market.

ACKNOWLEDGEMENTS

I would like to express gratitude to the Editor and the Arbitrators. They offered extremely valuable suggestions or improvements. The GOVCOPP Research Center of the University of Aveiro supported the author and ISCTE – Instituto Universitario de Lisboa and Business Research Unit (BRU-Iscte), Lisbon, Portugal

REFERENCES

Aleem, A., Loureiro, S. M. C., & Bilro, R. G. (2024). Luxury fashion consumption: A review, synthesis and research agenda. *Spanish Journal of Marketing - ESIC*, *28*(2), 144–164. DOI: 10.1108/SJME-06-2021-0105

Alim, M. A., Halkias, D., & Levitt, K. (2022). An integrative literature review of sustainable luxury fashion consumption through a circular economy business model. *International Journal of Competitiveness*, *2*(3), 234–247. DOI: 10.1504/IJC.2022.127403

Alserhan, B. A., Bataineh, M. K., Halkias, D., & Komodromos, M. (2014). Measuring luxury brand consumption and female consumers' religiosity in the UAE. Journal of Developmental Entrepreneurship, 19(2 C7 - 1450009). https://doi.org/DOI: 10.1142/S1084946714500095

Amatulli, C., Costabile, M., De Angelis, M., & Guido, G. (2017). Introduction: Sustainability in Luxury Branding. In Palgrave Advances in Luxury (pp. 1-5). Springer Nature. https://doi.org/DOI: 10.1057/978-1-137-60159-9_1

Amatulli, C., De Angelis, M., & Donato, C. (2021). The atypicality of sustainable luxury products. *Psychology and Marketing*, *38*(11), 1990–2005. DOI: 10.1002/mar.21559

Amatulli, C., De Angelis, M., Peluso, A. M., Soscia, I., Bagozzi, R. P., & Guido, G. (2016). How to Make Better Consumers in Luxury: The Role of Shame and Empathy. In Developments in Marketing Science: Proceedings of the Academy of Marketing Science (pp. 529-533). Springer Nature. https://doi.org/DOI: 10.1007/978-3-319-29877-1_108

Amatulli, C., de Angelis, M., & Spataro, V. (2021). Luxury and sustainability: How consumer-related characteristics may influence the effectiveness of different sustainability dimensions. *Micro and Macro Marketing*, *30*(1), 89–112. DOI: 10.1431/100338

Amatulli, C., & Guido, G. (2012). Externalised vs. internalised consumption of luxury goods: Propositions and implications for luxury retail marketing. *International Review of Retail, Distribution and Consumer Research*, *22*(2), 189–207. DOI: 10.1080/09593969.2011.652647

Aouina-Mejri, C., Partouche, J., & Mo, T. (2020). Self-Gift, Luxury Consumption, and Materialism: The Way to Happiness! An Abstract. In Developments in Marketing Science: Proceedings of the Academy of Marketing Science (pp. 211-212). Springer Nature. https://doi.org/DOI: 10.1007/978-3-030-39165-2_91

Byun, S. E., Long, S., & Mann, M. (2020). Drivers and dynamics of brand prominence preferences among the Chinese little emperors residing in the US. *Journal of Fashion Marketing and Management*, *24*(1), 66–82. DOI: 10.1108/JFMM-01-2019-0007

Chen, Q., Wang, Y., & Ordabayeva, N. (2023). The Mate Screening Motive: How Women Use Luxury Consumption to Signal to Men. *The Journal of Consumer Research*, *50*(2), 303–321. DOI: 10.1093/jcr/ucac034

Correia, A., & Kozak, M. (2023). Luxury product and brand purchasing behavior: A conceptual perspective. *Journal of Global Scholars of Marketing Science: Bridging Asia and the World*, *33*(3), 327–331. DOI: 10.1080/21639159.2020.1808823

Creevey, D., Coughlan, J., & O'Connor, C. (2022). Social media and luxury: A systematic literature review. *International Journal of Management Reviews*, *24*(1), 99–129. DOI: 10.1111/ijmr.12271

Dinh, T. M., Le Hoang, Q. C., Vu Hoang, H. D., Lao, T. K. L., & Pham, T. H. T. (2024). Do luxury brands have to trade off for sustainability? Journal of Global Fashion Marketing. https://doi.org/DOI: 10.1080/20932685.2024.2346845

Donato, C., De Angelis, M., & Amatulli, C. (2020). Sustainable Luxury: The Effect of Corporate Social Responsibility Strategy on Luxury Consumption Motivations. In Palgrave Advances in Luxury (pp. 123-146). Springer Nature. https://doi.org/DOI: 10.1007/978-3-030-25654-8_6

Donvito, R., Aiello, G., Godey, B., Pederzoli, D., Wiedmann, K. P., Hennings, N., . . . Chen, C. R. (2016). Are You Like Me? I Will Be Attached to You. Empirical Findings from an International Research About Consumer, Brand and Store Personality Congruence in Luxury Sector. In Developments in Marketing Science: Proceedings of the Academy of Marketing Science (pp. 295-304). Springer Nature. https://doi.org/DOI: 10.1007/978-3-319-24184-5_79

Firouznia, M., Brochado, A., & Wood, C. (2024). The Influence of Social Media Communications on Consumer-Brand Relationships in the Luxury Brand Context: A Bibliometric Review. Marketing Innovation Strategies and Consumer Behavior, 243-265. DOI: DOI: 10.4018/979-8-3693-4195-7.ch011

Ganesh, B. E., Jain, V., Belk, R., & Roy, S. (2018). Understanding the Luxury Consumption During Weddings in Southern India: An Abstract. In Developments in Marketing Science: Proceedings of the Academy of Marketing Science (pp. 75-76). Springer Nature. https://doi.org/DOI: 10.1007/978-3-319-99181-8_23

Gasulla Tortajada, E., Moreira, A. C., Duarte, P., & Silva, S. C. (2024). Circular Economy and Sustainability in Luxury Fashion Consumer Behavior: A Review and Research Agenda. *International Journal of Consumer Studies*, *48*(5), e13089. DOI: 10.1111/ijcs.13089

Haddaway, N. R., Page, M. J., Pritchard, C. C., & McGuinness, L. A. (2022). PRISMA 2020: An R package and Shiny app for producing PRISMA 2020-compliant flow diagrams, with interactivity for optimized digital transparency and Open Synthesis. *Campbell Systematic Reviews, 18*(2), e1230. DOI: 10.1002/cl2.1230 PMID: 36911350

Hennigs, N., Wiedmann, K. P., Klarmann, C., & Behrens, S. (2015). The complexity of value in the luxury industry: From consumers' individual value perception to luxury consumption. *International Journal of Retail & Distribution Management, 43*(10-11), 922–939. DOI: 10.1108/IJRDM-07-2014-0087

Hudders, L. (2012). Why the devil wears Prada: Consumers' purchase motives for luxuries. *Journal of Brand Management, 19*(7), 609–622. DOI: 10.1057/bm.2012.9

Husain, R., Paul, J., & Koles, B. (2022). The role of brand experience, brand resonance and brand trust in luxury consumption. *Journal of Retailing and Consumer Services, 66*, C7–C102895. DOI: 10.1016/j.jretconser.2021.102895

Jain, V., & Schultz, D. (2017). Structured Abstract: Discovering Relationships Between Indian Luxury Brands and Indian Consumers. In Developments in Marketing Science: Proceedings of the Academy of Marketing Science (pp. 1093-1099). Springer Nature. https://doi.org/DOI: 10.1007/978-3-319-45596-9_202

Jiang, L., Gao, H., & Shi, L. H. (2021). The effect of power distance beliefs on the inconspicuous versus conspicuous consumption of luxury accessories in China and the USA. *Journal of Marketing Management, 37*(15-16), 1459–1489. DOI: 10.1080/0267257X.2021.1913214

Joy, A., Belk, R. W., Wang, J. J., & Sherry, J. F. (2020). Emotion and consumption: Toward a new understanding of cultural collisions between Hong Kong and PRC luxury consumers. *Journal of Consumer Culture, 20*(4), 578–597. DOI: 10.1177/1469540518764247

Kang, Y. J., & Park, S. Y. (2016). The perfection of the narcissistic self: A qualitative study on luxury consumption and customer equity. *Journal of Business Research, 69*(9), 3813–3819. DOI: 10.1016/j.jbusres.2015.12.073

Kim, J., Park, J., & Septianto, F. (2022). The impact of socioeconomic status on preferences for sustainable luxury brands. *Psychology and Marketing, 39*(8), 1563–1578. DOI: 10.1002/mar.21671

Kim, S., & Chang, H. J. J. (2023). Mechanism of retail therapy during stressful life events: The psychological compensation of revenge consumption toward luxury brands. *Journal of Retailing and Consumer Services, 75*, C7–C103508. DOI: 10.1016/j.jretconser.2023.103508

König, J. C. L., Wiedmann, K. P., Hennigs, N., & Haase, J. (2016). The legends of tomorrow: A semiotic approach towards a brand myth of luxury heritage. *Journal of Global Scholars of Marketing Science: Bridging Asia and the World, 26*(2), 198–215. DOI: 10.1080/21639159.2016.1143155

Lee, S., Baumgartner, H., & Winterich, K. P. (2018). Did They Earn It? Observing Unearned Luxury Consumption Decreases Brand Attitude When Observers Value Fairness. *Journal of Consumer Psychology, 28*(3), 412–436. DOI: 10.1002/jcpy.1028

Lee, S., & Bolton, L. E. (2020). Mixed signals? Decoding luxury consumption in the workplace. *Journal of Business Research, 117*, 331–345. DOI: 10.1016/j.jbusres.2020.06.011

Lim, C. M., & Kim, Y. K. (2015). Luxe-Bargain Shopping: Relationships Among Perceived Values, Satisfaction, and Future Intentions. In Developments in Marketing Science: Proceedings of the Academy of Marketing Science (pp. 337). Springer Nature. https://doi.org/DOI: 10.1007/978-3-319-10873-5_193

Liu, Y. (2023). Digital Transformation in The Luxury Industry: Strategies, Challenges, And Opportunities. Highlights in Business. *Economics and Management, 23*, 650–656. DOI: 10.54097/xgftec52

Ma, M. H., & Coelho, A. (2024). Luxury Consumption Tendency: A Comparative Study Between Chinese and Portuguese Consumers. *Journal of Global Marketing*, •••, 1–19. DOI: 10.1080/08911762.2024.2350926

Madinga, N. W., Maziriri, E. T., Chuchu, T., & Mototo, L. (2021). The LGBTQAI+ community and luxury brands: Exploring drivers of luxury consumption in South Africa. *African Journal of Business and Economic Research, 16*(1), 207–225. DOI: 10.31920/1750-4562/2021/v16n1a9

Moraes, M., Gountas, J., Gountas, S., & Sharma, P. (2019). Celebrity influences on consumer decision making: New insights and research directions. *Journal of Marketing Management, 35*(13-14), 1159–1192. DOI: 10.1080/0267257X.2019.1632373

Mostafa, M. M., & Arnaout, J. P. (2020). What drives Kuwaiti consumers to purchase luxury brands? *International Review of Retail, Distribution and Consumer Research, 30*(1), 86–102. DOI: 10.1080/09593969.2019.1626259

Nazarani, M. R., & Suparna, G. (2021). The effect of luxury brand, brand image, and product quality on purchase intention. *American Journal of Humanities and Social Sciences Research, 5*(1), 290–295.

Razmus, W., Czarna, A. Z., & Fortuna, P. (2023). Luxury consumption and the dark triad of personality. *Journal of Business Research, 169*, C7–C114246. DOI: 10.1016/j.jbusres.2023.114246

Rosário, A., & Casaca, J. (2023). Relationship marketing and customer retention - A systematic literature review. *Studies in Business and Economics, 18*(3), 44–66. DOI: 10.2478/sbe-2023-0044

Rosário, A., Moreira, C., & Macedo, P. (2021). Competitive dynamics of strategic groups in the Portugueses Banking Industrry, Cuadernos de Gestión, 21(2), 1-15. ISSN: 1131-6837. DOI: <ALIGNMENT.qj></ALIGNMENT>10.5295/cdg.180975ac

Rosário, A. T., Lopes, P. R., & Rosário, F. S. (2023). Metaverse in Marketing: Challenges and Opportunities. In Khang, A., Shah, V., & Rani, S. (Eds.), *Handbook of Research on AI-Based Technologies and Applications in the Era of the Metaverse* (pp. 204–227). IGI Global., DOI: 10.4018/978-1-6684-8851-5.ch010

Roux, E., Tafani, E., & Vigneron, F. (2017). Values associated with luxury brand consumption and the role of gender. *Journal of Business Research, 71*, 102–113. DOI: 10.1016/j.jbusres.2016.10.012

Seo, Y., & Buchanan-Oliver, M. (2019). Constructing a typology of luxury brand consumption practices. *Journal of Business Research, 99*, 414–421. DOI: 10.1016/j.jbusres.2017.09.019

Sestino, A., & Amatulli, C. (2024). The challenge of integrating "intelligent" technologies in luxury shopping contexts: The role of brand personality appeal and consumers' status consumption orientation. *Journal of Retailing and Consumer Services, 76*, C7–C103488. DOI: 10.1016/j.jretconser.2023.103488

Sharda, N., & Bhat, A. K. (2018). Austerity to materialism and brand consciousness: Luxury consumption in India. *Journal of Fashion Marketing and Management, 22*(2), 223–239. DOI: 10.1108/JFMM-03-2017-0025

Soni, N., & Kumar, S. (2024). What drives new luxury consumption? Application of schema congruity theory and heuristic systematic framework. *Asia Pacific Journal of Marketing and Logistics, 36*(9), 2213–2233. DOI: 10.1108/APJML-04-2023-0319

Statista Market Insights. (2024). Luxury Goods – Worldwide. Statista. https://www.statista.com/outlook/cmo/luxury-goods/worldwide

Sun, H., Guo, Z., & Qian, H. (2024). The self on display: The impact of self-objectification on luxury consumption. *Psychology and Marketing*. Advance online publication. DOI: 10.1002/mar.22061

Tafani, E., Vigneron, F., Azoulay, A., Crener, S., & Zahid, A. (2024). The Influence of Culture and Gender in Luxury Brand Consumption: A Comparison Across Western and Eastern Culture Consumers. *Journal of International Marketing*. Advance online publication. DOI: 10.1177/1069031X241235629

Timperio, G., Tan, K. C., Fratocchi, L., & Pace, S. (2016). The impact of ethnicity on luxury perception: The case of Singapore's Generation Y. *Asia Pacific Journal of Marketing and Logistics, 28*(2), 217–233. DOI: 10.1108/APJML-04-2015-0060

Tsai, W. S., Yang, Q., & Liu, Y. (2013). Young Chinese consumers' snob and bandwagon luxury consumption preferences. *Journal of International Consumer Marketing, 25*(5), 290–304. DOI: 10.1080/08961530.2013.827081

Wang, Y. (2022). A conceptual framework of contemporary luxury consumption. *International Journal of Research in Marketing, 39*(3), 788–803. DOI: 10.1016/j.ijresmar.2021.10.010

Zhan, L., & He, Y. (2012). Understanding luxury consumption in China: Consumer perceptions of best-known brands. *Journal of Business Research, 65*(10), 1452–1460. DOI: 10.1016/j.jbusres.2011.10.011

Zhang, J., Chen, M., Xie, Z., & Zhuang, J. (2022). Don't fall into exquisite poverty: The impact of mismatch between consumers and luxury brands on happiness. *Journal of Business Research, 151*, 298–309. DOI: 10.1016/j.jbusres.2022.07.010

Zhang, X., Aw, E. C. X., Wei-Han Tan, G., & Ooi, K. B. (2024). The pursuit of splendour: A recipe of psychological motivations driving conspicuous luxury consumption. *International Journal of Retail & Distribution Management, 52*(5), 565–579. DOI: 10.1108/IJRDM-06-2023-0375

ADDITIONAL READINGS

Aleem, A., Loureiro, S. M. C., & Breazeale, M. (2024). Luxury fashion brand coolness: Niche versus mass cool. *Spanish Journal of Marketing - ESIC, 28*(2), 165–186. DOI: 10.1108/SJME-04-2023-0086

Aleem, A., Loureiro, S. M. C., & Martinho, J. (2024). From tech to touch: Self-concept and testimonials in AR try-on versus website. *Journal of Research in Interactive Marketing, 18*(3), 446–462. DOI: 10.1108/JRIM-07-2023-0222

Aleem, A., Loureiro, S. M. C., Schivinski, B., & Aguiar, M. (2024). What if utilitarian products are regarded as high-status? The moderate role of iconic and popular as two dimensions of brand coolness. *Journal of Marketing Communications, 30*(4), 508–528. DOI: 10.1080/13527266.2022.2152077

Kallevig, A., Ozuem, W., Willis, M., Ranfagni, S., & Rovai, S. (2022). Managing creativity in the age of data-driven marketing communication: A model for agencies to improve their distribution and valuation of creativity. *Journal of Advertising Research*, *62*(4), 301–320.

Loureiro, S. M. C., Jiménez-Barreto, J., Bilro, R. G., & Romero, J. (2024). Me and my AI: Exploring the effects of consumer self-construal and AI-based experience on avoiding similarity and willingness to pay. *Psychology and Marketing*, *41*(1), 151–167.

Loureiro, S. M. C., Rodrigues, A., & Martins, C. (2023). Love power: From identification to advocacy in fashion sportswear in the social media context. *Journal of Creative Communications*. Advance online publication. DOI: 10.1177/09732586231190267

Ozuem, W., Willis, M., Howell, K., Ranfagni, S., & Rovai, S. (2024). Examining user-generated content, service failure recovery and customer–brand relationships: An exploration through commitment-trust theory. *Internet Research*, *34*(3), 784–809.

Pasquinelli, C., Rovai, S., & Bellini, N. (2023). Linking place brands and regional innovation: Sustainable business strategies leveraging heritage. *Regional Studies*, •••, 1–17.

Rodrigues, M. B., Loureiro, S. M. C., & Romero, M. I. R. (2024). Luxury fashion games are so cool! Predicting awareness, perceived quality, and loyalty. *Journal of Retailing and Consumer Services*, *77*, 103668. DOI: 10.1016/j.jretconser.2023.103668

KEY TERMS AND DEFINITIONS

Artificial Intelligence: Is a set of technologies that enable computers to perform a variety of advanced functions, including the ability to see, understand and translate spoken and written language, analyze data, make recommendations, and more.

Augmented Reality: Is the integration of digital information with the user's environment in real time.

Brand Image: Refers to how audiences perceive your brand and how customers feel about their experience with you.

Brand Luxury: Are more than just the goods, because they give people the chance to live a dream.

Circular Economy: Is a model of production and consumption, which involves sharing, leasing, reusing, repairing, refurbishing and recycling existing materials and products as long as possible.

Conspicuous Consumption: Conspicuous consumption is the act of displaying ostentatious wealth.

Culture Dimensions: Cultural dimensions summarize the extent to which cultural groups are found empirically to differ from one another in terms of psychological attributes such as values, beliefs, self-construals, personality, and behaviors.

Ethical Consumption: Is all about choosing goods that are ethically sourced, ethically made and ethically distributed.

Influence Luxury: Individuals who influence consumer behavior towards luxury products and brands.

Sustainability: Is a social goal for people to co-exist on Earth over a long period.

Chapter 3
Luxury Fashion Industry Through the Lenses of Artificial Intelligence

Anubha Anubha
https://orcid.org/0000-0002-2719-7697
Jaipuria Institute of Management, Ghaziabad, India

ABSTRACT

Artificial Intelligence (AI) is transforming industries, and the luxury fashion industry is no exception. Its influence is stronger than ever, transforming design processes, boosting sustainability, and enhancing customer experiences. With AI tools like generative design platforms, brands can develop innovative designs faster and more efficiently. New technologies, like AI-powered design platforms and chatbots, are helping the fashion industry become more sustainable, personalized, and secure. The luxury fashion industry, known for its long history and exclusive appeal, is now using new technologies like artificial intelligence (AI) to improve customer experiences and to stay ahead of the competition. Accordingly, the present chapter aims to explore the potential of AI in improving the performance of luxury fashion brands. This study will bring significant insights to researchers and organizations by exploring the potential benefits of AI in transforming luxury fashion brands.

DOI: 10.4018/979-8-3693-8422-0.ch003

1. INTRODUCTION

The global luxury fashion market size was valued at USD 245.5 billion in 2023 and is projected to reach from USD 260.4 billion in 2024 to USD 410.6 billion by 2032, registering a CAGR of 5.8% during the forecast period (2024-2032) (Straits Research, 2024) There is hardly any industry which remains untouched by the potential of AI. AI offers more efficient and effective operational methods via innovative technology solutions to almost all industries including luxury fashion (Evangelista, 2019; Jin & Shin, 2021). The luxury fashion industry can get valuable consumer and industry data with the click of a mouse due to AI developments (Joy, et al. 2022; Jin & Shin, 2021). Global perspective is changing rapidly and in such a scenario, organizations that harness the power of AI will have competitive edge over others. Initially the luxury fashion industry was skeptical about the usage of AI as the industry is governed by artistic expression and exclusivity. However, later on, it become evident that the luxury fashion industry is having more substantial growth and revenue in the presence of AI solutions as compared to traditional approaches. The impact of AI in luxury fashion industry is huge ranging from enhanced design processes and improved customer experiences (Sestino, 2024). At the same time, AI is helping luxury fashion industry to attain sustainability (Nermain, Thanasi-Boçe, & Ali, 2022; Kong et al., 2021, Wang et al., 2021; Peric, 2024). At one end, AI makes trend forecasting easier for luxury fashion industry, at another, it helps in personalized marketing contributing to more memorable customer experiences (Sestino, 2024). AI has ensured a more secured, personalised and sustainable future for luxury fashion industry on account of many innovative applications like AI driven chatbots and generative design platforms (Hofmann, Jacob, & Pizzingrilli, 2022; Sharma, 2023; Ozuem & Willis, 2024). AI does not only impact the design and production of luxury fashion but has a significant influence on its shipping, marketing and sales. The impact of AI is not limited to only design and production of luxury fashion but it extends to its shipping, marketing and sales. In a nutshell, AI has transformed the luxury fashion industry by altering the way luxury fashion is designed, developed, transported, marketed and sold (Luce, 2018; Dennis, 2019; Nermain, Thanasi-Boçe, & Ali, 2022). For example, AI tools like Stable

Diffusion, Uizard and Midjourney enable luxury fashion designers to develop multiple design variations without the need to developing a physical one. These tools enable them to develop innovative ideas and to envisage preferences of consumers (Jin & Shin, 2021). AI-driven automation has made the production of luxury fashion more efficient and sustainable (Arantes & Barbosa Costa, 2024; Hofmann, Jacob, & Pizzingrilli, 2022). Further, AI enables luxury fashion marketers to access the huge amount of data based on algorithms using which they can optimize their marketing strategies and offer personalised shopping experience to their customers (Kong et al., 2021; Wang et al., 2021; Sestino, 2024; Sharma, 2023). Thus, AI is changing the luxury fashion industry by improving how designs are made, supporting sustainability, and enhancing customer experiences (Luce, 2018; Dennis, 2019; Nermain, Thanasi-Boçe, & Ali, 2022; Arantes & Barbosa Costa, 2024).

Although, luxury fashion brands were initially slow to embrace digital changes, they are now quickly becoming leaders in innovation. Technologies, like Blockchain and AI are helping luxury marketers with important business goals, such as making supply chains more transparent, protecting intellectual property, personalizing customer experiences, and using data to predict trends (de Boissieu, et al., 2021; Evangelista, 2019; Sestino, 2024; Ozuem, & Willis, 2024). By adopting these technologies, luxury brands are adding value and improving efficiency. The luxury fashion industry is experimenting with AI in a variety of ways, from Maison Meta's AI Fashion Week 2023 to Casablanca's AI-powered SS23 campaign. AI helps luxury fashion designers to suggest novel designs based on the review of past collections. Collina Strada, for instance, combined conventional methods with AI-generated designs to produce a novel Spring/ Summer 2024 collection (Srivastava, 2024; Sahota, 2024). Calvin Wong, a professor from Hong Kong, introduced AiDA, the first designer-led AI system, in 2022. It can create complex designs from simple sketches and colour combinations. AI tools like Google's DeepDream and IBM's Watson have also helped designers create innovative materials and patterns. Indian designers such as Falguni & Shane Peacock and Gaurav Gupta have incorporated IBM's Watson into their fashion show planning and production process, drawing inspiration from historical themes (Long, 2024). Hence, AI has become a part and parcel of today's luxury fashion industry. Accordingly, the present study aims to explore the potential of AI in improving the performance of luxury fashion brands. This study will bring significant insights to researchers and organizations by exploring the potential benefits of AI in transforming luxury fashion brands. The chapter will also discuss the constraints that a luxury fashion marketers may face in the implementation of AI. To attain these objectives, this study aims to answer the following research questions:

> RQ1: How the challenges of luxury fashion industry can be mitigated by AI?
> RQ2: What are the various applications of AI in today's luxury fashion industry?
> RQ3: What are the potential benefits of AI that has brought transformation in the luxury fashion industry?
> RQ4: What are the various AI techniques and technologies available for luxury fashion industry?
> RQ5: What are the challenges in the adoption of AI by the luxury fashion industry?

2. AI AND LUXURY FASHION INDUSTRY: WHAT CHALLENGES CAN BE MITIGATED?

In the luxurious world of high-end brands, a subtle transformation is happening, where the enduring appeal of fashion meets the precise capabilities of artificial intelligence (AI). This collaboration is not only changing the way luxury brands function but is also redefining what exclusivity and personalization mean (Ozuem & Willis, 2024). From Louis Vuitton to Gucci, AI is emerging as the invisible craftsman, altering the fabric of luxury. However, such a transformation did not happen instantly, rather a series of challenges were the driving force behind such transformation. This section discusses these challenges. It also deliberates the role of AI in mitigating these challenges:

Figure 1. Challenges of Luxury Fashion Industry

The first challenge in front of luxury fashion is that the fashion trends are changing very rapidly. Due to this luxury fashion marketers fail to estimate the preferences of their consumers. This volatility may result in waste due to over production leading to excess inventory. The next challenge faced by the luxury fashion retailers is the poor management of inventory. Either, they face the situation of excess inventory or they find themselves in the position of stockouts. The first situation brings them loss as their capital is tied to the inventory whereas the second situation results in lost sales. The next challenge faced by the luxury fashion marketers is to offer customised products and experiences. Such a personalised approach in the absence of sophisticated methods is very expensive and time taking. Marketing and advertising are another big challenge faced by these luxury fashion marketers. In an era characterised by the digitalised world with multiple social media platforms, it becomes quite challenging to target the correct audience with effective and efficient marketing strategies. The next big challenge before luxury fashion industry is to embrace sustainability (Peric, 2024). Ethical manufacturing practices with waste reduction and use of sustainable materials are the most significant challenges which today's luxury fashion industry is dealing with (Arantes & Barbosa Costa, 2024; Hofmann et al., 2022). As consumer behaviour is influenced by many factors, demand forecasting becomes a big challenge for luxury fashion marketers (Savolainen, 2023; Ozuem & Willis, 2024). The most significant challenge in front of the luxury fashion marketers is counterfeiting which weaken their real brand integrity.

The luxury fashion industry can address these challenges with the power of that has become a significant tool to solve problems in the luxury fashion industry. AI driven applications can offer more growth to luxury fashion marketers that help them to get success in such a highly competitive luxury fashion industry. AI enables luxury fashion marketers in making data driven decisions to improve their competitiveness. AI can also help them in waste reduction which will enhance their productivity and will make them more competitive. AI powered techniques enable luxury fashion marketers to keep abreast with the latest trends (Savolainen, 2023). Luxury fashion industry cannot ignore the possibilities offered by artificial intelligence making it their integral part.

3. APPLICATIONS OF AI IN LUXURY FASHION INDUSTRY

The role of AI has become huge in luxury fashion industry due to its wide applications. This section discusses these applications in luxury fashion industry in detail:

3.1 Luxury Fashion Business Operations

Trend Forecasting and Buying

Historically, qualitative methods including street fashion, pop culture, fashion influencers and runway shows like Paris Fashion week and Lakme fashion week are used by fashion trendsetters and forecasters to forecast trends (Srivastava, 2024; Savolainen, 2023; Long 2024). They even use to consider the impact of culture of a particular country and geopolitics on the world to predict trends (Srivastava, 2024; Savolainen, 2023).

Today, Artificial intelligence (AI) tools can predict luxury fashion trend more accurately, efficiently and effectively by analysing the vast data-sets from sales, global influences, fashion shows, search engines, social media and fashion blogs (Savolainen, 2023; Long, 2024). Now a days, luxury fashion retailers use various AI enabled platforms like Heuritech & Trendalytics that leverage "data from search, social media, and Google Trends to predict emerging and peaking trends"[1]. These platforms enable luxury fashion retailer to be more competitive. Let us discuss the example of Tommy Hilfiger that capitalises on 'Reimagine Retail'- a project that utilises AI to rationalize the design process according to the prevailing trends[2].Using social media listening, this project comprehends how former products have been received and make alterations in the upcoming designs of luxury fashion products (Gera, 2018). It is very essential for luxury fashion retailers like Tommy Hilfiger that they should be able to predict the items going to be in vogue in the near future to remain competitive in the market (Boileau, 2023; Guha et al., 2021; Chandramana, 2022).

Merchandising and Analysis

Effective merchandising is necessary for luxury fashion marketers to boost sales and at the same time to engage the customers. Great merchandising is an ever-staying trend. It becomes more important in luxury fashion industry on account of its being dynamic and digital. Right merchandising is a key to success and a tool to have competitive advantage over other competitors in the industry. Merchandising requires many skills with respect to fabulous retailing like expertise on products, price, place, promotion, quantities, timing, replenishment and consumer behaviour (Barrelet et al., 2023). AI tools enable luxury fashion marketers to decide effective & efficient merchandising. AI makes it easier to plan products and manage inventories. It looks at a lot of data, including sales numbers, past trends, and customer preferences, to decide on the best product mix, quantity, and store placement. This data-driven strategy prevents inventory from expiring, reduces overstock, and ultimately increases the profitability of luxury fashion enterprises. For instance, brands like Louis Vuitton have integrated AI into its operations which is primarily used for inventory management, demand forecasting and exclusivity of products present in the market (Kochar, 2024).

Product Design and Development

The design and development of luxury fashion products is being benefitted by the various AI applications. These AI application as such motivate fashion designers to improve design patterns by optimizing resource utilization (Tan & Luhrs, 2024). These tools enable them to develop virtual prototypes of fashion items in different styles and colours (Almaz, et al., 2024; Tan & Luhrs, 2024). These virtual prototypes can be easily tested with the target group of customers using Generative AI. Based on their feedback, improvements and changes could be incorporated without actually developing physical items. This could save crores of rupees which were earlier wasted in the absence of AI. This will also accelerate the process of developing final products.

Companies like Zara, H&M and Tommy Hilfiger had restructured their entire supply chain processes recently to keep up with the market demands. The big retailers are now able to get the latest apparel into the markets within weeks of production but the majority of items take anywhere between six to twelve months which leads to a lot of lost sales. For example, Tommy Hilfiger has joined hands with the IBM and Fashion Institute of Technology (FIT) on a project called "Reimagine Retail". This collaboration equips Tommy Hilfiger with AI powered skills to speed up its supply chain process. With this alliance, FIT students were given access to the AI facilities of IBM which include access to their computer vision (CV) labs, natural language understanding (NLU) and deep learning methods specifically trained on fashion data. Using these techniques, FIT students created entirely novel designs by incorporating 15000 product images of Tommy Hilfiger, 1 million patterns collected from fabric sites and 6 million publicly images, collected from varied fashion shows (Dar, 2018)

Styling and Visual Merchandising

Physical presentation of products is known as merchandising which is also termed as "Silent Selling" (Akhilendra & Aravendan, 2023; Razak et al. 2021). Merchandising is very important to portray the right image of company's product with the trendy look of online and offline store. Furthermore, the progress in self-service retailing has further fueled the growth of visual merchandising. Visual merchandising helps luxury fashion marketers to appeal, engage, and stimulate their consumers for actual purchase. For luxury fashion industry, the efficient merchandising is a way to improve their store image which will have a favourable impact on their retail revenue. Presenting products in an eye-catching manner is the aim of visual merchandising, both online and in physical locations. AI helps by suggesting styles and enhancing the visual presentation. AI analyses consumer preferences and fashion trends to recommend product styling and display. This makes shopping more engaging and personalized for customers by offering virtual try-ons, product pairings, and outfit recommendations (Ozuem & Willis, 2024).

3.2 Luxury Fashion E-Commerce

Customised Recommendations for Luxury Fashion

In luxury fashion e-commerce, offering personalized product recommendations is key to improving the shopping experience (Kuksa, Kent, & West, 2024; Karlsson & Ryberg, 2024). AI algorithms are crucial in this process, as they analyze a shopper's browsing and purchase history. By understanding a customer's tastes and past choices, AI can recommend products that are highly relevant to them (Chung et al., 2020; Landim et al., 2022). These personalized suggestions increase the likelihood of a purchase and build customer loyalty by showing that the brand values the shopper's unique style and preferences (Evangelista, 2019; Khamoushi & Kalantari, 2025)

Search for Luxury Products

The most critical aspect in online retail of luxury fashion is searching a product effectively and efficiently. Here is where AI play a pivotal role via AI- powered search engines which helps luxury fashion customers to search products more accurately and more efficiently. Natural Language Processing (NLP) making this task easier for customers (Piris & Gay, 2021; Liu, Shin, & Burns, 2021). One more technique that is useful for product search is visual search (Beeg, 2021; Liu et al., 2021). Now a days, consumers can search a particular product by uploading its picture. This can also be done by narrating a product in the form of words. More often, the voice commands are also used by customers to search a product of their own choice. All this is happening because of AI.

Customer Service

The success of e-commerce lies in offering exceptional customer service. Such an exceptional service can be offered effectively using AI enabled solutions (Evangelista, 2019). AI-driven solutions contribute significantly to this goal. Today's luxury fashion e-commerce is equipped with chatbots and virtual assistant that can provide effective solutions to customer inquiries (Chung et al., 2020; Landim et al., 2022). These virtual assistants and chatbots not only inform customers about various products but also help them in shopping (Shahzad et al., 2024; Chung et al., 2020; Landim et al., 2022). They are able to handle almost all common queries. These chatbots act as guides in the purchase process of customers (Sidlauskiene, Joye, & Auruskeviciene, 2023; Landim et al., 2022). They can even offer personalised guidance based on customised preferences of luxury customers (Chung et al., 2020; Landim et al., 2022). All these will help luxury fashion marketers in improving efficiency. They can reduce their response time in handing queries of customers which will enhance customer satisfaction, the much-needed attribute in luxury fashion industry (Prusova, 2023; Zeng, Vignali, & Ryding, 2023).

3.3 Luxury Fashion Retail

Enhancing Shop Floor Efficiency

AI can help luxury fashion marketers in optimization of time at the shop floor level. This is possible as AI is able to analyse the foot fall in a particular retail store and also at a particular time period. AI is capable of tracking the busiest shopping time and hence can help luxury fashion retailers to meet the growing demand of busiest period by allocating more employees.

Integrated Shopping Experience

Today's luxury customers do not purchase only in online store but in offline too. Sometimes, they are using both channels to close a purchase (Karadag & Erdogmus, 2020; Lim, 2024). These customers aspire for a seamless experience in both the modes (Amatulli et al., 2021). Any kind of discrepancies in terms of price, size, variant, promotion, discount or availability will lead to unpleasant shopping experience. Such a seamless shopping experience can be delivered with the help of AI (Lim, 2024; Pangarkar, Arora, & Shukla, 2022). AI helps luxury fashion retailers in integrating their online stores with physical ones to offer omnichannel experience to their customers in shopping so that they get personalised and consistent products, services, offers and communication across all touchpoints including both offline and online (Silva, Silva, & Dias, 2024; Lim, 2024). Such an integrated shopping experience enhances customer engagement (Ozuem & Willis, 2024). French luxury fashion house Chanel offers omnichannel experience using marketing experts and technology (Peishan & Yufei, 2021; Kochar, 2024; Kaushik, 2025).

Virtual Try-Ons

Virtual try-ons have radically changed the face of luxury fashion retail. It helps the customers to reduce their future cognitive dissonance as now with the help of virtual reality (VR) (Loureiro, 2023; Song & Bonanni, 2024).), they can see whether a particular fashion item will suit on them before they purchase an actual one. This is possible as VR technology generates a 3D illustration of the customer so that they can view how they will look with a luxury fashion product (Loureiro, 2023; Song & Bonanni, 2024).). This will improve customer satisfaction and the incidence of product return will be fewer (Prusova, 2023).

3.4 Luxury Fashion Marketing

Personalised Ad Campaigns

Luxury fashion marketing has become more efficient with its integration with AI that is capable to track customer browsing and transaction history on luxury fashion's app or website. Accordingly, luxury fashion marketers can launch personalised ad campaigns to motivate the customers to purchase (Jain, Paul, & Shrivastava, 2021). These personalised ad campaigns include showing the advertisements of those fashion items which they earlier searched on app or website but did not purchase (Misra, Aggarwal, & Taneja, 2024; Jain et al., 2021). AI is capable of showing only relevant ads as per the customers' interests which may increase the likelihood of final purchase. AI can track the preferences, likings and history of customers transaction on a particular luxury fashion app or website, and can offer customised rewards and discounts.

3.5 The AI and Luxury Fashion Supply Chain

Supply Chain Optimization

In any fashion industry, supply chain optimization is needed as it has direct influence on the overall cost of delivering fashion items (de Boissieu et al., 2021; Shen et al., 2020). Further, such a supply chain optimization also has an impact on the timely delivery of fashion products (Bindi et al., 2023; Shen et al., 2020). AI by analysing diverse datasets of inventory levels and past sales is able to manage inventory more efficiently. AI is capable of forecasting demand precisely which enables luxury fashion marketers to rationalise the overall logistics processes. For instance, with AI, luxury fashion marketers will be in a position to decide not only the inventory level but when to reorder (Shen et al., 2020). This's will save them from both, overstock and stockout. Such development in supply chain management improves the overall efficiency of luxury fashion marketers and helps them in the minimization of waste. All this in turn will improve the profitability of luxury fashion marketers (de Boissieu et al. 2021; Karaosman et al., 2020).

Automated Product Tagging

AI has streamlined operations in the luxury fashion sector via AI powered automated product tagging[3] which has also helped in enhancing customer satisfaction and experiences (Choi et al., 2023; Varshney, 2023). This transformation has enabled the luxury fashion retailers to tag their fashion items with precision that makes the information on each item consistent. It has got twin advantages. First, it enables luxury fashion marketers to manage inventory efficiently by deciding the optimal level of stocks[4]. Second, it facilitates the accurate product search and recommendation for luxury fashion consumers. All this leads to greater customer experience.

Fashion Sustainability and Ethical Sourcing

Consumers are becoming more ecofriendly and are more inclined towards products which are produced ethically including luxury fashion (Lim et al., 2023; Kong et al., 2021, Wang et al., 2021). This is true with luxury fashion items. Before purchasing and consuming, consumers are interested in knowing the origins of the products they want to purchase, here is where AI helps. With the AI- driven solutions, the origins of fashion items can be known with accuracy by tracing the supply chain. AI can also help consumers in verifying the ethical and sustainable claims made by luxury fashion supplier (Lim et al., 2023; Arantes & Barbosa Costa, 2024; Hofmann et al., 2022) AI can also help in monitoring whether that marketer follows fair labour practice. AI powered solutions can also be used to see whether luxury fashion marketers are complying with environmental regulations or they are sourcing material responsibly. If not, the AI can assist luxury fashion marketers in selecting the sustainable materials via its algorithms. These algorithms can access the impact of materials on environment and hence can help luxury fashion marketers meet the demand of sustainable luxury fashion (Lim et al., 2023; Arantes & Barbosa Costa, 2024; Kong et al., 2021; Wang et al., 2021, Hofmann et al., 2022).

Further, fabric waste reduction is the most crucial sustainability goal of luxury fashion marketers, here the contribution of AI driven waste reduction strategies is manyfold (Peric, 2024; Kong, Witmaier, & Ko, 2021). AI can analyse the quality control data and can surface the inefficiencies in real time basis. This will help luxury fashion manufacture in knowing the areas where wastes can be eliminated. This all will assist them in reducing the negative impacts of their manufacturing processes on environment.

3.6 Luxury Fashion Personalization

Personalised Marketing

With the advancement of technology, the today's marketers are opting for personalised marketing including luxury fashion marketers (O'Rourke et al., 2025). The role of AI is very huge in implementing such personalised marketing as AI can access the purchase and browsing history of customers including their geographical location (Choi et al., 2022; Kaur, Singh, & Singh, 2022; Tam & Lung, 2025). The marketers can develop highly personalized marketing campaigns using AI driven techniques. These campaigns are then targeted to the specific customers. All these campaigns are tailored as per the customer preferences via AI enabled tools (Clerkin, 2024). AI can share target ads, personalised emails and recommend fashion items based on consumer's past purchases, interests apart from their search and browsing history. By such type of personalization, AI and VR have revolutionised the luxury fashion industry and in turn, has offered immersive shopping experiences that has led to increased customer engagement (Kochar, 2024; O'Rourke et al., 2025). Such an engagement amplifies the likelihoods of conversions, and improves brand loyalty (Khamoushi & Kalantari, 2025).

Customized Fashion Items

Luxury fashion brands have been progressively embracing digital technology like AI to enhance customer experience, loyalty and engagement (Kong et al., 2021; Wang et al., 2021; Choi et al., 2022; Khamoushi & Kalantari 2025). Among various applications, luxury fashion industry is using AI to offer customization to attract their customers to purchase customised fashion brand and thus, improves their satisfaction (Choi et al., 2022; Brunello, 2024; Moreau et al., 2020).

With the help of AI techniques, it is now possible for customers to customise their own clothing and fashion accessories on luxury fashion websites. Consumers are now empowered to select from a vast array of personalise alternatives, like they can choose, fabric, colour and can design their own luxury fashion clothes5. All this could be possible due the generative AI. Now, with AI, consumers can develop one of its kind products that fits well with their persona, lifestyle and interests. Furthermore, AI tools and techniques enable consumers to customize professionally designed fashion items using online toolkits based on limited design decisions (Choi et al., 2022). For instance, Louis Vuitton offers customization to its customers to personalize leather items using their initials[6]. Similarly, Louis Vuitton's fine jewellery collections (Maison) can also be personalised by engraving a customised message, though this service is available exclusively in Louis Vuitton stores[7]. With the help of AI, the process of customization for users. becomes user friendly and seamless. It serves as a guide to choose the design and offers visual preview of the final item before it is actually made for them. All these improves customer experience (CX) and provides scope for self-expression in luxury fashion (Choi et al., 2022; Brunello, 2024; Moreau et al., 2020). Therefore, AI powered customization is a win-win situation for both the luxury fashion marketers and luxury customers. For marketers it is a tool to differentiate their products whereas for customers it offers increased satisfaction (Choi et al., 2022).

3.7 Fashion Security

Anti-Counterfeiting

E-commerce, though offers huge opportunities and advantages for luxury fashion industry, however, it has also paved the path of counterfeiting the luxury fashion items (Lee, & Kim, 2024). The counterfeiting leads not only brings economic damage to luxury fashion industries but results in huge brand losses too (Alhosni, Masengu, & Tsikada, 2025; Alhosni et al., 2024; Ciurel, 2024). The damage is not limited to the luxury fashion industry, but goes far away to impact the luxury customers who in their pursuit of have an exclusive authentic masterpiece, end up with a fake item. Therefore, the luxury fashion companies are leveraging latest technologies like AI to identify and detect counterfeit luxury fashion items (Lamptey, Mensah, & Korankye, 2024; Thanasi-Boçe, AL-Issa, & Ali, 2022). The AI algorithms can verify the authenticity of a luxury fashion item by analysing various attributes of an item including its image and label (Lee, & Kim, 2024). AI technologies like predictive analytics, image recognition, natural language processing and machine learning can safeguard luxury fashion marketers against such fraudulent activities. This will also improve the trust of customers in the luxury fashion brands (Ziccardi, 2020; Lall, 2023; Lamptey et al., 2024; Thanasi et al., 2022; Lee & Kim, 2024).

Loss Prevention: Luxury Fashion Industry Perspectives

As the problems of theft and loss has increased exponentially in luxury fashion retail outlets, the luxury fashion marketers are trying to harness the power of AI and blockchain to overcome this (Reydellet, 2022; Singh et al., 2024). Given their high-value inventory they carry, these outlets are more prone to robberies and thefts (Shalev, 2024). Luxury fashion brands are known for their exclusivity and craftmanship and the most important is the attached high price tag which leads to more losses in terms of theft and shoplifting (Reydellet, 2022; Singh et al., 2024). Further, luxury fashion items are produced in limited quantities only, emphasizing the worth of each item. As each exclusive item has a very premium price tag attached to it, the loss or theft of even a single item can have a noteworthy bearing on the luxury fashion retailer's profit and revenue (Shalev, 2024). A study was conducted by communication specialists to know the prevailing rate of theft and losses of Luxury fashion retailers with total annual sales of $ 3.1 billion in South America, USA, Europe, Africa and Asia (ibid.). The results revealed that 62 percent of respondents anticipated that by the year 2026, losses due to the theft of luxury fashion items will increase significantly (ibid.). When inquired about the current level of security, most of them were quite satisfied with the kind of security systems in their retail outlets, however, only 24 percent claimed it to be excellent. Further, this study also revealed that most of them will increase their spending to have more better security in their retail outlets. Accordingly, it is expected that there will be an increase of 28- 40% in the overall security budget of luxury fashion retailer by the year 2026 (Reydellet, 2022). They would like to have more secured AI and blockchain enabled security solutions which will help them to prevent the abovementioned losses on account of theft (Singh et al., 2024). These AI powered surveillance systems use advanced computer vision technology which can help luxury fashion marketers enhance overall security in their retail outlets. As such, this technology helps them in the monitoring the store environment in real time, hence they are in a position to track any suspicious move in their store. On identifying anything suspicious like unauthorized access to restricted areas or shoplifting, these AI algorithms can promptly alert store security personnels (Reydellet, 2022; Singh et al., 2024). Further, the luxury fashion marketers can also harness the power of RFID (Radio Frequency Identification) to reduce the cases of theft and losses (Shalev, 2024). RFID when combined with AI offers extraordinary benefits to retailers against these types of theft and losses, for example via tracking an item or predicting the purchaser behaviour[8].

Loss Prevention: Luxury Fashion Consumers' Perspectives

The luxury fashion brands are doubling down on the usage of trendy technologies like AI and blockchain to deliver a real impact on their profitability and brand equity (Hirschmiller, 2024). For this, they are collaborating with *Vaultik*, a luxury fintech which is actually a bank for customers' luxuries[9]. This platform is based on *triple-factor authentication.* Vaultik works directly via Web3 protocols and includes the Hedera distributed ledger[10]. Vaultik works with Avata[11], an insurtech firm to deliver integrated insurance protection and certificates of ownership. Let us understand this with an example. The luxury watch market have started using Vaultik's technology. London-based start-up NIX Time, a specialist of customised watches from famous luxury brands like Rolex has partnered with Vaultik. Vaultik, in this partnership, has powered digital product passports with integrated insurance. These passports include original serial number of each watch, additional warranty and authentication. This technology has safeguard luxury customers against their major challenge of loss and theft of their luxury possession (Hirschmiller, 2024) .

4. THE INTEGRATION OF AI WITH LUXURY FASHION DESIGN CYCLE

AI can make significant contribution in the fashion design process by optimizing resource allocation, automating repetitive tasks and providing data-driven insights that enable luxury fashion marketers improve decision making and efficiency. The integration of AI with the fashion design cycle of luxury fashion businesses can offer more responsive, customised and innovative design cycle. This section discussed the role of AI in handling the various challenges which are faced by luxury Fashion businesses during various stages of the design process.

The first and foremost challenge during the fashion design lifecycle is to identify the sources from where the inspiration of novel luxury fashion designs come and how these luxury fashion businesses can keep up with the swiftly shifting trends and changing preferences of luxury consumers (Srivastava, 2024; Savolainen, 2023; Cabigiosu & Cabigiosu,2020). In this case, AI based applications can analyse online forums, fashion blogs and social media to detect evolving trends (Akhtar, 2023). AI using machine learning and programming can understand the various preferences of customers based on their search and purchase history, hence help luxury fashion brands in market research. The second challenge during fashion design lifecycle is related with concept development (Zhang & Liu, 2024; Arda, 2024). Sometimes, it becomes very challenging to convert abstract concepts into tangible ideas[12]. Here also, the AI powered tools can develop various iterative designs on the basis of input keywords (Almaz, et al., 2024; Tan & Luhrs, 2024). Thus, AI enables luxury fashion designers to explore various design options and refine their designs before selecting the final one. The third major challenge before luxury fashion brands is to streamline the process of product design with in the stipulated time, as launching the new luxury fashion items as first mover always provide luxury fashion brands a competitive edge over others. Now, the role of AI becomes more crucial as it can handle all the repetitive tasks using automation[13]. A recent study revealed that around 62 percent of UX designers are using AI to automate repetitive tasks that improves productivity (Bharadwaj, 2025; Patel, et al., 2024). This allows luxury fashion designers to concentrate on creativity which differentiate luxury from mass fashion items[14] (Adeleye, 2024; Sreenivasan & Suresh, 2024).

The next pressing challenge for luxury fashion designers in the design cycle is to identify the right material that that fits within the decided budget and also aligns with the design vision[15,16]. AI powered algorithms can analyse the historic data related with the availability, costs and performance of material performance and accordingly, can suggest appropriate opportunities, enabling the luxury fashion designers to take optimal decision with reference to material selection[17]. The next challenge in the design cycle, faced by luxury fashion marketers is to control the quality (Dou, 2024). This task is also simplified by AI. AI powered computer vision systems can assure the quality in the design cycle by identifying inconsistencies and defects using automate quality control (Nair & Trivedi, 2024). One more significant challenge faced by luxury fashion marketers is to develop engaging marketing contents. The integration of AI with the luxury fashion will also help in creating those marketing contents which will help them in attracting and engaging luxury customers (Rathore, 2017; Robinson, 2023).

The most pressing challenge before luxury fashion producers is balance the speed of production as per the demand without compromising the quality (Patil, 2024; Alam, Islam, & Shil, 2023) This challenge is also mitigated by AI as AI powered applications can minimise disruptions in the production process and improve the overall production efficiency. This is due to the fact that AI helps luxury fashion manufactures in optimizing resource allocation and optimising production scheduling (Dalal et al., 2024; Del Gallo et al., 2023). Lastly, the AI helps luxury fashion industry to understand and respond the feedback given by their customers efficiently and effectively by analyzing the eWOM, online reviews, comments and feedback (Bilal et al., 2024; Rane, Choudhary, & Rane, 2024). Through sentiment analysis AI enables luxury fashion marketers to analyse the success of their fashion items (Oc et al., 2023; Rane, Choudhary, & Rane, 2024).

5. BENEFITS OF AI-LUXURY FASHION INTEGRATION

The integration of luxury fashion with AI has resulted into numeration benefits which these luxury brands can pass to their customers to engagement and win them. The benefits of AI in the luxury fashion industry are varied and comprehensive. From improving customer experience to enhancing customer satisfaction to optimizing operational efficiency to reducing costs and to promoting sustainability, AI has turned out to be indispensable for luxury fashion industry striving to succeed in a progressively dynamic and hyper competitive market. This section discusses these benefits in detail.

The first advantage is that with the help of AI, luxury fashion marketers are able to personalise their luxury items as per the needs and preferences of customers (Kuksa, Kent, & West, 2024; Karlsson & Ryberg, 2024). This feature of personalisation is more appealing to customers who wants to be distinguished and classy in their social circle (Karlsson & Ryberg, 2024). Secondly, with AI integration, inventory management becomes very efficient for luxury fashion marketers (Boileau, 2023; Guha et al., 2021). They now can manage their inventories optimally. Based on the sales data, AI is able to predict with accuracy the items which are currently trendy among luxury customers. Based on this, the luxury marketers can align their inventory level strategically with the prevailing trend (Chandramana, 2022). Thirdly, as mentioned above also that, AI offers tremendous help to luxury fashion designers in the design process (Harreis et al.,2023; Zhang & Liu, 2024; Arda, 2024). AI assists as a valuable design collaborator. AI can suggest various design based on current trends and preferences which will make luxury fashion designer to access without actually developing one (Hughes, Zhu, & Bednarz, 2021). This will save millions of rupees which designers invest in developing varied designs in the absence of AI tools (Yan et al., 2022). Fourthly, AI enables luxury fashion industry to achieve their goal of sustainability by optimising their production and supply chain processes (Peric, 2024; Kong, et al., 2021; Bindi et al., 2023; Shen et al., 2020). AI also helps luxury fashion marketers to be more efficient in producing luxury fashion items by identifying the areas where improvement can be made and wastes can be reduced (Abdelmeguid et al., 2024). Next, the integration with AI enables luxury fashion manufactures to remove inconsistencies and defects in their processes. AI powered quality control techniques help luxury marketers to have high product quality which increases customer satisfaction and loyalty (Kong et al., 2021). Among other benefits, offered by AI, the most significant ones are keeping abreast with the latest trends which makes luxury fashion marketers more competitive.

6. AI TOOLS AND TECHNIQUES IN LUXURY FASHION

The luxury fashion industry is harnessing the power of AI to transform its operations, from design to customer experience to customer loyalty. Accordingly, this section provides a snapshot of the tools and techniques of AI which have been embraced by the luxury fashion industry to be more competitive.

The first such technology is Machine Learning (ML). The machine learning algorithms can recognize the objects and patterns within the images. Hence, ML can be used in identifying colours, and styles which may be in trend. Further, it may help in the detection of counterfeit fashion items. The second is Natural Language Processing (NLP) that can analyse the textual data efficiently and effectively. Hence, luxury fashion industry can apply NLP to comprehend customer online reviews, sentiments and feedback which then, can be used to improve further. The third technique is Reinforcement learning that is used in recommendation systems. Reinforcement learning is also used by virtual stylists. In this technique, AI gets input from customer interactions and uses this to offer more relevant product and style suggestions.

The next useful technology is computer vision which makes visual search possible. Customers can search for a particular luxury fashion items either by uploading a picture or by taking a picture. Computer vision analyses the picture to identify the product characteristics and accordingly, recommend visually similar items. This simplifies the product search process for luxury customers. The next significant technology is Virtual try-ons which enables to try an item virtually which otherwise was possible only after actual purchase. Computer vision powers augmented reality (AR) and virtual reality (VR) applications that allows luxury customers to try and experience any fashion item including makeup, accessories and clothing without purchasing them actually (Idrees, Vignali, & Gill, 2023; Mekonnen, 2024).This technology can offer may realistic simulation based on body size and shape. Product recognition is another valuable technique of AI which helps in categorising the luxury fashion items. This technique can also automate the product tagging. Such an automated categorisation and tagging enables luxury fashion industry to manage their inventory more accurately and efficiently. They become more capable to list their products on e-commerce platforms swiftly.

One very important AI technique useful for luxury fashion sector is Automated authentication which can detect counterfeit fashion items accurately. Hence, authenticity of luxury fashion items can be ensured fully. One such AI powered solution is Entrupy[18] that ensures authenticity based on a database of counterfeit and genuine item images. The next important technique is Generative AI which includes techniques like Generative Adversarial Networks (GANs). GANs has two sets of neural networks—a generator and a discriminator. These two sets collaborate and develop distinctive and innovative fashion styles, designs, and sometimes even whole outfit.

Deep learning is one more valuable technique of AI which can be used by luxury fashion industry to forecast fashion trends. Deep learning enables luxury fashion marketers to predict emerging fashion trends by analysing influencer activities along with social media posts. Deep learning models use neural networks and can identify the colours, styles and other design elements that have high possibility of becoming a trend. Using this, the luxury fashion marketers can make data-driven decisions based on budding customer preferences. This makes them more competitive in the ever-dynamic fashion landscape. AI driven Chatbots and virtual assistants have offered the next level comfort to the luxury fashion retailers in providing quick and prompt solution to the queries, questions and complaints of luxury customers. One emerging AI technology is Voice commerce which enables customers to use voice commands for searching and purchasing luxury fashion items.

7. CHALLENGES IN THE ADOPTION OF AI BY LUXURY FASHION INDUSTRY

Each technology has two aspects: positive and negative. Though positive side of AI can be understood with its contribution in luxury fashion industry which ranges from predicting trends to refining product design to improving operations to reducing wastes to optimizing supply chain to personalization industry and many more. However, it has negative aspects too which is related with the challenges of AI adoption. This section details these challenges.

The adoption of AI in luxury fashion industry poses significant challenges which are worth mentioning. The first one being data security and privacy. As AI is based on extensive data which causes a possibility that some sensitive information may be leaked. Furthermore, the AI recommendation system works on consumers' personal details, search and purchase history which may raise the concern of their security. This may make people worry about keeping that data private and secure. Complying with data protection laws, like India's Digital Personal Data Protection Act (DPDPA) is really difficult for luxury while using AI (Anubha, 2024). To obey the DPDPA and similar laws and regulations globally, luxury fashion businesses require a deep understanding of these laws and regulations to assure and ensure that their AI systems maintain data privacy rights of their consumers. Second significant challenge is cybersecurity risk. AI algorithms collect and process a huge amount of personal data which may be a soft target for cyberattacks (Walters & Novak, 2021). Therefore, keeping the personal data safe and secured with in AI powered luxury fashion industry is an enduring challenge. Hence, luxury fashion marketers need to invest a significant amount in cybersecurity measures. They should continuously monitor their systems for any possibility of any vulnerability. The luxury fashion marketers need to be agile to the changing tactics of cybercriminals (Dou, 2024).

8. CONCLUSION

The influence of Artificial Intelligence (AI) in the luxury fashion industry is stronger than ever, transforming design processes, boosting sustainability, and enhancing customer experiences (Abdelmeguid et al., 2024). With AI tools like ML, NLP, GANs and Deep learning, brands can develop innovative designs faster and more efficiently. New technologies, like AI-powered design platforms and chatbots, help luxury fashion industry to become more sustainable, personalized, and trendy in dealing with the hypercompetitive luxury landscape. By using AI luxury fashion industry can become more agile and can predict trends accurately. This chapter

discusses how luxury fashion industry is using AI to be more efficient and effective. This chapter explores the challenges of luxury fashion marketers which can be mitigated by the use of AI. This chapter also discusses various AI applications in luxury fashion industry, for example product design and development, styling and visual merchandising, customised recommendations for luxury fashion, enhancing shop floor efficiency, omnichannel shopping experience, virtual try-ons, personalised marketing, supply chain optimization, automated product tagging, anti-counterfeiting, to name few. This chapter also details AI tools and techniques that are currently being used by luxury fashion marketers to be more competitive. The chapter, in the end, discusses the potential challenges of AI which must be addressed carefully by the luxury fashion industry in order to capitalize on the power and potential of AI.

REFERENCES

Abdelmeguid, A., Tsironis, G., Afy-Shararah, M., Tsagarakis, K. P., & Salonitis, K. (2024). Insights into sustainability and circular economy trends in luxury fashion: A LinkedIn topic modelling study. *Cleaner and Responsible Consumption*, *15*, 100228.

Adeleye, I. O. (2024). The Impact of Artificial Intelligence on Design: Enhancing Creativity and Efficiency. *Journal of Engineering and Applied Sciences (Asian Research Publishing Network)*, *3*(1), 1–13.

Akhilendra, S. P., & Aravendan, M. (2023). A review on apparel fashion trends, visual merchandising and fashion branding. *Intelligent Information Management*, *15*(3), 120–159.

Akhtar, W. (2023). Digital innovations in fashion: mapping the co-evolution of technological advancements and fashion industry. *JYU Dissertations*. DOI:DOI: 10.13140/RG.2.2.25336.66564

Alam, M., Islam, M. R., & Shil, S. K. (2023). AI-Based predictive maintenance for US manufacturing: Reducing downtime and increasing productivity. *International Journal of Advanced Engineering Technologies and Innovations*, *1*(01), 541–567.

Alhosni, R. H., Masengu, R., & Tsikada, C. (2025). Leveraging Artificial Intelligence to Detect Counterfeit Luxury Products: A Systematic Review of Machine Learning, Natural Language Processing, and Image. In Masengu, R., Tsikada, C., & Garwi, J. (Eds.), *AI and Machine Learning Applications in Supply Chains and Marketing* (pp. 237–256)., DOI: 10.4018/979-8-3693-6760-5.ch010

Almaz, A. F., El-Agouz, E. A. E. A., Abdelfatah, M. T., & Mohamed, I. R. (2024). The Future Role of Artificial Intelligence (AI) Design's Integration into Architectural and Interior Design Education is to Improve Efficiency, Sustainability, and Creativity. *Sustainability, and Creativity*, *3*(12), 1749–1772.

Amatulli, C., De Angelis, M., Sestino, A., & Guido, G. (2021). Omnichannel shopping experiences for fast fashion and luxury brands: An exploratory study. In *Developing successful global strategies for marketing luxury brands* (pp. 22–43). IGI Global.

Anubha, A. (2024). RegTech: An Effective Way to Regulatory Compliance. In *Integrating RegTech Solutions for Industry 4.0* (pp. 1-14). IGI Global.

Arantes, L., & Barbosa Costa, S. (2024). Culture and Sustainability in the Luxury Market: An Analysis of Adaptive Practices in Global Contexts. *Journal of International Consumer Marketing*, •••, 1–15.

Arda, D. (2024). *Investigation of Artificial Intelligence Tools in Design Process and Creativity* (Master's thesis, Middle East Technical University).

Barrelet, D., Chapman, M., Eklöw, E., Huang, J., & Yankelevich, H. (2023). Great merchandising never goes out of fashion. Available at: https://www.mckinsey.com/industries/retail/our-insights/great-merchandising-never-goes-out-of-fashion#/

Beeg, L. (2021). Revolutionising E-Commerce: Visual Search for Improved User Experience. Available at: https://blog.marketingblatt.com/en/visual-search-how-to-use-this-trend-for-your-marketing

Bharadwaj, C. (2025). 10 Ways AI is Disrupting Traditional Digital Product Design Practices, Available at: https://appinventiv.com/blog/ai-in-product-design/

Bilal, M., Zhang, Y., Cai, S., Akram, U., & Halibas, A. (2024). Artificial intelligence is the magic wand making customer-centric a reality! An investigation into the relationship between consumer purchase intention and consumer engagement through affective attachment. *Journal of Retailing and Consumer Services*, *77*, 103674.

Bindi, B., Bandinelli, R., Fani, V., & Pero, M. E. P. (2023). Supply chain strategy in the luxury fashion industry: Impacts on performance indicators. *International Journal of Productivity and Performance Management*, *72*(5), 1338–1367.

Boileau, W. (2023, October). AI in Retail Industry: Valuable Insights that Improve Profitability and Drive Growth. In *Proceedings of the Future Technologies Conference* (pp. 332-342). Cham: Springer Nature Switzerland.

Brunello, S. (2024). Assessing the effects of customization on luxury perception and consumer behaviour: Analysing the differences between in-store and online shopping experiences. University of Padova. Ph.D. Thesis., Retrieved from https://thesis.unipd.it/h andle/20.500.12608/54514/, Retrieved February 09, 2025, from.

Cabigiosu, A., & Cabigiosu, A. (2020). An overview of the luxury fashion industry. *Digitalization in the luxury fashion industry: Strategic branding for Millennial consumers*, 9-31.

Chandramana, S. (2022). AI in Retail Industry: Reshaping Shopping Experience and Business Profitability. *Ushus Journal of Business Management, 21*(4).

Choi, D., Seo, Y., Septianto, F., & Ko, E. (2022). Luxury customization and self-authenticity: Implications for consumer wellbeing. *Journal of Business Research, 141*, 243–252.

Choi, W., Jang, S., Kim, H. Y., Lee, Y., Lee, S. G., Lee, H., & Park, S. (2023). Developing an AI-based automated fashion design system: Reflecting the work process of fashion designers. *Fashion and Textiles, 10*(1), 39.

Chung, M., Ko, E., Joung, H., & Kim, S. J. (2020). Chatbot e-service and customer satisfaction regarding luxury brands. *Journal of Business Research, 117*, 587–595.

Ciurel, A. (2024). Opportunities and challenges for fashion companies in the use of blockchain technology as a tool for product authentication and counterfeit prevention. *Journal of Intellectual Property Law and Practice*, jpae104. https://doi.org/DOI: 10.1093/jiplp/jpae104

Clerkin, A. (2024). Personalize luxury brand marketing strategies for lasting loyalty. Available at: https://www.luxurydaily.com/personalize-luxury-brand-marketing-strategies-for-lasting-loyalty/

Dalal, S., Lilhore, U. K., Simaiya, S., Radulescu, M., & Belascu, L. (2024). Improving efficiency and sustainability via supply chain optimization through CNNs and BiLSTM. *Technological Forecasting and Social Change*, *209*, 123841.

Dar, P. (2018). IBM, Tommy Hilfiger and FIT Using AI to Collaborate and "Reimagine Retail". Available at: https://www.analyticsvidhya.com/blog/2018/01/ibm-tommy-hilfiger-fit-using-ai-collaborate-reimagine-retail/

de Boissieu, E., Kondrateva, G., Baudier, P., & Ammi, C. (2021). The use of blockchain in the luxury industry: Supply chains and the traceability of goods. *Journal of Enterprise Information Management*, *34*(5), 1318–1338.

Del Gallo, M., Mazzuto, G., Ciarapica, F. E., & Bevilacqua, M. (2023). Artificial intelligence to solve production scheduling problems in real industrial settings: Systematic Literature Review. *Electronics (Basel)*, *12*(23), 4732.

Dennis, C. A. (2019). AI-generated fashion designs: Who or what owns the goods. *Fordham Intellectual Property. Media & Entertainment Law Journal*, *30*, 593.

Dou, J. (2024). The application and challenges of artificial intelligence in the fashion and luxury industry. *Applied and Computational Engineering*, *42*, 90–96.

Evangelista, P. N. (2019). Artificial intelligence in fashion: how consumers and the fashion system are being impacted by AI-powered technologies. https://hdl.handle.net/10589/167521

Guha, A., Grewal, D., Kopalle, P. K., Haenlein, M., Schneider, M. J., Jung, H., & Hawkins, G. (2021). How artificial intelligence will affect the future of retailing. *Journal of Retailing*, *97*(1), 28–41.

Harreis, H., Koullias, T., Roberts, R., & Te, K. (2023). Generative AI use cases in fashion. Available at: https://www.mckinsey.com/industries/retail/our-insights/generative-ai-unlocking-the-future-of-fashion

Hirschmiller, S. (2024). How Luxury Brands Are Leveraging Blockchain and AI For Business Impact. Available at: https://www.forbes.com/sites/stephaniehirschmiller/2024/02/12/how-luxury-brands-are-leveraging-blockchain-and-ai-for-business-impact/

Hofmann, K. H., Jacob, A., & Pizzingrilli, M. (2022). Overcoming growth challenges of sustainable ventures in the fashion industry: A multinational exploration. *Sustainability*, *14*(16), 10275.

Hughes, R. T., Zhu, L., & Bednarz, T. (2021). Generative adversarial networks–enabled human–artificial intelligence collaborative applications for creative and design industries: A systematic review of current approaches and trends. *Frontiers in Artificial Intelligence*, *4*, 604234.

Idrees, S., Vignali, G., & Gill, S. (2023). Sustainable Mass-Customisation Business Model by Incorporating Virtual Fitting Room Marketing Tools in Fashion E-Commerce: A Study of the Luxury Unstitched Market. In *The Garment Economy: Understanding History, Developing Business Models, and Leveraging Digital Technologies* (pp. 259–285). Springer International Publishing.

Jain, G., Paul, J., & Shrivastava, A. (2021). Hyper-personalization, co-creation, digital clienteling and transformation. *Journal of Business Research*, *124*, 12–23.

Jin, B. E., & Shin, D. C. (2021). The power of 4th industrial revolution in the fashion industry: What, why, and how has the industry changed? *Fashion and Textiles*, *8*(1), 31.

Joy, A., Zhu, Y., Peña, C., & Brouard, M. (2022). Digital future of luxury brands: Metaverse, digital fashion, and non-fungible tokens. *Strategic Change*, *31*(3), 337–343.

Karadag, G. M., & Erdogmus, I. E. (2020). Digitization of luxury fashion by building an omnichannel dream. In *Managing customer experiences in an omnichannel world: Melody of online and offline environments in the customer journey* (pp. 233–256). Emerald Publishing Limited.

Karaosman, H., Perry, P., Brun, A., & Morales-Alonso, G. (2020). Behind the runway: Extending sustainability in luxury fashion supply chains. *Journal of Business Research, 117*, 652–663.

Karlsson, J., & Ryberg, A. (2024). The Power of Customization: Exploring the impact of customized design and fit on user experience and perceptions of garments.

Kaur, J., Singh, S., & Singh, R. (2022). AI and Customer Experience in the Fashion Industry. In *Adoption and Implementation of AI in Customer Relationship Management* (pp. 127–138). IGI Global.

Kaushik, A. (2025). Omnichannel Marketing: A Complete Guide for 2025 and Beyond. Available at: https://www.moengage.com/blog/omnichannel-marketing/

Khamoushi, S. S., & Kalantari, D. H. (2025). Enhancing loyalty in luxury fashion with AI: The mediation role of customer relationships. *Asia-Pacific Journal of Business Administration.*

Kochar, S. (2024) Luxury Fashion Brands in 2025: Navigating Change and Growth. Available at: https://www.iiad.edu.in/the-circle/luxury-fashion-brands-navigating-change-and-growth/

Kong, H. M., Witmaier, A., & Ko, E. (2021). Sustainability and social media communication: How consumers respond to marketing efforts of luxury and non-luxury fashion brands. *Journal of Business Research, 131*, 640–651.

Kuksa, I., Kent, A., & West, H. (2024). Pathways to green personalisation: Reducing consumption through design. *The Design Journal*, *27*(5), 823–842.

Lall, M. M. (2023). *IN BLOCKCHAIN WE TRUST? The examination of an anti-counterfeiting solution* (Doctoral dissertation, City, University of London).

Lamptey, L., Mensah, R. O., & Korankye, V. (2024). Prevalence of counterfeit fashion goods in a West African Country: Crime in perspective. *Deviant Behavior*, •••, 1–21.

Landim, A. R. D. B., Pereira, A. M., & Vieira, T., de B. Costa, E., Moura, J. A. B., Wanick, V., & Bazaki, E. (2022). Chatbot design approaches for fashion E-commerce: An interdisciplinary review. *International Journal of Fashion Design, Technology and Education*, *15*(2), 200–210.

Lee, G., & Kim, H. Y. (2024). Human vs. AI: The battle for authenticity in fashion design and consumer response. *Journal of Retailing and Consumer Services*, *77*, 103690.

Lim, L. (2024). Making omnichannel work for luxury retail. Available at: https://hbr.org/2024/09/making-omnichannel-work-for-luxury-retail

Lim, X. J., Cheah, J. H., Ngo, L. V., Chan, K., & Ting, H. (2023). How do crazy rich Asians perceive sustainable luxury? Investigating the determinants of consumers' willingness to pay a premium price. *Journal of Retailing and Consumer Services*, *75*, 103502.

Liu, X., Shin, H., & Burns, A. C. (2021). Examining the impact of luxury brand's social media marketing on customer engagement: Using big data analytics and natural language processing. *Journal of Business Research*, *125*, 815–826.

Long, C. (2024). Up close and personalised. Paris Fashion Week| Designers explored ideas about the essence of couture, mixing the elevated and the more everyday. By Carola Long. *The Financial Times*, 5-5.

Loureiro, S. M. C. (2023). Artificial intelligence and extended reality in luxury fashion retail: Analysis and reflection. In *Augmented reality and artificial intelligence: The fusion of advanced technologies* (pp. 323–348). Springer Nature Switzerland.

Luce, L. (2018). *Artificial intelligence for fashion: How AI is revolutionizing the fashion industry*. Apress.

Mekonnen, A. (2024). Augmented reality (AR) in retailing: customers' experience in luxury fashion. In *Digital Transformation for Fashion and Luxury Brands: Theory and Practice* (pp. 91–106). Springer International Publishing.

Misra, R., Aggarwal, E., & Taneja, C. (2024). Examining the impact of the 3Cs: Content, collaboration and customisation of social media marketing on luxury fashion brand perception. *The Retail and Marketing Review*, *20*(2), 135–153.

Moreau, C. P., Prandelli, E., Schreier, M., & Hieke, S. (2020). Customization in luxury brands: Can Valentino get personal? *JMR, Journal of Marketing Research*, *57*(5), 937–947.

Nair, G. G., & Trivedi, V. (2024). Application of AI And ML in Quality Control Department of Textile and Apparel Industry. *International Conference on Sustainable Design Practices*

Nermain, A. I., Thanasi-Boçe, M., & Ali, O. (2022). Boosting luxury sustainability through blockchain technology. *Blockchain Technologies in the Textile and Fashion Industry*, 17.

O'Rourke, A. M., Lin, J., Sung, B., & Septianto, F. (2025). Social dynamics of luxury customization: The unique impact of name personalization. *Psychology and Marketing*, *42*(2), 493–513.

Oc, Y., Plangger, K., Sands, S., Campbell, C. L., & Pitt, L. (2023). Luxury is what you say: Analyzing electronic word-of-mouth marketing of luxury products using artificial intelligence and machine learning. *Psychology and Marketing*, *40*(9), 1704–1719.

Ozuem, W., & Willis, M. (2024). Artificial Intelligence and Predictive Analytics: Towards a Praxis of Personalised Shopping Experiences. In *Digital transformation for fashion and luxury brands: Theory and practice* (pp. 3–26). Springer International Publishing.

Pangarkar, A., Arora, V., & Shukla, Y. (2022). Exploring phygital omnichannel luxury retailing for immersive customer experience: The role of rapport and social engagement. *Journal of Retailing and Consumer Services*, *68*, 103001.

Patel, K., Beeram, D., Ramamurthy, P., Garg, P., & Kumar, S. (2024). Ai-enhanced design: Revolutionizing methodologies and workflows. [IJAIRD]. *Development*, *2*(1), 135–157.

Patil, D. (2024). Artificial Intelligence-Driven Predictive Maintenance In Manufacturing: Enhancing Operational Efficiency, Minimizing Downtime, And Optimizing Resource Utilization. *Minimizing Downtime, And Optimizing Resource Utilization (December 11, 2024).*

Peishan, S., & Yufei, W. (2021, December). Luxury Brands Culture and Marketing: How Does Chanel Stay popular. In *2021 3rd International Conference on Economic Management and Cultural Industry (ICEMCI 2021)* (pp. 1438-1442). Atlantis Press.

Peric, M. (2024). Leveraging AI for sustainability in the fashion industry: anticipated and unanticipated consequences. http://hdl.handle.net/10400.14/45023

Piris, Y., & Gay, A. C. (2021). Customer satisfaction and natural language processing. *Journal of Business Research, 124*, 264–271.

Prusova, D. (2023). Key B2C Luxury Brand Marketing Strategies to Establish Strong Relationships with the Modern Consumer of Luxury Fashion.

Rane, N., Choudhary, S., & Rane, J. (2024). Artificial intelligence, machine learning, and deep learning for sentiment analysis in business to enhance customer experience, loyalty, and satisfaction. In *Trustworthy Artificial Intelligence in Industry and Society* (pp. 233–261). Deep Science Publishing.

Rathore, B. (2017). Exploring the intersection of fashion marketing in the metaverse: Leveraging artificial intelligence for consumer engagement and brand innovation. *International Journal of New Media Studies: International Peer Reviewed Scholarly Indexed Journal*, *4*(2), 51–60.

Razak, M. I. M., Ariffin, Z. Z., Yahaya, M. N., & Ismail, I. (2021). An overview of personal luxury brands consumption in Malaysia. *The Sciences, 11*(3), 566–573.

Reydellet, H. (2022).Security: a growing problem for luxury brands. Available at: https://luxus-plus.com/en/security-a-growing-problem-for-luxury-brands/

Robinson, K. (2023). How generative AI can boost consumer marketing. Available at: https://www.mckinsey.com/capabilities/growth-marketing-and-sales/our-insights/how-generative-ai-can-boost-consumer-marketing

Sahota, N. (2024). Weaving Elegance with Intelligence: How Luxury Brands are Embracing AI. Available at: https://www.forbes.com/sites/neilsahota/2024/03/15/weaving-elegance-with-intelligence-how-luxury-brands-are-embracing-ai/

Savolainen, P. (2023). *The use of AI for demand and trend forecasting in fashion and the potential of these methods for sustainable brands* (Bachelor's thesis).

Sestino, A. (2024). The challenge of integrating "intelligent" technologies in luxury shopping contexts: The role of brand personality appeal and consumers' status consumption orientation. *Journal of Retailing and Consumer Services*, *76*, 103488.

Shahzad, M. F., Xu, S., An, X., & Javed, I. (2024). Assessing the impact of AI-chatbot service quality on user e-brand loyalty through chatbot user trust, experience and electronic word of mouth. *Journal of Retailing and Consumer Services*, *79*, 103867.

Shalev, L. (2024). Luxury Retail Security Concerns Are on the Rise, Can RFID Be the Answer? Available at: https://www.chainlane.io/blog/rfid-for-luxury-brands

Sharma, M., Shail, H., Painuly, P. K., & Kumar, A. S. (2023). AI-powered technologies used in online fashion retail for sustainable business: AI-powered technologies impacting consumer buying behavior. In *Sustainable Marketing, Branding, and Reputation Management: Strategies for a Greener Future* (pp. 538-561). IGI Global.

Shen, B., Minner, S., Chan, H. L., & Brun, A. (2020). Logistics and supply chain management in the luxury industry. *Transportation Research Part E, Logistics and Transportation Review*, *143*, 102095.

Sidlauskiene, J., Joye, Y., & Auruskeviciene, V. (2023). AI-based chatbots in conversational commerce and their effects on product and price perceptions. *Electronic Markets*, *33*(1), 24.

Silva, S. C., Silva, F. P., & Dias, J. C. (2024). Exploring omnichannel strategies: A path to improve customer experiences. *International Journal of Retail & Distribution Management*, *52*(1), 62–88.

Singh, O., Singh, N., Singh, A., & Vinoth, R. (2024). AI, IoT, and Blockchain in Fashion: Confronting Industry Applications, Challenges with Technological Solutions. *International Journal of Communication Networks and Information Security*, *16*(4), 393–410.

Song, X., & Bonanni, C. (2024). AI-Driven Business Model: How AI-Powered Try-On Technology Is Refining the Luxury Shopping Experience and Customer Satisfaction. *Journal of Theoretical and Applied Electronic Commerce Research*, *19*(4), 3067–3087.

Sreenivasan, A., & Suresh, M. (2024). Design Thinking and Artificial Intelligence: A Systematic Literature Review Exploring Synergies. *International Journal of Innovation Studies.*, *8*(3), 297–312.

Srivastava, A. (2024). AI in Luxury Fashion: Redefining Creativity and Customer Experience. Available at: https://www.fibre2fashion.com/industry-article/10054/ai-in-luxury-fashion-redefining-creativity-and-customer-experience

Straits Research. (2024). Luxury Fashion Market Size, Share & Trends Analysis Report By Product Type (Apparel, Footwear, Accessories), By End-User (Men, Women, Children), By Generation (Gen X, Millennials and Gen Z, Baby Boomer and Silent Gen), By Distribution Channel (Online, Mono Brand Stores, Specialty Stores, Departmental Stores, Off-Price Stores, Airports) and By Region (North America, Europe, APAC, Middle East and Africa, LATAM) Forecasts, 2024-2032. Available at: https://straitsresearch.com/report/luxury-fashion-market

Tam, F. Y., & Lung, J. (2025). Digital marketing strategies for luxury fashion brands: A systematic literature review. *International Journal of Information Management Data Insights*, *5*(1), 100309.

Tan, L., & Luhrs, M. (2024). Using Generative AI Midjourney to Enhance Divergent and Convergent Thinking in an Architect's Creative Design Process. *The Design Journal*, •••, 1–23.

Thanasi-Boçe, M. AL-Issa, N., & Ali, O. (2022). Combating Luxury Counterfeiting Through Blockchain Technology. In *Blockchain Technologies in the Textile and Fashion Industry* (pp. 1-16). Singapore: Springer Nature Singapore.

Varshney, N. (2023). Automatic Fashion Product Tagging: Technology that makes catalogue management easier for brands. Available at: https://apparelresources.com/technology-news/retail-tech/automatic-fashion-product-tagging-technology-makes-catalogue-management-easier-brands/

Walters, R. J., & Novak, M. (2021). Cyber Security. Springer eBooks, pp.21–37.

Wang, H., Ko, E., Woodside, A., & Yu, J. (2021). SNS marketing activities as a sustainable competitive advantage and traditional market equity. *Journal of Business Research*, *130*, 378–383.

Yan, H., Zhang, H., Liu, L., Zhou, D., Xu, X., Zhang, Z., & Yan, S. (2022). Toward intelligent design: An ai-based fashion designer using generative adversarial networks aided by sketch and rendering generators. *IEEE Transactions on Multimedia*, *25*, 2323–2338.

Zeng, N., Vignali, G., & Ryding, D. (2023). Understanding the Application of AI-enabled Chatbots in Luxury Fashion Retailing. In *The Garment Economy: Understanding History, Developing Business Models, and Leveraging Digital Technologies* (pp. 369–388). Springer International Publishing.

Zhang, Y., & Liu, C. (2024). Unlocking the Potential of Artificial Intelligence in Fashion Design and E-Commerce Applications: The Case of Midjourney. *Journal of Theoretical and Applied Electronic Commerce Research*, *19*(1), 654–670.

Ziccardi, G. (2020). Wearable technologies and smart clothes in the fashion business: Some issues concerning cybersecurity and data protection. *Laws*, *9*(2), 12.

ENDNOTES

1 https://www.crunchbase.com/organization/trendalytics

2 https://www.crunchbase.com/organization/trendalytics

3 https://sciative.com/research-articles/the-impact-of-ai-tagging-on-online-shopping

4 https://www.syte.ai/blog/ecommerce-trends/why-deep-tagging-is-crucial-for-your-fashion-company/

5 https://www.accenture.com/content/dam/accenture/final/a-com-migration/pdf/pdf-166/accenture-retail-fashion-personalization-pov.pdf

6 https://in.louisvuitton.com/eng-in/stories/personalisation#leathergoods

7 https://in.louisvuitton.com/eng-in/stories/personalisation#leathergoods

8 https://cybra.com/how-rfid-and-ai-can-work-together/

9 https://www.vaultik.com/

10 https://hedera.com/learning/distributed-ledger-technologies

11 https://www.avata.gg/

12 https://community.openai.com/t/ai-driven-framework-for-translating-abstract-concepts-into-structured-models/1109560

13 https://appinventiv.com/blog/ai-in-product-design/

14 https://newo.ai/insights/revolutionizing-design-the-impact-of-ai-on-creative-processes/

15 https://blog.refabric.com/optimizing-fabric-selection-with-ai-in-fashion/

16 https://www.leewayhertz.com/ai-use-cases-in-fashion/

[17] https://newo.ai/insights/revolutionizing-design-the-impact-of-ai-on-creative-processes/

[18] https://www.entrupy.com/

Chapter 4
AI in the Luxury Market and Its Impact on India's Economic Development

Prabhuram Tripathy
https://orcid.org/0000-0002-7325-0583
Sri Sri University, India

ABSTRACT

The application of Artificial Intelligence (AI) in the luxury market is driving a transformative shift in how premium products are produced, marketed, and consumed. In the Indian context, this technological integration intersects with a rapidly evolving economy, a growing middle and upper class, and increasing digital penetration. This paper examines the role of AI in enhancing customer personalization, streamlining operations, and enabling data-driven strategies within the luxury sector in India. It further analyses the broader economic implications, including the stimulation of AI-focused Luxury Market, Hyper-Customer Engagement and Personalization, Smart Cities, job creation in high-tech and retail sectors, and the rise of digital consumerism and Technologies like Augmented Reality, and Immersive Virtual experiences are enabling luxury brands

DOI: 10.4018/979-8-3693-8422-0.ch004

to offer innovative, high-touch experiences. The paper assesses how AI is not only redefining luxury consumption but also acting as a catalyst for India's economic development.

1. INTRODUCTION

In recent years, artificial intelligence (AI) has emerged as a transformative force across industries, and the luxury market is no exception. Global industry transformation is being largely attributed to artificial intelligence (AI), with the luxury market and the growth of developing nations such as India experiencing the fastest transformations (Mondal and Chakrabarti, 2021). With a rapidly growing affluent class and increasing digital penetration, the country is becoming a key player in the global luxury landscape (KPMG, 2022). AI has had a significant impact on the luxury market by enabling previously unheard-of levels of personalisation, efficiency, and innovation in operational procedures and client involvement (Ellahi,2025). Simultaneously, As AI is accelerating innovations in infrastructure, healthcare, financial inclusion, agriculture, and other areas that are vital to India's rapid growth, it is transforming the country's overall economic development (Sandra,2025). Traditionally associated with craftsmanship, exclusivity, and high-touch experiences, the luxury sector is now undergoing a quiet yet powerful revolution driven by intelligent technology. AI is helping luxury brands reimagine the way they engage with consumers (Deloitte, 2023). From personalized shopping experiences to supply chain optimization and data-driven customer insights, AI is reshaping how luxury brands connect with their audience. In the Indian context, this shift holds particular significance. As one of the fastest-growing consumer markets in the world, India presents a unique blend of rising affluence, digital adoption, and a young, aspirational population. The integration of AI into the luxury segment not only enhances consumer engagement but also contributes to broader economic growth—fuelling innovation, generating employment, and attracting global investment.

2. AI IN THE LUXURY MARKET

The luxury market, long known for its exclusivity, craftsmanship, and personal touch, is experiencing a quiet but powerful transformation driven by Artificial Intelligence (AI). Far from replacing the human element, AI is enhancing the core values of the luxury experience by enabling brands to connect more deeply and meaningfully with consumers. From creating personalized shopping experiences to optimizing back-end operations, AI is helping luxury brands adapt to an increasingly digital and data-driven world (Ellahi,2025). One of the most impactful contributions of AI in the luxury sector is personalization at scale (Dou, 2024). By analysing vast amounts of consumer data—such as browsing habits, purchase history, social media interactions, and even emotional cues—AI can offer tailored recommendations, content, and product suggestions that feel intuitive and curated for the individual (McKinsey & Company, 2023). For instance, luxury fashion houses now use machine learning algorithms to suggest outfits based on a customer's past purchases, lifestyle, and current trends, creating a bespoke digital shopping experience that mirrors in-store VIP treatment (Dhiwar, 2024).

AI also plays a crucial role in enhancing customer service. AI-powered chatbots and virtual shopping assistants, which use natural language processing (NLP), can provide real-time support and guidance to customers across global time zones (Fanni et al, 2023). These tools ensure that luxury clients receive the prompt, attentive service they expect—anytime and anywhere—without compromising on quality (Accenture, 2022). Some high-end retailers have even begun integrating AI into physical spaces, using facial recognition and smart mirrors to offer tailored suggestions in brick-and-mortar stores. Beyond customer-facing applications, AI is transforming operational efficiency and decision-making. In an industry where supply chains are global and product availability is often limited, AI helps brands better forecast demand, manage inventory, and streamline logistics (Deloitte, 2023). This not only reduces waste and costs but also ensures that exclusive products are available to the right customer at the right time—essential for maintaining the brand's prestige and reliability (Sweeney and Swait, 2008).

Furthermore, AI has become a critical tool in combating counterfeiting, a major challenge for luxury brands. AI-powered image recognition and blockchain integration are being used to verify product authenticity and track items throughout the supply chain, preserving the integrity of high-value goods (PwC, 2023). This fosters greater trust among consumers and protects brand reputation in a competitive market. While some may worry that AI could dilute the "human touch" that defines luxury, many brands are discovering that technology, when used thoughtfully, can enhance the emotional and experiential aspects of luxury. It allows brands to be more responsive, more intuitive, and more aligned with the evolving expectations of today's affluent, tech-savvy consumers (Grandi and Bruni, 2024).

3. HYPER-CUSTOMER ENGAGEMENT AND PERSONALIZATION

In today's digital-first world, customer expectations are higher than ever. Consumers no longer want just a product or service—they crave personalized experiences that reflect their preferences, behaviours, and lifestyles Iqbal, A., Farooq and Gillani, 2025). This has given rise to the era of hyper-customer engagement, where brands go beyond traditional interactions to build deeper, data-driven, and emotionally resonant relationships with their audiences. At the heart of this transformation is personalization powered by technology, particularly Artificial Intelligence (AI) and data analytics. These AI-driven solutions allow brands to cater to the sophisticated tastes of their customers, ensuring that each interaction feels unique and exclusive, thus enhancing customer satisfaction and driving higher sales conversion rates (Sinha, 2020). Hyper-customer engagement refers to a brand's ability to maintain continuous, meaningful interactions with consumers across multiple touchpoints—whether online, in-store, on social media, or through customer service channels. It's about creating a 360-degree view of the customer, and then using that insight to deliver relevant content, timely communication, and tailored offers. This approach not only enhances customer satisfaction but also builds trust and long-term brand loyalty (Salesforce, 2022). AI is playing a key role in making this level of engagement possible. By processing large volumes of customer data in real time, AI can help brands understand not just what customers are buying, but why they're buying—and what they're likely to want next. For instance, Netflix's content recommendations, Amazon's product suggestions, and Spotify's curated playlists are all prime examples of personalization in action, made possible through intelligent algorithms (Accenture, 2023). In the luxury market and high-end retail, personalization is even more nuanced. Here, AI is used to track customer behaviour, analyse preferences, and even detect emotional responses to marketing content. These insights help brands deliver tailor-made experiences, such as personalized messages, curated product collections, early access to exclusive items, and even one-on-one consultations with brand experts (McKinsey & Company, 2023). In stores, some brands are using AI-powered tools like smart mirrors and facial recognition to offer personalized product suggestions based on previous interactions.

Beyond product recommendations, hyper-engagement also means proactive customer service. Brands can now anticipate when a customer may need help—such as tracking a shipment, needing a size exchange, or running low on a recurring product—and reach out before the customer even asks. This kind of predictive, anticipatory service creates a feeling of being truly seen and valued, which is central to the success of hyper-personalization (Gartner, 2022). However, with great personalization comes great responsibility. Consumers are becoming increasingly concerned about data privacy and want to know how their information is being used. Transparency, consent, and ethical data practices are critical for maintaining trust in an environment where personalization is deeply data-driven (PwC, 2023). Striking the right balance between personalization and privacy is one of the most important challenges brands face today.

4. AUGMENTED REALITY (AR), AND IMMERSIVE EXPERIENCES IN THE BROADER LUXURY MARKET

The luxury market, once reliant on in-store experiences and face-to-face service, is undergoing a digital transformation that is both radical and refined. Technologies like Artificial Intelligence (AI), Augmented Reality (AR), and immersive virtual experiences are enabling luxury brands to offer innovative, high-touch experiences that replicate—and in some ways surpass—the exclusivity and intimacy of traditional luxury shopping (Mekonnen, 2024). This is particularly important in India, where the rise of e-commerce has transformed consumer behaviour, and luxury shoppers now demand more innovative digital experiences and contributing to the growing preference for digital luxury experiences in India, offering a significant competitive edge to brands that adopt these AI tools (Balachandran, 2021). At the core of this transformation is AI-driven virtual shopping, which is redefining convenience and personalization. With the help of AI, online shopping platforms can now offer personalized recommendations, interactive chatbots, virtual stylists, and real-time product suggestions based on consumer behaviour and preferences (Accenture, 2023). These tools aren't just functional—they're designed to make the digital experience feel luxurious, thoughtful, and custom-made. Brands like Gucci and Chanel are integrating AI into their online stores to replicate the feel of a high-end boutique, complete with style consultants powered by machine learning algorithms.

Augmented Reality (AR) takes the luxury experience to the next level by allowing consumers to virtually "try on" products. Whether it's trying on designer sunglasses, testing out luxury makeup shades, or previewing how a high-end handbag looks with different outfits, AR bridges the gap between physical and digital retail (Deloitte, 2022). For example, Dior's AR makeup filters let users see how products would appear on their faces in real time, offering a seamless blend of technology and beauty. Similarly, Rolex and Cartier use AR apps to let customers visualize how watches look on their wrist—without ever stepping into a store. These innovations aren't just about aesthetics—they're about deepening emotional engagement. Immersive technologies such as Virtual Reality (VR) and metaverse-style showrooms are providing new environments for storytelling, brand heritage, and customer interaction (Patel, 2024). Luxury fashion houses like Balenciaga and Louis Vuitton have experimented with virtual fashion shows and digital art experiences, creating spaces where customers don't just buy—they explore, experience, and connect with the brand's ethos (McKinsey & Company, 2023).

The potential of these technologies goes far beyond novelty. They are reshaping the consumer journey by enabling phygital (physical + digital) experiences—blending real-world quality with digital convenience. As luxury consumers increasingly value personalization and innovation, these immersive tools help brands deliver memorable experiences while also gathering invaluable data on preferences and engagement (PwC, 2023). Furthermore, immersive tech is proving to be a smart investment. A growing number of affluent, digitally-savvy consumers—particularly Gen Z and Millennials—expect luxury brands to innovate (Weiss,2018). According to a Salesforce (2022) report, 57% of consumers say they're more likely to buy from brands that offer personalized and interactive digital experiences. For luxury companies, this means AI and AR are not just enhancements; they're strategic necessities.

5. SUPPLY CHAIN OPTIMIZATION AND INVENTORY MANAGEMENT

In the modern business landscape, where speed, efficiency, and customer expectations are at an all-time high, supply chain optimization and inventory management have become vital for both operational excellence and customer satisfaction. For luxury brands, where exclusivity and quality are non-negotiable, these functions are even more critical. They must balance limited production runs, high-value products, and global demand—without compromising on service quality or brand image (Kapferer, 2012). Thanks to digital transformation, technologies like Artificial Intelligence (AI), machine learning, and real-time data analytics are now enabling brands to optimize their supply chains and manage inventory with greater precision and agility. AI-driven image recognition tools can also detect fake products being sold online, protecting both the brand's reputation and the consumer's trust (Aithal & Kumar, 2021).

5.1 The Complexity of Luxury Supply Chains

Unlike mass-market retailers, luxury brands often work with artisanal suppliers, custom production timelines, and tightly controlled product releases. This complexity makes the supply chain more sensitive to disruptions and inefficiencies. Late deliveries, excess inventory, or stockouts can all impact customer satisfaction and brand credibility (Deloitte, 2023). Moreover, luxury consumers expect seamless service, whether they're shopping in Paris, Mumbai, or online. Ensuring global availability without overproducing is a delicate balancing act (Brandao et al, 2021).

5.2 AI and Predictive Analytics in Inventory Management

AI-powered tools are transforming the way brands forecast demand and manage inventory. By analyzing a mix of historical sales data, current market trends, seasonal behavior, and external variables like economic conditions or social media sentiment, predictive algorithms can anticipate future demand with remarkable accuracy (McKinsey & Company, 2022). This allows brands to stock precisely what is needed—no more, no less—minimizing excess inventory and reducing the risk of markdowns or waste. Luxury brand Louis Vuitton, for example, has adopted AI solutions to anticipate product demand at a regional level, which helps improve product allocation and reduce missed sales opportunities (Bain & Company, 2023). These tools also help manage slow-moving stock and optimize replenishment schedules, ensuring a smoother supply chain flow from production to point-of-sale.

5.3 Real-Time Visibility and Transparency

Modern inventory management systems, powered by cloud technology and IoT (Internet of Things), offer real-time visibility into the entire supply chain—from raw materials to store shelves. This transparency enables quicker decision-making, better supplier collaboration, and more responsive customer service. For instance, if a specific handbag model is selling faster than expected in one region, stock can be redirected from other areas where demand is lower, avoiding shortages and excess inventory simultaneously (PwC, 2022). Additionally, technologies such as blockchain are being explored for luxury supply chains to ensure product authenticity and traceability. This is especially important in preventing counterfeits and preserving brand integrity—key concerns in the high-end market (Accenture, 2023).

5.4 Sustainability Through Smarter Supply Chains

Sustainability is increasingly important to luxury consumers. Brands are now expected not only to deliver high-quality goods but to do so in environmentally responsible ways. AI and data analytics help identify inefficiencies, reduce waste, and support more sustainable sourcing and logistics practices. Smarter routing, consolidated shipping, and optimized production schedules contribute to a smaller carbon footprint—without compromising on service or exclusivity (Gartner, 2022).

6. AI-TRANSFORMED CUSTOMER SERVICE FOR LUXURY BRANDS

In the luxury sector, customer service is not just a support function—it's part of the brand promise. Personalized attention, exclusivity, and exceptional responsiveness are foundational to the luxury experience (Samanta et al., 2024). As customer expectations evolve and digital channels become more dominant, luxury brands are increasingly turning to Artificial Intelligence (AI) to elevate their service offerings. Rather than replacing the human touch, AI is being used to augment and enhance it, enabling luxury brands to deliver consistent, high-quality service across every channel and time zone.

6.1 AI as a Digital Concierge

AI-driven customer service tools are enabling brands to provide round-the-clock support without compromising on the sophistication their clientele expects. Intelligent chatbots, for instance, now use natural language processing (NLP) to understand and respond to complex customer queries in a conversational tone. These digital concierges can assist with everything from recommending new arrivals based on personal taste, to managing returns, checking availability, and booking personalized shopping sessions (Accenture, 2023). Luxury brands such as Burberry and Louis Vuitton have successfully deployed AI chatbots on platforms like WhatsApp and WeChat to engage customers in real time—delivering fast, polished assistance that mimics the attentiveness of in-store service (McKinsey & Company, 2022).

6.2 Hyper-Personalization through Predictive AI

One of AI's greatest strengths is its ability to learn from data. By analysing purchase history, online behavior, and even customer sentiment, AI systems can anticipate needs and preferences with remarkable accuracy. This enables a level of hyper-personalization that was once only possible in face-to-face interactions (Gkikas and Theodoridis, 2021). For example, AI can detect when a loyal customer is likely to run low on a favourite skincare product and prompt a timely reminder or offer. It can also personalize messages and recommendations down to the preferred color, style, or size, making each interaction feel uniquely crafted (Salesforce, 2023). This not only improves customer satisfaction but deepens emotional engagement with the brand.

6.3 Multilingual and Multichannel Excellence

Luxury brands operate globally, which means offering seamless service in multiple languages across various channels—online stores, mobile apps, social media, and physical boutiques (Deloitte, 2023). AI tools enable real-time language translation, sentiment analysis, and channel optimization to ensure a smooth and culturally attuned customer experience, no matter where the client is or how they choose to interact (Rane et al., 2024). By centralizing data across channels and using AI to interpret it, brands can maintain continuity in conversations. A client who browses online and later visits a store can be greeted by a staff member who already knows their preferences and recent activity—thanks to AI-powered CRM systems (Gartner, 2022).

6.4 AI Supporting Human Service Teams

Importantly, AI is not replacing luxury service professionals; it's empowering them. Virtual assistants can handle routine inquiries, freeing up human staff to focus on more nuanced or high-touch interactions. AI also provides insights and recommendations that staff can use to better understand their clients and provide even more exceptional service (Song and Bonanni, 2024). Brands like Chanel are using AI-driven customer service platforms to assist their sales associates with real-time data and predictive suggestions, allowing them to tailor conversations and services with more relevance and confidence (PwC, 2023).

7. AI IN MARKETING AND CONSUMER INSIGHTS

In today's data-driven world, businesses are no longer relying on guesswork to understand their consumers. With the rise of Artificial Intelligence (AI), marketers now have the tools to uncover real-time insights into customer behaviours, preferences, and motivations—at a scale and speed that would have been unimaginable just a decade ago (Gkikas and Theodoridis, 2021). AI is revolutionizing how brands connect with their audiences, offering a more targeted, relevant, and personalized approach to marketing.

7.1 From Data to Understanding: AI's Role in Consumer Insight

Every digital interaction—from clicks and likes to purchases and reviews—leaves behind a trail of valuable data. But data alone isn't enough; it's the ability to interpret and act on it that makes the difference. That's where AI comes in. Using machine learning and natural language processing (NLP), AI systems can comb through vast datasets to identify patterns, trends, and even emotional cues in consumer behaviour (Deloitte, 2023). This has enabled marketers to shift from broad demographic targeting to micro-segmentation, where campaigns are tailored for niche groups—or even individuals. For instance, AI can analyse a customer's browsing history, purchase frequency, and even their social media activity to predict what product they might be interested in next (Salesforce, 2023). This level of insight drives hyper-personalization, which significantly boosts engagement and conversion rates.

7.2 Predictive Analytics: Anticipating Needs Before They Arise

AI doesn't just explain past behaviour—it helps forecast future actions. Predictive analytics, powered by AI, allows brands to anticipate consumer needs, recommend products or services in advance, and optimize marketing spend. For example, e-commerce platforms use AI to recommend products based on not just past purchases but on what similar profiles are buying, and even on external factors like weather or local events (McKinsey & Company, 2022). In the luxury sector, brands like Gucci and Prada are using AI to determine which customer segments are most likely to respond to certain campaigns, enabling more precise and cost-effective marketing strategies (Bain & Company, 2023).

7.3 Content Creation and Optimization

AI is also playing a growing role in content creation and testing. AI tools can generate headlines, product descriptions, and social media posts tailored to resonate with specific audiences (Ahmed and Ganapathy, 2021). More importantly, AI can A/B test content in real time and instantly analyse what works best, adjusting campaigns dynamically. This ensures that marketing messages are not just creative, but also effective (Accenture, 2023).

7.4 Emotional and Sentiment Analysis

Understanding how consumers feel about a brand is just as crucial as knowing what they do. AI-powered sentiment analysis tools can scan thousands of online reviews, social media mentions, and customer support chats to gauge public opinion and emotional tone (Srivastava, 2024). This helps brands spot emerging issues, identify brand advocates, and fine-tune messaging to align with the audience's values and mood (PwC, 2022). For luxury brands, which trade heavily on emotional connection and brand storytelling, this level of insight is invaluable.

7.5 Ethical Use and Data Privacy

With all the power AI provides in marketing, ethical considerations are increasingly important. Consumers are more aware and concerned about how their data is collected and used. Transparency, consent, and compliance with regulations like GDPR are essential. Brands that use AI responsibly—by prioritizing ethical data use and respecting consumer privacy—will stand out and earn trust in the long run (Gartner, 2023).

8. AI AND SMART CITIES

As urban populations grow and the demand for efficient, sustainable living increases, Artificial Intelligence (AI) has become a cornerstone in the development of smart cities. These urban areas are designed to use data and technology to improve the quality of life for citizens while optimizing resource use and infrastructure (Srihith et al, 2022). AI, in this context, acts as both a brain and a nervous system, powering everything from traffic management and energy distribution to public safety and citizen engagement.

8.1 Transforming Urban Infrastructure with AI

One of the most significant contributions of AI to smart cities lies in infrastructure optimization. AI systems can analyses data from sensors embedded in roads, bridges, and buildings to predict maintenance needs, detect faults, and optimize operations. For instance, predictive maintenance powered by AI can help cities avoid costly infrastructure failures by addressing issues before they escalate (McKinsey & Company, 2023). Moreover, AI can help manage public transportation systems in real-time, adjusting routes based on traffic patterns, weather, and rider demand. Cities like Singapore and Barcelona are already using AI to optimize bus and metro schedules, reducing wait times and improving commuter satisfaction (Deloitte, 2023).

8.2 AI in Traffic and Mobility Management

Traffic congestion is a major urban challenge. AI-powered traffic systems analyse data from cameras, GPS devices, and traffic sensors to optimize signal timings, reroute vehicles, and predict congestion hotspots before they happen. Smart traffic lights, for example, adapt in real-time to traffic flow, reducing unnecessary delays and improving fuel efficiency (PwC, 2022). Additionally, AI is central to the future of autonomous vehicles, which are expected to reduce accidents, lower emissions, and make transportation more accessible for elderly and disabled populations (Khayyam et al, 2019).

8.3 Public Safety and Emergency Response

AI technologies are being used to improve public safety by enabling real-time surveillance, facial recognition, and behavioural pattern analysis. While this raises important ethical and privacy considerations, when used responsibly, AI can help detect threats, track missing persons, and respond more effectively to emergencies. Cities like Dubai and London are experimenting with AI-powered crime prediction tools that analyse historical crime data to anticipate potential incidents, allowing for proactive law enforcement deployment (Gartner, 2022).

8.4 Environmental Monitoring and Sustainability

Smart cities are also leveraging AI to combat climate change and promote sustainability. AI can help monitor air and water quality, manage energy consumption, and predict pollution patterns. By analysing environmental data, cities can issue early warnings, enforce regulations more effectively, and plan better for long-term sustainability goals (Al-Raeei, 2025). For example, AI systems can analyse usage patterns to optimize energy grids, integrating renewable sources and reducing waste. This helps cities meet their carbon neutrality targets more efficiently (Accenture, 2023).

8.5 Citizen Engagement and Inclusivity

AI is also being used to improve citizen services. Chatbots and virtual assistants on municipal websites allow residents to access services 24/7, from paying utility bills to reporting potholes. AI can also analyze feedback from citizens to identify common concerns and guide decision-making (Kuziemski and Misuraca, 2020). Smart city initiatives that include AI-powered language translation and accessibility tools also help make city services more inclusive for diverse populations, including non-native speakers and people with disabilities.

8.6 Challenges and Ethical Considerations

Despite the promise of AI in smart cities, there are important challenges. Data privacy, algorithmic bias, and digital exclusion are major concerns. Cities must ensure transparency in how data is collected and used, and involve communities in decisions about surveillance and automation. There must also be a focus on equitable access to technology, so that all residents—regardless of income or education—can benefit from smart city innovations (Voda and Radu, 2019).

9. CONCLUSION

AI is rapidly transforming both the luxury market and India's broader economic landscape. In the luxury sector, AI enables hyper-personalized experiences, improves operational efficiencies, and enhances customer engagement, positioning India as a growing player in the global luxury market. At the same time, AI is driving economic development by improving agricultural productivity, healthcare outcomes, financial inclusion, and urban infrastructure. As India continues to integrate AI into its key industries, it is crucial to address the challenges of data privacy, workforce reskilling, and the digital divide. As AI continues to shape the future of urban living, it will be crucial to adopt ethical frameworks, transparency protocols, and inclusive policies to ensure that smart cities truly live up to their potential as equitable, sustainable, and human-centered spaces. By doing so, AI can become a powerful tool for driving both luxury market growth and inclusive economic development, helping India achieve its long-term development goals.

REFERENCES

Accenture. (2022). *Luxury customer experience in the age of AI.* https://www.accenture.com

Accenture. (2023). *AI and sustainability in smart cities.* https://www.accenture.com

Accenture. (2023). *Luxury customer engagement reimagined: The AI advantage.* https://www.accenture.com

Accenture. (2023). *Personalization pulse check: How companies are meeting customer expectations.* https://www.accenture.com

Accenture. (2023). *Redefining Luxury Retail: Personalization at the Speed of AI.* https://www.accenture.com

Accenture. (2023). *Reinventing marketing with AI: The new age of personalization.* https://www.accenture.com

Accenture. (2023). *Supply chain reinvention in luxury: The role of AI and transparency.* https://www.accenture.com

Accenture. (2023). *The ethical use of AI in smart cities.* https://www.accenture.com

Ahmed, A. A. A., & Ganapathy, A. (2021). Creation of automated content with embedded artificial intelligence: A study on learning management system for educational entrepreneurship. *Academy of Entrepreneurship Journal, 27*(3), 1–10.

Aithal, P. S., & Kumar, P. M. (2021). Blockchain Technology and AI in Luxury Product Authentication. *International Journal of Applied Engineering Research: IJAER, 16*(1), 150–162.

Al-Raeei, M. (2025). The smart future for sustainable development: Artificial intelligence solutions for sustainable urbanization. *Sustainable Development, 33*(1), 508–517.

Bain & Company. (2023). *AI and the future of luxury marketing.* https://www.bain.com

Bain & Company. (2023). *How luxury brands can unlock value with smarter supply chains*. https://www.bain.com

Balachandran, A. (2021). Augmented Reality and Virtual Reality in Luxury Shopping: A Case Study of India. *Journal of Digital Commerce*, *4*(3), 40–52.

Brandao, M. S., Godinho Filho, M., & Da Silva, A. L. (2021). Luxury supply chain management: A framework proposal based on a systematic literature review. *International Journal of Physical Distribution & Logistics Management*, *51*(8), 859–876.

Deloitte. (2022). *The AR Opportunity in Luxury Retail*. https://www2.deloitte.com

Deloitte. (2023). *Elevating luxury with AI-driven customer service*. https://www2.deloitte.com

Deloitte. (2023). *How AI is powering the future of urban mobility*. https://www2.deloitte.com

Deloitte. (2023). *Tech Trends 2023: Emerging technologies in luxury markets*. https://www2.deloitte.com/global/en.html

Deloitte. (2023). *The future of the luxury supply chain: Agile, intelligent, and customer-centric*. https://www2.deloitte.com

Dhiwar, K. (2024, January). Artificial Intelligence and Machine Learning in Fashion: Reshaping Design, Production, Consumer Experience and Sustainability. In *2024 ASU International Conference in Emerging Technologies for Sustainability and Intelligent Systems (ICETSIS)* (pp. 1766-1775). IEEE.

Dou, J. (2024). The application and challenges of artificial intelligence in the fashion and luxury industry. *Applied and Computational Engineering*, *42*, 90–96.

Ellahi, A. (2025). AI and Its Importance in the Development of the Luxury Market. In *Innovative Trends Shaping Food Marketing and Consumption* (pp. 395–418). IGI Global Scientific Publishing.

Fanni, S. C., Febi, M., Aghakhanyan, G., & Neri, E. (2023). Natural language processing. In *Introduction to artificial intelligence* (pp. 87–99). Springer International Publishing.

Gartner. (2022). *Customer service trends in the age of AI*. https://www.gartner.com

Gartner. (2022). *Predictive engagement: The next frontier in customer experience*. https://www.gartner.com

Gartner. (2022). *Smart cities: Trends and technologies for urban innovation*. https://www.gartner.com

Gartner. (2022). *Sustainable supply chains: Trends and technologies shaping the future*. https://www.gartner.com

Gartner. (2023). *AI governance: Ethical considerations for smart cities*. https://www.gartner.com

Gartner. (2023). *Responsible AI in marketing: What leaders need to know*. https://www.gartner.com

Gkikas, D. C., & Theodoridis, P. K. (2021). AI in consumer behavior. In *Advances in Artificial Intelligence-based Technologies: Selected Papers in Honour of Professor Nikolaos G. Bourbakis—Vol. 1* (pp. 147–176). Springer International Publishing.

Gkikas, D. C., & Theodoridis, P. K. (2021). AI in consumer behavior. In *Advances in Artificial Intelligence-based Technologies: Selected Papers in Honour of Professor Nikolaos G. Bourbakis—Vol. 1* (pp. 147–176). Springer International Publishing.

Grandi, L. C., & Bruni, S. (2024). Will the Artificial Intelligence Touch Substitute for the Human Touch? *NeuroSci*, *5*(3), 254–264. PMID: 39483277

. Iqbal, A., Farooq, A., & Gillani, S. M. A. H. (2025). Business in Digital World. *Algorithmic Training, Future Markets, and Big Data for Finance Digitalization*, 1.

Kapferer, J. N. (2012). Abundant rarity: The key to luxury growth. *Business Horizons*, *55*(5), 453–462.

Khayyam, H., Javadi, B., Jalili, M., & Jazar, R. N. (2019). Artificial intelligence and internet of things for autonomous vehicles. In *Nonlinear approaches in engineering applications: Automotive applications of engineering problems* (pp. 39–68). Springer International Publishing.

KPMG. (2022). India's luxury landscape: Growth and transformation. https://home.kpmg/in/en/home.html

Kuziemski, M., & Misuraca, G. (2020). AI governance in the public sector: Three tales from the frontiers of automated decision-making in democratic settings. *Telecommunications Policy*, *44*(6), 101976. PMID: 32313360

McKinsey & Company. (2022). *Digital supply chain transformation: Lessons from global brands*. https://www.mckinsey.com

McKinsey & Company. (2022). *Ethics of AI in urban planning: Challenges and solutions*. https://www.mckinsey.com

McKinsey & Company. (2022). *Redefining customer experience in luxury through digital transformation*. https://www.mckinsey.com

McKinsey & Company. (2022). *The impact of AI on marketing performance*. https://www.mckinsey.com

McKinsey & Company. (2023). *Next in personalization 2023: The future of customer engagement*. https://www.mckinsey.com

McKinsey & Company. (2023). *Smart cities and AI: The path forward*. https://www.mckinsey.com

McKinsey & Company. (2023). *The State of Fashion Technology Report*. https://www.mckinsey.com

McKinsey & Company. (2023). *The State of Fashion: How technology is redefining luxury*. https://www.mckinsey.com

Mekonnen, A. (2024). Augmented reality (AR) in retailing: customers' experience in luxury fashion. In *Digital transformation for fashion and luxury brands: Theory and practice* (pp. 91–106). Springer International Publishing.

Mondal, A., & Chakrabarti, A. B. (2021). Information and communication technology adoption strategies of emerging multinationals from India. [JGIM]. *Journal of Global Information Management*, *29*(5), 161–175.

Patel, K. (2024). Revolutionizing Customer Experience: Integrating Blockchain with AR and VR in Retail. In *Augmenting Retail Reality, Part B: Blockchain, AR, VR, and AI* (pp. 1-22). Emerald Publishing Limited.

PwC. (2022). *Inventory management and AI: Navigating the next wave of efficiency*. https://www.pwc.com

PwC. (2022). *Smart cities and the digital divide: Ensuring equitable access to AI*. https://www.pwc.com

PwC. (2022). *The power of sentiment analysis in brand strategy*. https://www.pwc.com

PwC. (2022). *Urban transformation with AI: Smarter, safer cities*. https://www.pwc.com

PwC. (2023). *AI in customer service: Elevating the luxury client experience*. https://www.pwc.com

PwC. (2023). *Consumer Intelligence Series: Trusted tech*. https://www.pwc.com

PwC. (2023). *Future of Customer Experience: Immersive Technology and AI*. https://www.pwc.com

PwC. (2023). *The power of AI in retail and luxury: Transforming customer experience and operations*. https://www.pwc.com

Rane, N., Choudhary, S., & Rane, J. (2024). Artificial intelligence, machine learning, and deep learning for sentiment analysis in business to enhance customer experience, loyalty, and satisfaction. *Available at SSRN* 4846145.

Salesforce. (2022). *State of the Connected Customer (5th ed.)*. https://www.salesforce.com

Salesforce. (2023). *State of the Connected Customer (6th ed.)*. https://www.salesforce.com

Salesforce. (2023). *Trends in AI-powered marketing*. https://www.salesforce.com

Samanta, P., Amir, M., Maira, S., Barakoti, A., Chopra, M., & Shrivastava, V. (2024, December). Analyzing the Transformative Effects of AI-Powered Influencer Marketing on Consumer Decision-Making. In *2024 1st International Conference on Advances in Computing, Communication and Networking (ICAC2N)* (pp. 1236-1241). IEEE.

. Sandra, A. (2025). Leveraging AI and Technology to Address the Challenges of Underdeveloped Countries.

Sinha, P. (2020). AI and Hyper-Personalization in the Indian Luxury Market. *Luxury Business Review*, *8*(1), 56–75.

Song, X., & Bonanni, C. (2024). AI-Driven Business Model: How AI-Powered Try-On Technology Is Refining the Luxury Shopping Experience and Customer Satisfaction. *Journal of Theoretical and Applied Electronic Commerce Research*, *19*(4), 3067–3087.

Srihith, I. V. D., Kumar, I. V. S., Varaprasad, R., Mohan, Y. R., Srinivas, T. A. S., & Sravanthi, Y. (2022). Future of Smart Cities: The Role of Machine Learning and Artificial Intelligence. *South Asian Research Journal of Engineering and Technology*, *4*(5), 110–119.

. Srivastava, A. (2024). AI-Powered Data Collection and Analysis. *Utilizing AI Tools in Academic Research Writing*, 114-140.

Sweeney, J., & Swait, J. (2008). The effects of brand credibility on customer loyalty. *Journal of Retailing and Consumer Services*, *15*(3), 179–193.

Voda, A. I., & Radu, L. D. (2019). How can artificial intelligence respond to smart cities challenges? In *Smart cities: Issues and challenges* (pp. 199–216). Elsevier.

Weiss, C. (2018). RETHINKING RESEARCH METHODS IN A DIGITALLY SAVVY WORLD. In *INTED2018 Proceedings* (pp. 7225-7230). IATED.

Chapter 5
Metamorphosing Luxury:
Role of Artificial Intelligence (AI) in Development of Luxury Market

Ipseeta Satpathy
https://orcid.org/0000-0002-0155-5548
KIIT School of Management, KIIT University, India

Arpita Nayak
https://orcid.org/0000-0003-2911-0492
KIIT School of Liberal Studies, KIIT University, India

Vishal Jain
https://orcid.org/0000-0003-1126-7424
School of Engineering and Technology, Vivekananda Institute of Professional Studies, New Delhi, India

ABSTRACT

Artificial Intelligence (AI) is revolutionizing the luxury market by improving personalization, marketing, product design, supply chain, customer experience, fraud prevention, sustainability, and customer loyalty. AI algorithms create personalized recommendations, using customer infor-

DOI: 10.4018/979-8-3693-8422-0.ch005

mation to ensure a tailored shopping experience. Chatbots and virtual assistants provide timely customer attention, while AI-based customer segmentation targets customers based on preferences and age. AI aids in product development, design, and sustainable practices, while also ensuring timely supply chain and inventory management. AI prevents infringement of luxury brands and fraudulent practices, and contributes to customer retention and loyalty programs. The advancement of AI could lead to revolutions in the luxury industry.

I. INTRODUCTION

Luxury refers to firms that offer high-end items, products, or services. The luxury industry includes companies that are known for their high quality, rarity, aesthetic appeal, and high price. It's a vast business, and luxury brands come in many kinds and sizes, from fashion labels to automobiles, hotel resorts, and whisky brands, all catering to affluent consumers. Luxury firms are facing rising tensions as consumer activists criticize them for a lack of supply-chain transparency and accuse them of animal and labor mistreatment. In response, the luxury industry is gradually realising its duties and possibilities to promote sustainability in sourcing, production, and marketing (Athwal et al.,2019). The concept of luxury dates back to ancient times, when goods such as expensive diamonds were used to differentiate persons as belonging to the upper classes or elites. These products, which were often constructed of expensive materials or masterfully created, were objects of delight rather than everyday use, or articles of luxury. The notion of luxury has endured throughout history, and luxury items or services are distinguished by their high quality, exclusivity (not everyone may own them), and high price. (Chandon et al.,2016). As a class of products and services that denote status, selectness, and quality, luxury goods are one of the oldest known classes of goods. The mandates of the luxury market can be dated back to antiquity when luxurious objects were linked with kings, queens, noble persons, and other privileged beings. These goods were made from materials that were considered to be very unique and expensive, and hence the possession of such goods meant that one was powerful, wealthy, and had the requisite status. Luxury consumption dates back to ancient civilization; the Egyptian king and elite used ornaments of gold and gemstones. Likewise in Ancient Rome, the élite was proclaimed by luxurious residences evidenced by the luxurious villas, fine wines, and delicious banquets. As a result, the luxury products in these civilizations were required not only to persuade the buyers to buy products for comfort and to decorate the rooms but also to convince the clients about their status and the possibility of having a strong impact on others (McNeil & Riello,2016). the conception of luxury went through some changes; the Renaissance played an important role in European history regarding this aspect. In this period there appeared powerful dynasties of merchants, and one of them – the Medici family from Florence – stimulated the development of art, fashion, and architectural decoration corresponding to the epoch's richness. Another beneficial con of the Renaissance was that it created luxury brands, meaning that the artisans and craftsmen who created them were finally respected for their fine work. Venetian glass craftsmen and French flower makers became famous for their best-quality articles that created the basic template for luxury. New changes to the luxury market emerged from the Industrial Revolution in the 18th and 19th centuries. The availability of the products increased due to mass production but still, luxury products were easily identifiable by the quality of work, less number produced, and brand image. Among the cultures that gradually involved luxury brands, the creation of everlasting and famous brands like Louis Vuitton, Cartier, and Chanel made the concept of luxury connected with the concept of brand. These brands not only signed the ultimate quality but also identified with the quality of life of the consumers (Elgebali et al.,2023). While the notion of luxury as reflecting the greatest quality items, goods, or experiences exists, and for some, it will always be true, the consumer landscape has evolved, and so has the definition of luxury.

Luxury has traditionally meant obtaining the most sought-after, expensive things or experiences, but it is now more about the experience economy and a preferred way of life. Globalization and technological advancements are influencing consumer choices and values.

Economic expansion has increased disposable money, making luxury more accessible. As a result, rich consumers are increasingly seeking new and unique experiences, where luxury is no longer simply about acquiring stuff but also about achieving an idealized lifestyle or state of being. In today's digital world, where everything is at our fingertips, luxury has become synonymous with convenience, particularly among the younger generation. Whatever a brand sells must be easily available to be deemed valuable (Chechi, 2022). Over the last few decades, the global luxury goods market has grown and changed dramatically. The expansion of the middle class in developing economies, notably in China, India, Brazil, and Russia, has led to more discretionary incomes and a greater need for luxury commodities and products. As a result, these rising markets have become key actors in the luxury goods business as shown in Table 1.

Table 1. Global Luxury Goods Market Size by Type, 2022-2032 (USD Billion)

Year	Goods
2022	342.1
2023	354.8
2024	366.2
2025	383.3
2026	399.4
2027	412.2
2028	421.6
2029	437.2
2030	451.3
2031	468.0
2032	487.6

Source: https://market.us/report/luxury-goods-market/

AI has had an influence on several businesses, including the luxury goods market. Technological advancements and improvements have changed corporate practices as well as customer expectations. The industry's performance and expectations reflect this developing transformation. The luxury goods industry is estimated to reach 365 billion euros by 2025, with an expected annual growth rate of 3-5% each year. Companies in this market must carefully plan their strategies to effectively comprehend, excite, and engage their customers. Consumer sentiments, as well as a desire for prestige and social approval, generally motivate the purchase of luxury products. Luxury merchants are using technology tools including chatbots, machine learning, voice recognition, and picture identification to improve personalized consumer connection. As an example, Burberry employs AI to identify counterfeit merchandise, while Prada uses AI to improve customer comprehension and strengthen their marketing efforts (Munoz,2023). Luxury as a concept has always been closely related to exclusivity, material quality, and brand identity which has a historic reference point; yet, the incorporation of AI into the industry has brought about certain changes. In the age of new technologies and determinative global consumption trends, more and more, luxury brands are trying to introduce into their Companies AI solutions to improve the value proposition, effectiveness of processes, and the development of new forms of appeal that orient to the modern wealthy client. The use of AI in the development of the luxury market is multidimensional and affects various aspects of this industry. The use of AI has been one of the most profound in one area of luxury: personalization. Clearly, in the context of a highly competitive, luxury-driven, and personalized industry, AI becomes instrumental in providing strong differentiated solutions that can satisfy each of the consumer's requirements. Given this, there is the promise of great effectiveness in using AI to probe into large quantities of data to generate insights about patterns of use, thus allowing brands to target their products with pinpoint accuracy. The highly-rated luxury fashion firms employ algorithms developed through artificial intelligence to decode a customer's previous purchases, social media posts, and even their surfing habits; all in a bid to offer the customer products that match their expectations. Such a level of customization also applies to virtual shopping, in which case such tools as chatbots and virtual assistants offer individual consultations to the customer, increasing the overall experience (Sahne,2023). Technology, and most specifically, AI is also disrupting the design and manufacturing solutions within luxury. In the past, luxury products could be defined as those items that are produced using the highest level of craftsmanship and detailing. Although these qualities define the luxury brand, it is evident that AI plays a role in enhancing creativity by offering novelties to the designers. Besides the improvement of design, another significant aspect that is also being dominated by the adoption of AI in the luxury market is the supply chain management and increasing efficiency of production. Luxury products are mostly expensive and can only be produced in small quantities, therefore adequate measures are required to be taken for managing stocks. Thus, the use of AI to analyze data helps brands to predict consumers' demand and adjust their stocks and losses effectively. AI can assist in minimizing the costs of production by analyzing the weaker areas and recommending ways to optimize them with the goal of meeting the customers' high expectations of the luxury sector (Hindolia & Arya,2022). AI is not only revolutionizing the way luxury brands communicate with buyers but is also guaranteeing the sanctity and credibility of these brands. Piracy is a major problem in luxury products since many counterfeit products are likely to harm brand image and reduce customer loyalty. Current innovations in AI technologies include; machine learning and block blockchain technologies; these are being used to reduce counterfeiting by increasing product trackability and identification. The integration of AI into the luxury market also transferred to in-store experience where it is currently utilized to improve customers' experiences. Thus, while today luxury brands' purchases are more digital and are aimed at establishing a presence on social networks and creating applications, it must be recognized that the physical stores still play a crucial role in their sales and AI is helping to connect the two. AI is now being used for the creation of luxury market and its innovation, customization and operational performance. This means that luxury brands can stringently track trends ahead of time, increase their market personalization and innovation, and fit into consumers' shifting needs and expectations through the involvement of AI. As the development of AI progresses, it is explicable that the change it brings to the luxury market will be enhanced to form a decisive structure that corresponds to luxurious values such as consumers' privacy, better quality, tradition, and sustainability.

II. RESEARCH QUESTIONS

- How Artificial Intelligence (AI) helps in development of luxury market?

- What are the various factors that AI impact in development of luxury market?

III. RESEARCH OBJECTIVES

- To understand the role of AI in the development of the luxury market.
- To comprehend various factors that AI would impact the development of the luxury market.

IV. RESEARCH METHODOLOGY

The study involves a comprehensive literature review conducted across three primary databases: for instance, Scientific Direct, Web of Science, and Google Scholar among others. These databases were chosen because they all provide substantial coverage of scholarly articles regardless of the disciplinary focus. The rationale for this study is to obtain up-to-date and relevant information on the role of AI in the development of the luxury market. To embark on this exercise, proper subjection of relevant keywords across these databases to subjects such as luxury market, Artificial Intelligence, AI, customer fraud detection and security, and supply chain, etc., Thus, articles identified in the search process were further narrowed down according to the type of study, relevancy, year of publication, and any other constraints set by the inclusion criteria. Specifically, the articles proposed for the reviewing step had to be related to the study subject, and not older than five years. The articles not related to the study topics such as news clipping and research papers not related to the topics are excluded. The focus of this search was to establish works offering a comprehensive analysis of the part played by the effect of AI on the development of the luxury market. Thus, after passing through the inclusion and exclusion criteria, a total of 36 articles were selected for further analysis. Some of those identified journals were critically analyzed, extracting the findings, methods, and theories concerning the role of AI in the development of the luxury market. The findings were synthesized and the focus was made on the patterns, principles, and perspectives that can demonstrate the influence of learning analytics concerning talent management.

V. ARTIFICIAL INTELLIGENCE (AI) DRIVEN PRODUCT DEVELOPMENT AND DESIGN: BOOSTING THE LUXURY MARKET

The strategy of both product design and development in the luxury market is to come up with products that reflect glamour, detailing, quality, and the use of modern technology. This process starts with the post-conceptualization process that involves identifying the target consumer, their wants, needs, and how they live, which in turn leads to the generating of ideas for products that not only have utility but also appeal to the consumers' emotions. During the design process, the most importance is on creativity, and the products are often made by local artisans utilizing techniques borrowed from the digital age to create products that are as classic as they are innovative. It is a process of creating luxury products with a meticulous focus on details that relate to the material used, as well as the fine touch given to prototypes as they undergo various improvements, all in a bid to represent the brand's history that is associated with quality. The end product is usually in small batches which increases its demand due to the scarcity of the product. During the course, sustainability and ethical issues gain significance with luxury brands' attempts to combine innovation with sustainability. The aim of product design and development in the luxury market is to come up with items that call for fashion, are symbolic, qualitative, and have an inside story (Barile et al.,2024). AI is a rapidly advancing tool that is enhancing the processes of product design and production, especially in luxury goods. The luxury industry, which has always focused on exclusivity, innovation, and the quality-hungry clientele is using AI to substantially increase creative output, optimize the processes, and match the new craving of the consumers. AI has intervention in product design and development processes taken through the different steps of designing, developing, manufacturing, and marketing, thus affecting the evolution of the luxury business. The application of AI in product design can be assessed based on the following key aspects: Data analysis is one of the main functions through which AI is revolutionizing the processes of product design in the modern world. Luxury designers must know that in this market segment, trends are volatile and consumers' characteristics are complex, and with the help of AI, this information is rather valuable. Intelligent analysis of various types of information, including posts on social networks, market research materials, and customer feedback will help AI to define trends in consumption and predict further changes. This helps luxury brands to closely work with customers and in this way, they can make sure that their designs are in sync with the consumer. The prediction approach that is accorded to AI also helps brands avoid risk when introducing a new design because the AI can predict which designs can be successful (Polese et al.,2018). AI is also contributing to the ability to design creatively since it provides designers with new tools and procedures to work with. Besides, this saves time in the design process and offers the opportunity to envision designs that would not have been previously conceived of. Also, as the luxury market focuses on innovation and individuality, a machine's capacity to create completely new designs falls under AI's advantages. Since it is possible to deliver highly customized solutions to consumers, AI can help designers continue the tradition of luxury goods production for clients (Maglio & Lim,2018). In the material selection and testing phases also AI is stepping up for its contributions to the development phase of products. The selection of the material in a luxury market is vital since it defines the general feel and outlook of the good. AI will help in making the best decisions of choosing the materials by their properties and their ability to perform in certain conditions (Rahman et al.,2023). AI is also increasing creativity in the design process by availing new opportunities to improve the designer's process. An AI-based design tool can create multiple designs out of the design input given by the designer concerning certain parameters. This not only speeds up the design and construction work but also enables the designer to include new possibilities in their design ideas that they have not thought of before. Thus, in the luxury market space based on the principles of innovation and individualism, the function of generating new designs is critical for the application of AI. It means that designers, with the help of AI, can produce goods that correspond to specific customer's needs and desires, which stress the primary element of luxury – uniqueness. Also, during the Material Selection &testing step of product development, AI is a growing and essential contributor. The selection of fabrics is paramount when dealing with luxury goods because it is the face of the product. This is done by analyzing the properties and performance of the materials and their suitability in different conditions to arrive at the best materials to be used (Sharma,2023). AI is also reshaping the luxury market through changes in the creativity of product design and, of course, the choice of materials, but, first of all, through changes in prototyping and manufacturing processes. Conventional prototyping in the luxury industry has always called for a lot of time and has been very costly since the prototypes are usually produced after many cycles and require much handwork. Traditional techniques like modeling and molding have been made easier by AI technologies like generative designing and 3D printing concerning quicker and inexpensive prototyping. Generative design, which is premised on AI, can generate several thousand designs based on certain parameters laid down by the designers, this way the latter can easily sift through to the designs that are likely to give the best results. Once there is a choice of a particular design, 3D printing can quickly complete a set of prototypes and test them for improvement. It also promotes the fast development of new products, which is quite crucial because luxury brands can now introduce new products to the market much faster (Lee,2022). In other words, AI entails not only the physical characteristics of the product and its attributes in quality and functionality but also ones that are digital and experiential. In the luxury goods segment where the real focus is on the consumer touch point, the application of AI is being made to make the experience of the product more appealing. AI has started creating opportunities for luxury brands, where the brand new object can have smart features and thus the functionality of such an object is expanded. Watches and jewelry can be made to incorporate boosting AI that checks on the health status or is in communication with other smart products. In the future world of luxury fashion, one can consider such applications of AI as making the clothing item responsive to the body temperature and or the weather condition of the region the item is sworn in by immediately changing color. These innovations do more than help to demarcate luxury products from ordinary products but also serve as a sign that luxury brands are embracing future technologies. (Oc et al.,2023).AI is at the forefront of product design and development, particularly in the luxury segment and it has brought these changes that have been necessitated by innovation and creativity as well as pushing for sustainable development. Thus, the application of AI promises luxury brands to remain the leaders in terms of design, offer distinctive and individual solutions, as well as provide consumers with the ultimate shopping experience. Thus, can be concluded that AI has a stronger influence over the luxury market as it moves forward, this change will continue to reshape how the luxury products domain is perceived and developed in terms of the interaction with consumers.

VI. ARTIFICIAL INTELLIGENCE (AI) AS A CATALYST FOR SUSTAINABILITY AND ETHICAL PRACTICE THAT WOULD LEAD TO ETHICAL TRANSFORMATION IN THE LUXURY SECTOR.

The luxury market has always been surrounded by elegance, handwork, and use of the best materials possible. However, in recent years, the industry has come under pressure to address the sustainability and the ethical manner in which it operates. Customers with the new generation and tourists are paying attention to sustainability, hence applying pressure on luxury fashion brands. AI is fast becoming the solution, enabling luxury brands to usher in this change, by championing sustainable and ethical practices along the value chain, from production to consumption (Osburg et al.,2021). The supply chain is perhaps one of the areas of the grandest impact that AI has made in support of sustainability in the luxury market. Products of luxury brands involve the use of materials from different parts of the world, and this makes it very difficult to assess the origin and the level of ethics of these materials. A source of these problems is solved by Artificial Intelligence (AI) using blockchain technology that allows brands to follow the process of materials from the raw stage to the final product. This transparency guarantees that all materials used are naturally sourced without compromising the environment or ethical working standards (Athwal et al.,2019). However, there is still a significant position of AI in managing supply chains and more effectively predicting demands. The typical supply chain systems depend on conventional thinking and conventional mathematics and hence inspire overproduction. While traditional methods are overall okay, it's like trying to guess the result of a football match while AI on the other hand can analyze extremely large data in real-time for instance, market trends, consumer behaviour, and even weather forecasts to have a clearer picture of the demand. This gives luxury brands opportunities to manufacture only what is required to avoid adding to the pollution of the environment (Vahamme et al.,2021). That is why ethical sourcing is a vital consideration for luxury brands, or consumers expect to know where and how their goods are sourced. AI can help in guaranteeing the material in luxury products in terms of origin and sustainability to minimize cases of fake luxury products in the market. In the manufacturing process, it becomes possible to use AI in the automation of various processes without compromising labor standards. Of course, many people linked automatic technologies with the loss of jobs, which is not true here; instead, automation enhances human craftsmanship in the sphere of LIG. Due to this Artificial Intelligence (AI) can help to undertake boring and dangerous tasks thus validating that human experts are constrained to doing more creative and challenging tasks in the manufacturing processes. This also helps to guarantee quality work and is also economical in that it prevents exploitive practices on labor (Vahamme et al.,2021).AI also helps in ethical practices through the monitoring of the working conditions of factories. Things like unsafe working conditions, or infringement of labor rights can be flagged by AI-powered sensors and analytics, for a brand to act on as soon as possible. Such a level of supervision is even more relevant in the areas where labor legislation can be lax while coming out with finished products that are free of ethical violations. AI is also invading the market for luxury products by changing the methods of production, advertisement, and usage of the products. The buyers of the present generation are well-informed and selective, and they require information on the standings of organizations as sustainable and ethical. Using AI technologies in marketing communications, luxury brands can explain their values by presenting information about the product's origin, material, and manufacturing process. Some brands employ AI to develop an ecosystem to generate digital identification such as a passport of the product which can be read by the customer to get more information on the sustainability of the product. The use of artificial intelligence in the personalization of marketing messages and products to clients increases consumer interest. This also enhances the shopping experience of a consumer and at the same time, helps the consumers to make better choices (Ferm et al.,2023). Originally, AI systems were used for various forms of passive logging tools in sustainable material sourcing, but today AI systems are used for these as active tools that proactively forecast and assess the environmental costs of such material. Conventional luxury brands have not sourced adequate data to inform their sourcing most of the time they have depended on the face value of the material and its appearance. But AI can now take into account a much wider set of parameters, including the extraction of materials, as well as their disposal at the end of their lifespan. Of those, the most promising is the preparation of long-term ecological performance prediction of new materials through an AI system. Through the incorporation of these notions into the companies' sourcing practices, brands can make more informed choices regarding the aesthetic appeal of their products while sticking to sustainable developments (Rathore,2019). AI is thus assisting luxury companies to look for materials that are peculiar and unprecedented in the industry. For example, through data mining, AI can scour databases in an attempt to find connections of relations that may propound new ecological raw materials or ways of manufacturing. This might result in the identification of substitutes for the skins used in manufacturing leathers that could come from plant products or synthetic diamonds that were cultured in the laboratory to mimic natural ones. The former has not only decreased environmental costs in luxury products but has also come up with competitive advantages that are appealing in the current concepts of green consumers (Sahne,2023). Manufacturing industries do not deploy AI merely for automation and increased productivity of the line but to comply with the ethical standards in the production line. Over the years, the luxury industry has been accused of vices that are socially irresponsible especially concerning labor. Nevertheless, at present, AI can be employed much more efficiently for controlling and enforcing ethical norms. Intelligent systems can mine the working conditions in real time because it can be done with the help of various sensors and fabricated devices located in the operating factory environment. They can identify seven bullying behaviors and unsafe conditions for working such that management can be informed before things get worse. This real-time control is necessary to preserve ethical benchmarks, especially if the labor legislation of the nations is questionable (Nermain et al.,2022). Besides the monitoring factor, AI can also contribute towards a more reasonable distribution of tasks in factories to eliminate the exploitation of workers. For instance, through machine learning, one can have the work distribution done in such a way that it covers many workers so that an individual cannot be exploited or made to overwork. Moreover, AI also frees workers from those mundane and sometimes potentially fatal tasks and due to that makes workers work smarter by dedicating most of their time to the meaningful and creative part of the products, With the help of AI job satisfaction is increased and luxury products produced are very carefully designed (Giovanola et al.,2023). One of the more promising recent trends in the luxury industry is the use of AI in achieving the circular economy. The idea of closed-loop; products being built to be remanufactured, refurbished, or recycled; instead of the current model of disposal has become the topic of discussion for finding sustainable solutions. Such a vision is possible through the integration of AI that assists in improving the existing and future enhanced recycling processes. Luxury brands must use these insights gathered by AI to create products that can be disassembled and recycled. Using such content analysis, AI can recommend changes to materials and how they are placed that make the end product more recyclable without having to compromise on topic quality or appearance (Kang & Sung,2022).AI is helping to optimize the process of reverse logistics – the action that implies the return of products for recycling or use. AI brings the added advantage of being able to estimate times and places where products are likely to be returned hence arrangement and management of the returns can be done efficiently cutting on cost and the effect on the environment. This is true for luxury brands mainly because most of the branded products belong to the top-end category and their parts might be useful for manufacturing new units, refurbishment, etc (Akrout & Guercini, 2022). AI is also being used to bring sustainability and ethical consumption in luxury good industry through personalization functions. Whereas in the past, luxury was considered to be all about customizing individual needs to products and services by applying AI, it is now being used to link individual needs with sustainability and ethical considerations in luxury. Due to advanced machine learning, there are chances of personalization where the eating habits, values, and spending capabilities can all be considered and products can be recommended basing the criteria that the consumer supports environmentally and ethically.AI can help luxury brands and consumers have more openness of sustainability and their ethical profiles. Brands could use artificial intelligence combined with the blockchain to let the consumers know all the details regarding the origin, process of its production, and environmental consequences that the product they are using has. It is important to note that such transparency helps unlock trust and re-establishes the brand's ethical stance (Sudas et al.,2019). AI's position in market forecasting is also progressing with outstanding improvements and potentialities for luxury brands to coordinate their strategies in sustainability and ethics. The conventional methods of forecasting involve using past experiences and trends, hence are not good when it comes to implementing newer trends that customers may find worthy or when some environmental factor comes up. As for that, AI can operate on far more extensive data sets – mood on social media, reports on the state of the environment, or climate data, for example – for a more accurate market prediction. Of special interest, this capability can help entailing the early identification of the changing consumer sentiments regarding sustainability and ethics, and the subsequent adaptation of strategies. For instance, AI may look into the future and identify that there will be increased concern for vegan leather or gems that are sourced sustainably, and brands will buy these materials hoping for a trendy future. By embracing these trends, luxury brands will keep pace with such mindedness making themselves the epitome of sustainability and ethical compliance, good news to the conscience consumer. (Lopez et al.,2023).AI is set to transform the luxury industry, especially in matters to do with sustainability and the right practices to uphold in production, manufacturing, and even consumption. In using AI, luxury brands are not only in a position to meet the increasing consumer concern for sustainability and ethical practices, but the brands are also in a place to elevate the bar of that particular industry. Therefore, as the advancement of technology develops, so will the ability of AI to contribute to the positive change that could be a benefit for the luxury market, to be able to design a mature future for the luxury market that would be sustainable and ethical outcomes for the future concern of the luxury market.

VII. THE IMPACT OF ARTIFICIAL INTELLIGENCE (AI) ON SUPPLY CHAIN AND INVENTORY MANAGEMENT IN THE LUXURY INDUSTRY

Supply chain and inventory management are some of the areas that are not easy to handle due to increased scrutiny especially since luxury products have to be of high quality, exclusive, and made with a lot of workmanship. Consumers are now insisting on disclosure, sustainable sources of material, and the capability of products to be available in stores immediately, the traditional methods of manufacturing need to improve on its efficiency while retaining the luxurious feel. AI has now proved itself as an important enabler for this balancing act of driving sustainability while improving all elements of supply chain visibility, inventory management, etc. AI enables luxury brands to sustain their product differentiation while at the same time, satisfying emerging consumer needs (Lin & Yu,2023). Supply chain transparency is one of the most valuable impacts of AI on luxury products since it gives consumers a better understanding of the brand. Products associated with luxury are favorites of the complex supply chain, as some interrelated and interdependent materials are sourced from different locations and various stages of production may occur in different countries. These materials credited must be as it is, genuine, organically sourced, and manufactured in an environmentally friendly manner to preserve the integrity of the brand (Rathore,2019). Artificial intelligence and the use of blockchain technology are being used to enhance supply chain transparency as a record is created for every transaction and transfer in the supply chain. Due to this technology, luxury brands are in a position to track all the raw materials from the point of procurement to the final product and guarantee that all the materials used comply with the luxury brands' standards of quality and ethics (Brun & Karaosman, 2020).

Besides, authenticating the supply chain, AI supply chain visibility allows brands to navigate risks more efficiently. AI systems are capable of tracking activities around the global supply chain and help to ascertain prospective disruptions including earthquakes, political changes, and when suppliers are at risk of shutting down. Through this AI, vendors can forecast the effects of these disruptions on the supply chain; this way, AI makes recommendations on other supply routes and suppliers who can help deliver the products without much delay (Pawlicka & Bal,2022). Inventory management plays a special role in the luxury segment where the degrees of rationally-proved scarcity and real availability of goods can be either beneficial or detrimental to a brand. This is especially a challenge for luxury brands to produce the right numbers of brands that are in demand to at the same time not flood the markets such that people start to think that the brand is not as exclusive as they thought. AI has the most advanced techniques for the right stock amounts, so brands do not lose this balance (Sander,2020). Of all the approaches in inventory optimization, AI-driven demand forecasting is one of the most potent. Using previous sales data and trends in the market may be time-consuming in delivering results that respond to new changes in the market. AI, on the other hand, can process large amounts of data from social media, search trends, and even weather conditions in real-time, and can estimate the demand from the consumer more accurately. Also, by using AI, stock merchandising can be categorized according to their location, the consumer, and how they use the product. This makes it possible for luxury brands to be able to institute various patterns of inventory depending on and as required by the various markets. For example, a luxury car maker may employ AI systems to discover that the models of some expensive watches are preferred by Asian customers while they are not in Europe; hence minimizing the distribution of large proportions of unnecessary inventory (Modgill et al.,2022). Consumers nowadays are more environmentally receptive and responsible and thus luxury brands cannot avoid being environmentally responsible. Regarding this, the application of AI is critical in augmenting these endeavors by promoting the best practices in the supply chain and inventory management to minimize waste and enhance sustainability. The first manner in which and can enhance sustainability is by reducing overproduction. Overproduction among other problems results in increased inventory that can be sold at a loss or even buried and has a very severe impact on the environment. AI provides for efficient demand forecasting which ensures that luxury brands create new products on demand and not create a hull of unused products as is often seen. This is more relevant in the luxury sector where trend is formed by controlling the circulation of products to a certain market by destroying the excess to prevent competition. Another way that AI is useful in the promotion of sustainability is because it helps to minimize the wastage of the available resources in the supply chain. AI can guide brands to select fewer damaging materials and also compare the sustainability of various choices (Babu et al.,2022). Being part of the operation, the supply chain and inventory management can be considered as the application of AI from the financial perspective but it also improves customer satisfaction. In Fashion luxury AI, helps the brand to better target specific customers' needs and wants in the market thus increasing the efficiency in matching the supply within the market. The use of artificial intelligence in customer relationship management (CRM) allows the prediction of customer behavior based on past purchases, browsing, and social media activity and therefore builds the most accurate customer profile. This helps luxury brands to be capable of predicting the requirements of their client and be in a position to meet them systematically, making sure that the demanded products are constantly being supplied. For instance, if a customer always orders some specific type of luxury handbag, the brand can predict when the customer is likely to order again and make sure that the product is restocked (Brun et al.,2017). AI helps assist brands with relevance in the Personalized selection and presentation of Inventory concerning regional or cultural preferences. Using data analysis from different markets, AI can define which product is popular in those areas and manage the stock correspondingly. This not only enhances the level of satisfaction to the customer by ascertaining that the right products are availed on the shelves but also acts as a check to minimize on excess of slow-moving products, which ordinarily would have crowded the shelves under ADC. Artificial Intelligence (AI) technologies are making a tremendous impact in supply chains and inventory, especially in luxury industries; solutions help to improve visibility and efficiency, minimizing wastage and optimizing shipping. To satisfy the consumer demand of the rapidly growing market and keep the exclusivity and quality of their products, luxury brands can make use of AI. The application of AIS in the supply chain and inventory management of luxury brands will expand as the technology of AIS enhances in the future to support these brands for managing global supply chain systems and supplying quality products to consumers. Turning to the aspect of AI, it is possible to reveal the key phenomena and approaches that would help the luxury market to be both innovative and traditional, thus guaranteeing its further successful development in terms of response to the emergence of an ethically sustainable future.

CONCLUSION

The luxury market, which has always been associated with exclusivity, proper production, and history, is at the crossroads of a qualitative leap connected with the use of AI. AI is redefining all sectors of luxury business including supply chain and demand, stock transitioning and control, customerisation and sustainability. Through optimization, iTrust in operations, and improved consumer interaction, luxury brands are now able to meet the expectations of the new demands of socially awakened consumers. While luxury brands are using AI to increase efficiency, decrease costs, and invent unique services, and products, they are not eroding their over-brand luxury image but also are creating new standards for the market by showing how brands can be innovative and sustainable. This transformation is making AI as one of the essential catalysts for the future developments of the luxury industry and maintaining its proper ethical standards. Therefore, AI is not only the tool of modernization but the enabler for a new generation of luxury where references are to be blended with technology and the premium product is to be delivered with supporting intelligence. Over time, it is expected that the utility of AI is going to become mandatory to take the luxury business in a direction, where the management of luxury goods will not only be a matter of product quality, but it will be the amalgamation of intelligence and ethics that are going to be involved in the manufacturing and distribution of such products.

REFERENCES

Akrout, H., & Guercini, S. (2022). Sustainability in fashion and luxury marketing: Results, paradoxes and potentialities. Journal of global fashion marketing, 13(2), 91-100.

Athwal, N., Wells, V. K., Carrigan, M., & Henninger, C. E. (2019). Sustainable luxury marketing: A synthesis and research agenda. *International Journal of Management Reviews*, *21*(4), 405–426. DOI: 10.1111/ijmr.12195

Athwal, N., Wells, V. K., Carrigan, M., & Henninger, C. E. (2019). Sustainable luxury marketing: A synthesis and research agenda. *International Journal of Management Reviews*, *21*(4), 405–426.

Barile, S., Bassano, C., Piciocchi, P., Saviano, M., & Spohrer, J. C. (2024). Empowering value co-creation in the digital age. *Journal of Business and Industrial Marketing*, *39*(6), 1130–1143. DOI: 10.1108/jbim-12-2019-0553

Brun, A., Castelli, C., & Karaosman, H. (2017). A focused supply chain strategy for luxury fashion management. *Journal of Fashion Marketing and Management*, *21*(4), 544–563.

Brun, A., & Karaosman, H. (2020). Luxury supply chain management. In The Oxford Handbook of Luxury Business.

Chandon, J.-L., Laurent, G., & Valette-Florence, P. (2016). Pursuing the concept of luxury: Introduction to the JBR Special Issue on "Luxury Marketing from Tradition to Innovation.". *Journal of Business Research*, *69*(1), 299–303. DOI: 10.1016/j.jbusres.2015.08.001

Chechi, H. (2022, December 28). What is luxury marketing? Les Roches; Les Roches International School of Hotel Management. https://lesroches.edu/blog/what-luxury-marketing/

Dogan-Sudas, H., Kara, A., & Cabuk, S. (2019). The role of sustainable environment attributes in luxury product perceptions: Evidence from an emerging market. *Journal of Transnational Management*, *24*(1), 3–20.

Elgebali, M., & Zaazou, R. (2023). The Impact of Value Perception on Luxury Brand Consumption. *Open Journal of Business and Management*, *11*(5), 2288–2309.

Ferm, L. E. C., Shawky, S., Thaichon, P., & Quach, S. (2023). Ethical and Sustainability Issues of Artificial Intelligence (AI) in the Luxury Industry. In Luxury Marketing, Sustainability and Technology (pp. 37-52). Routledge.

Giovanola, B., Tiribelli, S., Frontoni, E., & Paolanti, M. (2023). Ethical implication of Artificial Intelligence in the Fashion Industry: A comprehensive analysis. *Fashion Highlight*, (2), 22–28.

Hindolia, A., & Arya, J. (2022). Hermeneutic approach in understanding the role of artificial intelligence: Fashion & apparel industry/luxury brand retailing. *Academy of Marketing Studies Journal*, *26*(2).

Kang, E. Y., & Sung, Y. H. (2022). Luxury and sustainability: The role of message appeals and objectivity on luxury brands' green corporate social responsibility. *Journal of Marketing Communications*, *28*(3), 291–312.

Khamoushi Sahne, S. S. (2023). The Impact of Artificial Intelligence on Customer Loyalty in the Luxury Market: Mediating Role of Customer Relationship. Available at *SSRN*.

Lee, Y. A. (2022). Leading edge technologies in fashion innovation: Product design and development process from materials to the end products to consumers. 1–16.

Lin, Y., & Yu, J. (2023). Study on the Modernization of Supply Chain Management of the Luxury Industry in the Context of the Digital Economy. *Academic Journal of Management and Social Sciences*, *4*(1), 5–11.

López, B., Rangel-Pérez, C., & Fernández, M. (2023). Sustainable strategies in the luxury business to increase efficiency in reducing carbon footprint. *Journal of Business Research*, *157*, 113607.

Maglio, P. P., & Lim, C. (2018). On the impact of autonomous technologies on human-centered service systems. Handbook of service dominant logic

Market. us. (2023). Luxury goods market share, size, trends, forecast 2023 | 2032 [Data set].

Mcneil, P., & Riello, G. (2016). *Luxury: A rich history*. Oxford University Press.

Modgil, S., Singh, R. K., & Hannibal, C. (2022). Artificial intelligence for supply chain resilience: Learning from Covid-19. *International Journal of Logistics Management, 33*(4), 1246–1268.

Mohiuddin Babu, M., Akter, S., Rahman, M., Billah, M. M., & Hack-Polay, D. (2022). The role of artificial intelligence in shaping the future of Agile fashion industry. *Production Planning and Control*, •••, 1–15.

Munoz, J. M. (2023, July 11). AI and technological sophistication in luxury companies. California Management Review. https://cmr.berkeley.edu/2023/07/ai-and-technological-sophistication-in-luxury-companies/

Oc, Y., Plangger, K., Sands, S., Campbell, C. L., & Pitt, L. (2023). Luxury is what you say: Analyzing electronic word-of-mouth marketing of luxury products using artificial intelligence and machine learning. *Psychology and Marketing, 40*(9), 1704–1719.

Osburg, V. S., Davies, I., Yoganathan, V., & McLeay, F. (2021). Perspectives, opportunities and tensions in ethical and sustainable luxury: Introduction to the thematic symposium. *Journal of Business Ethics, 169*, 201–210.

Pawlicka, K., & Bal, M. (2022). Sustainable Supply Chain Finances implementation model and Artificial Intelligence for innovative omnichannel logistics. *Management, 26*(1), 19–35.

Polese, F., Carrubbo, L., Caputo, F., & Megaro, A. (2018). Co-creation in action: An acid test of smart service systems viability. In Exploring Service Science: 9th International Conference (pp. 151–164). Springer International Publishing

Rahman, M. S., Bag, S., Hossain, M. A., Abdel Fattah, F. A. M., Gani, M. O., & Rana, N. P. (2023). The new wave of AI-powered luxury brands online shopping experience: The role of digital multisensory cues and customers' engagement. *Journal of Retailing and Consumer Services, 72*(103273), 103273. DOI: 10.1016/j.jretconser.2023.103273

Rathore, B. (2019). From Trendy to Green: Exploring AI's Role in Sustainable Fashion Marketing. *International Journal of New Media Studies: International Peer Reviewed Scholarly Indexed Journal*, *6*(2), 12–22.

Rathore, B. (2019). Artificial Intelligence in Sustainable Fashion Marketing: Transforming the Supply Chain Landscape. *Artificial Intelligence*, *8*(2).

Sharma, A. (2023). Product design and development using Artificial Intelligence (AI) techniques. *RE:view*.

Chapter 6

Household Consumption in the Midst of Poverty and Conspicuous Consumption:
The Role of Media and Household Characteristics

Shafiu Ibrahim Abdullahi
https://orcid.org/0000-0003-3471-4493
Department of Economics, Skyline University Nigeria, Kano, Nigeria

Ahmad Muhammad Tsauni
Bayero University, Kano, Nigeria

Amina Abubakar Ismail
Bayero University, Kano, Nigeria

Mansur Idris
Bayero University, Kano, Nigeria

DOI: 10.4018/979-8-3693-8422-0.ch006

ABSTRACT

Households in Kano metropolis, like in other developing parts of the world, made decision under poverty condition, poor information and a society wide low-education level. The ramification of poor economic development is felt in all sectors of the society. Unlike the rich, the living condition of the poor is constraint; his low purchasing power has restricted him to the fringe of society. Just like the rich of the advanced economies of the world who want to enjoy their mammoth wealth through extravagant expenditures, the rich of the less developed countries are also keen to imitate their rich world counterparts through conspicuous consumption. Households' inherent characteristics may have played a role in influencing how they perceived information. This study tries to find out the influence of information on households' consumption visa-vis other factors in Kano metropolis. Kano metropolis is a multi cultural environment that has in its mid people of all races, income groups and cultures.

INTRODUCTION

Just like the rich of the advanced economies of the world who want to enjoy their mammoth wealth through extravagant expenditures, the rich of the less developed countries are also keen to imitate their rich world counterparts through conspicuous consumption. From expensive vacations to flashy cars to huge mansions the very rich in the developing world are doing their best to compete with their rich world counterparts. Despite the rampant poverties in India and Nigeria, for example, they have some of their super rich listed in the exclusive Forbes billionaire club. But poverty is real in the developing world, the poor has struggled to meet his basic needs such as foods, shelter, good health and education. It is estimated that about 711 million people in the world live on less than two dollars a day. In Nigeria the percentage of the poor is very high, it is estimated that four in every ten Nigerian is extremely poor (NBS, 2019); while about 63% are categorized as multidimensionally poor (NBS, 2022). The middle class, going by the number of poor in Nigeria, is not that much in size compare with the middle class in other developing countries. Apart from the super rich and the rich, the middle class is the other group that manages from time to time to enjoy some form of luxury preserve for the rich. They enjoy affordable vacations, good cars, jewelries, fashionable attires, etc. The economic crises of recent years and poor economic policies on the part of the subsequent governments have managed to reduce the size of middle class in Nigeria. In recent years a number of retailers that serve the middle class and the rich have left Nigeria due to the dire economic condition and the reduced market for their goods and services. Major retailers and manufacturers such as Shoprite have all left Nigeria. Despite all these setbacks, the Nigerian rich and the middle class still want to make it up through constant travels to places such as Dubai in UAE and London in the UK to make their shopping and enjoy amenities that are not available at home. For the poor, he/she remains in Nigeria to make living in midst of poverty, unemployment, poor infrastructures and lack of social amenities.

Economic literature is richly endowed with works that tried to highlight the role of media in consumption especially in advertising. At the same time there are a number of gaps in the past studies on the role of media in consumption that are yet to be attended to. Information is an important variable in economic decision-making that influence success or otherwise of any undertaken. Information economics or the economics of information deals with how information and information systems affect an economy and economic decisions. According to Stigler (1961) information is a valuable resource: knowledge is power. Economic theory of information is in many respects a sophisticated theory of consumer and seller behavior, a theory that involves much more than search by consumers and advertising by sellers (Calfee and Ford, 1988). It focus has been on consumer search, price dispersion, the relation between price and quality, and the informational content of advertising. Large body of literature has dealt with market signaling and other theoretical solutions to the problems of cost and verification. It also deals with how consumers deal with the problems of extracting useful information from biased sources, i.e., sellers, and how sellers attempt to provide valuable information to consumers. Recently, the literature has focused on how modern media such as the internet and social media such as Facebook and YouTube affect how consumers make consumption decision. Other literatures have focused on the important role mobile media plays in providing households with information. The exponential growth in the use of mobile communication has not escaped the attentions of these studies. At the same time this was taking place, mobile commerce is also rapidly developing to serve as competitor to traditional commerce. Mobile commerce provides household with alternative means of meeting their consumption needs of luxury goods and services as well as day to day goods and services.

Information is considered money even before the advent of modern information technology (Goodhart, 1989). But in today information technology environment, the role of information in our lives has become more strategic than at any time before. Consumption is one such economic function that cannot do without information. Consumers need information as much as students need knowledge. This is where modern technology such as mobile technology becomes handy. These modern devices have provided consumers with information at their finger tips. For modern consumers, consumption of information alone is itself consumption. Just as income is important for consumption, information is also important for consumption. Another important factor that affects how consumers use information is culture and the environment the consumer is living in. For example, Chinese, Frances, Brazilian or Nigerian consumers shall not be expected to adopt internet/mobile media in the same manner, since they are influenced by different cultures and environments. Studies such as that of Plasse (2017), Wells, et al. (2012) and Harris, et al. (2005) have shown how cultures and environments differ in adopting mobile technology. Generally, media plays important role in consumption; a study on the effects of mass media on consumers' purchase of organic food shows that mass media is effective in influencing consumption (Fei and Yi, 2023). In a different study, Voramontri and Klieb (2019) discovered that social media influenced consumers purchase decision. They noted that consumers' purchase decisions involved significant brand differences, high consumer involvement and risk. Chunfang, et al (2023) analyzes the impact of Internet usage on household consumption in China. Their findings show that Internet usage significantly increases household consumption. In consumption, micro decision making involves such things as deciding what to use for consumption, how much to pay for particular items of consumption, where to get the money to pay for purchases of consumption goods and services, etc. Micro decision making involves aggregation of small day to day decisions that all together have combine (huge) impacts on economic lives of households. But, all these decision taking cannot be possible without quality information in the hand of the decision maker (the head of the household).

In modern age, media is arguably the most important source of information about consumption. But, while media is important in consumption other factors play different degree of role in how consumers process the information available to them. Factors such as education level of the consumer, cultural environment of the consumer and religion of the consumer all have role to play in how consumers process information. In case of technology adaptation, culture and environment also play prominent roles. Other variables that affect how consumers process information include age, gender and occupation of the consumer. This chapter aims to measure the influence of sources of information such as TV, Radio, print media, mobile media and the internet on consumption behavior of the rich and the poor. It, among others, looks at how consumers manage luxury expenditures. It also finds out how households' characteristics affect their ability to understand advertising information. The income of the consumer, whether he/she is rich or poor has central role in how consumer conducted his day to day live. This also takes us to the realm of culture and environment and their roles in determining how consumers use information and adopt technology. The study tests how variables such as age, gender, education and occupation affect consumers' perception of information in advertising, use of communication technology, etc. Advances in psychology and consumer behaviour studies have uncovered the surprising manner in which information influence consumers' behaviour. Considering the role of consumption in economic growth and development, any study that explains the factor that determines consumption has direct and indirect effects on economic growth itself. Studies such as that of Grigoreva (2021) have shown how young generation of consumers sourced information online through social media and the internet before making consumption decision. The study also shows that young consumers also called generation Z tend to make their consumption purchases online.

EMPIRICAL LITERATURE REVIEW

This section, among others, reviewed a number of works that deals with the influence of media on consumption. The media include traditional media and modern media such as social media and the internet. Kizgin, Jamal, Dey and Rana (2017) observed that social media has become a significant and effective means of endorsing activities and communications among peers, consumers and organizations. Previous studies have acknowledged the role of agents of cultural change, but largely remain silent on the role of social media in influencing consumption choices. The study uses self-administered questionnaire to collect data from 514 diverse respondents and examines how use of social media affects acculturation and consumption choices. The research shows that social media is a vital means of cultural change and a driver of acculturation strategies and consumption choices. Akbarov and Islamli (2021) investigate relationships between two socio-psychological concepts (self-esteem and public self-consciousness) and marketing concepts (symbolic consumption and brand consciousness). 274 questionnaires were collected through convenience sampling. The work applies structural equation modeling for analysis. The results show self-esteem has a positive influence on symbolic consumption, brand consciousness, and public self-consciousness. It also finds that individuals that evaluate themselves highly are more concerned about public opinion. Individuals who care about their presence in society will use products that reflect their lifestyle. Consumers who make purchasing that is congruent with their lifestyle and self are more brand-conscious.

A work by Bayat (2017) has studied the phenomenon of conspicuous consumption in the midst of poverty. The environment of the study South Africa is noted for its high income inequality and racial differences among other differences between classes. The study noted how the poor used their limited income on expenditures that do not help in alleviating their poverty but only increase their symbolic status. The study tried to measure the relationship that exists between conspicuous consumption and poverty in South Africa. It asked the question does conspicuous consumption increase poverty? Data from national income dynamic study (NIDS) 2008 to 2015 was used for the study. The finding shows that engaging in conspicuous consumption by the poor increase poverty. Other studies look at the use of modern technology as tool of consumption. The use of modern technology as source of information for household has been on the increased in recent decades. Technology has revolutionized how sellers interact with buyers; how buyers chose where to make their purchases. Traditional computers and modern mobile devices have featured prominently in studies concerning how household get their consumption information. The emergence of mobile technology has provided both sellers and buyers with more options at their disposal. Recent studies have examined the phenomenon of mobile marketing in Nigeria. Onana (2021) examined the effects of digital marketing brand equity of microenterprises in Nigeria. The study collected 400 responses from respondents who are active internet users. The findings indicated that mobile marketing and social media have likely positive effects on brand equity.

In a study on how Facebook advertisement affect consumers' response, Ng, Goh, Nisar, Ghumro and Lim (2023) observed that perceived usefulness, entertainment, informativeness, irritation, and privacy concern significantly affect consumers' attitudes. They also noted that they have positive effect on consumers' attitudes towards intention and behavioural response. Zhang (2020) investigated consumer online search and purchase patterns, as well as digital consumption behaviors and the potential implication for marketing. The results suggest that mobile phones attract consumers who have lower overall purchase interests. The study also noted that that there is a large segment of consumers who are highly price-sensitive and are willing to overpay to curb future consumption. Sama (2019) has noted that modern marketers invest in various media platforms to influence consumer behaviour. An online survey method was utilized for the study. Data were collected from 529 respondents. Cronbach alpha, exploratory factor analysis (EFA) and Kruskal–Wallis (K–W) test were used to analyze data. The results indicate that newspapers advertisements, TV and the Internets are statistically significant. The results also revealed that magazines and newspapers are effective in influencing behaviour of consumers. Jashari and Rrustemi (2017) analysed the impacts of social media on consumers' behaviour in Kosovo. The result show that consumers reported to have been pushed to make consumption decision, including unplanned decision. Social media friends decisions are also important variable in influencing their own decisions.

Alaimo (2014) investigated social media and the construction of digital consumers. He noted that not only are consumers immersed in an information mediated context - decoupled from physical and socio-cultural constrains - but they also experience other consumers and themselves differently, embracing the prescriptions of a technological medium made by algorithmic suggestions and software instructions." The study shows that technological information and software systems disassemble traditional practices of consumption and reassemble consumers in new and unseen ways. Sun (2005), analyze the promotion effect on consumption. Applying a test on packaged tuna and yogurt, he finds that endogenous consumption responds to promotion as a result of forward-looking and stockpiling behavior. Niazi, Siddiqui, Shah, and Hunjra (2012) examined relationship between effective advertising and consumer buying behavior. Research questionnaires were given to 200 respondents in twins' cities of Pakistan. Findings show moderate relationship. It shows that consumer purchase those brands they are emotionally attached. Ampofo (2014) examined the effects of advertising on consumer buying behaviour of cosmetic products in Bangalore India. Using sample of 100 respondents of mostly young, the study found that advertising influence purchase of cosmetics products. Other factors include consumer's income, price of the product, brand and referrals.

THEORETICAL FRAMEWORK

The rise in the phenomenon of conspicuous consumption in midst of poverty has been spectacular in recent decades. In her book "framing", Diana E. Kendall (2011) has discussed in detail how media represented wealth and poverty in America. How the media glorified the lives of the rich and demonized that of the poor. David Cloutier (1972) in his book "the Vice of luxury: economic excess in a consumer age", heavily criticize the life of excesses in the Western world. He sees luxury as destructive to both individual and society. According to scholars such as Kenneth Galbraith (1977) and Susan George (2010) there are a lot of academic studies on the poor, yet there were few studies on the rich. The rich and super rich shall also be studied extensively. This will go a long way in learning how to improve the lives of the oppressed poor. Kempf (2008) and others have argued that the consumption habit of the rich is behind the craze for unsustainable economic growth and rush for material things. Conspicuous consumption is simply expenditure of money on luxury goods and services to publically display one's income or wealth. Such a display of economic power is a means of showing social status (Veblen, 1899). Conspicuous consumption manifests from the urge to achieve social status by showing wealth through extravagant expenditures. In this scenario, "budget" brands are priced at insignificant cost, but "luxury" brands, though not inherently superior, are sold at higher prices to rich consumers seeking to advertise wealth (Bagwell and Bernheim, 1996).

Unlike the rich, the living condition of the poor is constraint; his low purchasing power has restricted him to the fringe of society. Thus, in the field of modern consumption the poor has no much room for maneuver. Poverty is one concept that has seen differing interpretations, depending on the angle the observer is coming from. The conventional view of poverty sees it as lack of sufficient income for securing basic needs. Poverty manifests in day to day life aspects such as education, food, health, accommodation, lifestyle and status in society. In term of consumption, the consumption of the poor is different from that of the rich. Some poor families cannot afford basic needs, talk-less of luxury things. Poverty is subdivided into absolute poverty, relative poverty and abject poverty. In some locations poverty has high correlation with gender, disability, race and ethnicity. The poor is more exposed to problems such as harmful environmental effects, climate change and natural disasters than the rich. Poverty is vicious and cyclical, as being poor tend to make a family more entrenched in poverty. All these factors combine to affect how the poor access vital information and available knowledge to better his life.

In marketing, consumer behavior is defined by Kotler (2003) as 'how individuals, groups, and organisations select, buy, use and dispose of goods, services, ideas or experiences to satisfy their needs and desires'. A consumer's buying behavior is influenced by cultural, social, personal and psychological factors. Cultural factors exert the broadest and deepest influence (Kotler, 2003). Consumer's wants and behavior are highly influenced by the culture he belongs to. In turn, those needs, wants, behaviors, and values are shaped by the society in which customers live (Anderson and Vincze, 2004). The consumer buying behaviour is not only restricted by social, political and economic opportunities, but also influenced by cultural frameworks of consumers' environments (Willer, 2006). Culture itself is made up of subcultures. Subcultures make it easier for marketers to target specific groups, since they provide more specific identification and socialization. Subcultures include nationalities, religions, racial groups and geographical regions. Through diversity marketing, marketers target subcultures that growth into a large market segment. Modern marketing, generally, sees customer loyalty and long-term profitability as the overarching goals for an organization. Culture profoundly influences all aspects of human behavior, including consumption. This means that few marketing researchers or practitioners can afford to ignore cultural differences in consumer psychology and behavior. Alsaad (2020) noted that the role of moral certainty has received relatively little attention. Moral certainty refers to the subjective sense of conviction or confidence one holds about his/her ethical judgment of an object.

Personal factors such as age, occupation, economic circumstances, lifestyle and personality also affect consumption decision. Family lifecycle also affect consumption decision. Other factors that affect consumption include occupation and economic circumstances, rich and high earning employees buy more luxurious goods than poor and lower earning employees who try to earn money for buying basic things. Marketers have over the years used researches on human behavior coming from the field of psychology. They recognized the effect of psychology on consumers buying behavior. Then there is perception, the process by which individuals chooses, organizes and interprets information around them. In marketing, perception is very important, marketers do not play with it, sometime it is more important to them than the reality around. But, the process of learning involves changes in individual's behavior through experience. People acquire beliefs and attitude about a particular products or services. Business must find out consumers who also serve as their customers. Hence, the reason why business learnt what customers want and act accordingly. The changing demands among consumers and changes in consumption habits are constant source of anxiety to a businessman. He must adapt his products to consumer preference (Lindholm and Driscoll, 1967). Marketers use advertising, branding, promotion and other marketing communication tools to create emotional bonds with consumers. How consumers make their purchase decisions has long been a popular research topic among marketing scholars all around the world.

On the traditional theory of consumption, there are well known theories in economics that tries to explain consumption. One theory that is relevant for this work is Hall's rational expectation theory of consumption. The Robert Hall's extension of the permanent-income hypothesis of consumption has important implication for this work. The permanent-income hypothesis shows that consumption depends on people's expectations. Robert Hall's (1978, 1987) work on consumption has combined this view of the consumer with the assumption of rational expectations. According to rational expectation theory people use all available information to make optimal forecasts of the future. Random walk hypothesis shows that changes in consumption over time should be unpredictable. Thus, consumption follows random walk. According Mankiw (2007), Changes in consumption reflect "surprises" about lifetime income; if consumers are optimally using all available information, they should only be surprised by events that were entirely unpredictable. This means that changes in consumption are unpredictable. Here the model takes into consideration uncertainty assumption about the income flow. The individual consumer maximizes

$$E(U) = E\left[\sum_{t=1}^{T}\left(C_t - \frac{a}{2}C_t^2\right)\right],$$

$$a > 0 \qquad (1)$$

It is assumed that marginal utility is positive and any debt is paid off at the end of life. Budget constraint is as in the equation under permanent income hypothesis above:

$$\sum_{t=1}^{T} C_t \leq A_0 + \sum_{t=1}^{T} Y_t \qquad (2)$$

Under this theory, the best forecast of consumption next year would be consumption this year. This is because changes in consumption are very hard to predict, hence consumers shall start their analysis with their current consumption. If consumers are very foresighted, they will change their consumption only when they learn something new about the future, such as increase or reduction in income, gift, inheritance, etc. But, by definition, such news cannot be predicted. At the end, all these cannot be possible without the information available from firms, media and other sources.

DATA AND METHODOLOGY

Data and Source

Data for the study was sourced through questionnaire survey conducted among household residing in Kano metropolis Kano state Nigeria. Kano is located in northern part of Nigeria (geographically it is in Savanna region of Africa) with population of about 5 million people. It is the second most populous metropolis in Nigeria after Lagos in the South West. It is also second most commercially strategic metropolis in Nigeria after the same Lagos. Kano has people from different tribal and religious backgrounds living their lives together. Hence, it is a kind of micro Nigeria. Thus, Kano is multicultural and ideal for study that tries to see how cultures and economic groups intermixed. Like other parts of Nigeria majority of its inhabitants are poor and literacy rate is low, though it is increasing gradually. The sampling process for the work is based on multistage sampling techniques where out of the eight local government of the metropolis four were selected then from that four two wards were selected from each local government making it eight wards. It is from these eight wards that respondents' opinions were collected using questionnaire. Hence, the data is micro level data suitable for short run analysis and multinomial modelling. The study paid special attention to variables that influence household consumption. It also looks at how household features affected its understanding and handling of information. The targeted respondents are head of households who are responsible for making decision for the household who are also mostly responsible for providing money needed to pay for consumption expenses. A household head can be a male or female. Household size in Nigeria is classified by NBS (2019) at average of 5.

Figure 1. Kano Metropolis

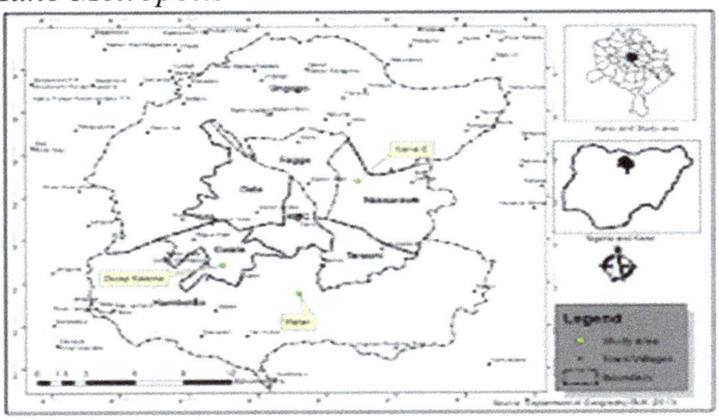

Source: Department of Geography BUK

Variables Definition

Consumption: Defined as spending for acquisition of utility (Black, Hashimzade, Myles, 2009). People are rational consumers; hence, they decide on what combinations of goods and services to buy based on their utility function and budget constraint. At the point of deciding which quantities of a particular commodity to buy, a consumer is assumed to possess all the necessary information needed for effective decision making. This information includes knowledge about the available goods and services, their prices, their applications and his budget. The consumer is assumed to choose among the available alternatives in such a way that the satisfaction he derives from consuming commodities is as large as possible (Henderson and Quandt, 2007).

Income: income here denotes the (average) amount of money household head makes in a month. In all the major consumption theories, income is the primary determinant of consumption. Because of difference in income the rich can afford things of luxury that the poor cannot afford. The very rich earn what the poor can only dream of; this give the rich the power to use his earning power the way its suit his way of living. While the poor because of low earning power is highly constraint in what he uses his money for. Hence, as far as determinants of consumption are concerned, all other variables come after income.

Trend/fashion: the urge to outdo your neighbours or follow the popular trend in a society made consumers to demand for more goods and services sometimes beyond what they may actually need. This is the main factor behind conspicuous consumption and some of the luxury expenditures one see around. The rich and the middle class want to outdo each other in term of luxury expenditure. The poor also participate to the extent that their income will allow them. Trend influence what people consume by making every household to follow what is in fashion (Bagwell and Bernheim, 1996; Akbarou and Islamli, 2021). Thus, the variable measures respondent degree of following the general trend.

Electronic media: Electronic media uses electronics or electromechanical means for the audience to access information (Sama, 2019). Electronic media include radio, television, video, telephone and game console; it is the main source of information in developing countries such as Nigeria. As source of information on different aspects of human life including consumption, it is variable of significance in this study. Here like in other areas of live, there are differences in term of the type of electronic media used by the rich and the poor. As usual the rich uses very expenses items such as plasma TV and costly handsets. The quality of the information received by each group may also differ. The rich and the middle class can afford to subscribe to sources of quality information for consumption such as pay TV which the poor cannot.

Print media: Broadly speaking, print media is any written or pictorial form of mass communication produced mechanically or electronically using printing, photocopying, or modern digital methods from which multiple copies can be made. They are news/information sources such as newspapers, magazines, journals, brochures and pamphlets. Print media are more effective in societies where the literacy rate is high (Sama, 2019). A lot of poor cannot afford to pay for print media, this limit the amount of information they get from this area. For the rich and the middle class they can afford to pay for any print media that meet their tests.

Mobile Media/Internet: Internet is a global wide area network that connects different types of computing systems. The computer lines are connected to major Internet hubs that distribute data to other locations, such as web servers and ISPs. Mobile media involves information sharing through handsets and other mobile devices. It includes internet accessed using handsets devices. Social media channels such as Facebook, Twitter and Whatapps are some of the important mobile internet channels of getting news. Other examples of mobile media devices are DVDs, CDs, USB drives, thumb drives, portable drives or discs, magnetic disks and digital memory. In many poor countries, the poor cannot afford to pay for internet access or pay for costly gadgets. This limits his access to fast changing news in the social media and the internet.

Gender: the variable gender shows whether respondent is male or female. Gender is theorized to affect household's consumption activities (Iyangbe and Orewa, 2009).

Age: age shows the current age of the respondent. Age of household heads matters a lot in consumption of the household in term of quality and quantity of goods and services consumed (Olasehinde and Olaniyan, 2017; Iyangbe and Orewa, 2009).

Education: the variable measures level of education of the respondent. Respondent level of educational attainment guides him on how he uses information available to him to conduct his/her consumption (Olasehinde and Olaniyan, 2017; Umoh, 1997). In poor countries, the rich and the middle class have upper hand in term of the quality of education they receive, when compared with the poor. This has effect on how the poor process the information coming to them. A lot of the poor in the developing world are illiterate or semi literate, while the vast majority does not have any qualification beyond secondary schooling. The rich can afford to send their wards to any part of the world to get the education needed to make them highly enlighten and qualified. This invariably has effect on shaping their tests and shopping habits.

Occupation: the variable measures formal or informal job of the respondent. Occupation which determines how much income households are getting within a particular time schedule is definitely very important variable in determining consumption (Olarewaju, 2018; Sekhampu and Niyimbanira, 2013). Occupation is also related to the level of knowledge and awareness of the respondent. The rich and the middle class get the juicy jobs while the poor is left with the not so desirable jobs (the hard labour) that pay less. This ultimately has effect on the nature of his consumption in term of luxury or basic necessities. Because the job in which the poor is employed is not paying much, the poor cannot be able to afford luxury he can only do with the necessities.

Advertising (information) Awareness; this variable measures how consumers perceive (analyze) the information they are receiving through media and other sources; an important consumption information source in this regard is advertising. Advertising is also discriminatory. Some advertising are targeted toward the rich while others are targeted toward the poor. It all depends on the goal the advertiser is willing to achieve.

Background Information and Descriptive Statistics

Male made up of 76.4% of the sample population while female made up 23.6%; in this part of the world male are expected to be head of households. The largest age group in the study is 36-50 with 45.1% of the respondents, followed by 51-72 age group and 18-35 group. In term of educational qualification, those with informal education made up the largest share (25.1%) followed by those with Degree or HND (23.6%), NCE/Diploma (18.2%), Secondary schooling (14.9%), Primary schooling (7.2%), Masters (6.3%), PhD (4.2%) and others (0.5%). In term of occupation, self-employed/artisan makes the majority with 31.6% followed by civil servant (27.8%) and business owner (24.2%). From the data, majority of the respondents are self employed. This is followed by those that are working for government and then business owners. This pattern of occupation can be explained by the fact that Kano is an important center of commerce Nigeria. Figure 2 provides details about the occupational distribution. Table 1 and 2 provide further details about background information and descriptive statistics.

Table 1. Background Information

Variable		Frequency	Percentage
Gender	Male	256	76.4
	Female	79	23.6
Age	18-35	85	25.4
	36-50	151	45.1
	51-72	89	26.6
	72-Above	10	2.9
Educational Qualification	Informal	84	25.1
	Primary School	24	7.2
	Secondary School	50	14.9
	NCE/Diploma	61	18.2
	First Degree/HND	79	23.6
	Masters	21	6.3
	PhD	14	4.2
	Others	2	0.5
Occupation	Self-Employed/Artisan	106	31.6
	Business Owner	81	24.2
	Civil Servant	93	27.8
	Private Sector Employee	25	7.5
	Student	13	3.9
	Unemployed	15	4.5
	Others	2	0.5
Marital Status	Married	251	74.9
	Single	84	25.1
Household Size	0-5	145	43.3
	6-15	148	44.2
	16-25	26	7.8
	26-35	6	1.8
	Above 35	10	2.9

continued on following page

Table 1. Continued

Variable		Frequency	Percentage
Accommodation	Rent	89	26.6
	Owner-Occupier	177	52.8
	Government House	15	4.5
	Family House	38	11.3
	Company House	0	0
	Friend/Neighbor/Community House	12	3.6
	Others	4	1.2

Source: Field Work (2023)

Figure 2. Occupational Distribution

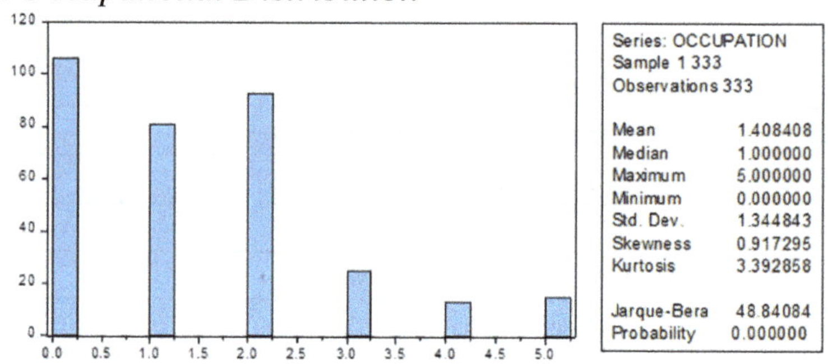

Source: Author's Analysis using Eviews (2023)

Key:

0 – Self-employed/Artisan, 1 – Business Owner, 2 – Civil Servant, 3 – Private Sector Employee, 4 – Student, 5 – Unemployed

The respondents spend most of their consumption income on the purchase of food items; it is followed by Entertainment/leisure/House furnishing, which is followed by Transportation/Utility Bills/House Rent. See figure 3 for details.

Figure 3. Distribution of Respondents' Expenditure Pattern

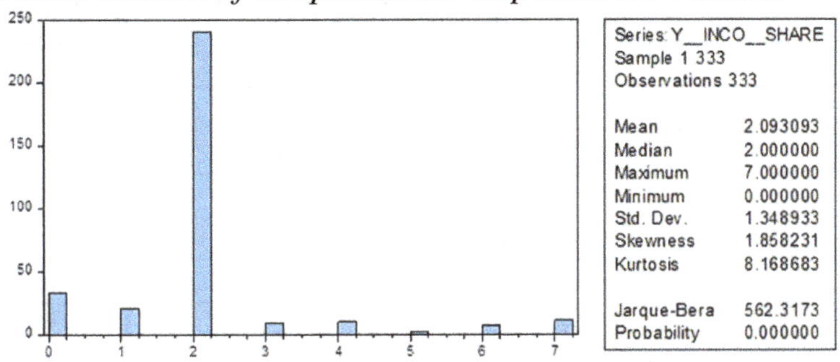

Source: Author's Analysis using Eviews (2023)

Key:

0 – Entertainment/leisure/House furnishing, 1 – Transportation/Utility Bills/House Rent, 2 – Food, 3 – Culture and Religious festival, 4 – Clothes and Footwear, 5 – Health, 6 – Education, Gifts and Charities

Table 2. General Summary Statistics of Responses

Variable	Obs	Mean	Std. Dev.	Min	Max
Consumption	333	0.949 (47500 Naira)	1.202	0 (27500 Naira)	4 (200000 Naira)
Income	333	1.051 (49723 Naira)	1.215	0 (22500 Naira)	4 (300000 Naira)
Food Expenditure	333	1.498 (53179 Naira)	1.179 (41819 Naira)	0 (10500 Naira)	4 (100000 Naira)
Age	333	1.063 (43 years)	0.795 (20.93 years)	0 (26.5 years)	4 (73 years)
Education	333	2.44 (Sec. Edu.)	1.809	0 (None/Informal)	6 (PhD)
Accommodation	333	1.18 (Owner Occupier)	1.211	0	4
Assets/Endowment	333	1.64	1.198	0	4
Cost of Energy	333	1.303	1.177	0	4
Charity	333	5.5%	0.562	0	50%
Electronic Media	333	0.483 (Radio & TV)	0.5	0	1
Fashion Trend	333	1.98 (Moderate)	1.153	0	4
Food Price	333	0.775	1.114	0	4
Gender	333	0.234	0.424	0	1
Household Size	333	0.753	0.870	0	4

continued on following page

Table 2. Continued

Variable	Obs	Mean	Std. Dev.	Min	Max
Information	333	1.381	1.564	0	4
Insecurity	333	1.513	1.046	0	4
Internet	333	0.691	0.463	0	1
Loan	333	2.763	1.501	0	5
Luxury/Leisure	333	1.895	1.199	0	4
Marital Status	333	0.258	0.452	0	1
Moderation	333	1.703	1.049	0	4
Occupation	333	1.408	1.345	0	5
Print Media	333	0.922	0.269	0	1
Social Security	333	3.501	1.726	0	5
Largest segment of consumption income	333	2.093 (Food)	1.349	0	7

Source: Author's Field Work (2023)

Method of Analysis

Binary Models

The Binary Outcome Models: Binary choice models assume that individuals are faced with a choice between two alternatives and that the choice depends on identifiable characteristics (Pindyck and Rubinfeld, 1998). Two standard binary outcome models are the logit and probit models. The models use maximum likelihood (ML) method. But, there is also another model called linear probability model by ordinary least square method.

Probit Model

Probit model uses cumulative distribution function (CDF) that follows normal distribution.

$$Zi = \alpha + \beta Xi \tag{3}$$

Where; Z = Z index, an unobservable utility index; X = explanatory variable; α, β = parameters

Let Y represent a dummy variable which equal 1 for high value of Z_i and 0 for lower value. They also represent choices among the two alternatives outcomes. Probit model solves the problem of how to obtain estimates for the parameters α and β while at the same time obtaining information about the underlying index Z. Z_i^* represents the critical cut off value which translates the underlying index into choices. Then,

$$\text{Individual choice} \begin{cases} 1st\ choice\ ifZi > Z_i^* \\ 2nd\ choice\ if\ Zi \leq Z_i^* \end{cases}$$

The probit model assumes thatZ_i^* *is* normally distributed random variable.

Logit Model

The model is based on cumulative logistic probability function.

$$\text{Li} = \ln\left(\frac{\text{P}}{1 - \text{P}}\right) = \beta 1 + \beta 2\text{Xi} + \mu\text{i} \tag{4}$$

The L shows log of the odds ratio.

Multinomial Models

Ordered Multinomial Logit Model

Ordered logit model is ordered regression model with ordered multiple categories. Here the dependent variable is ordinal. It is the extension of logistic regression model that allowed for more than two ordered response categories. Hence, the model is a multinomial model.

$$P(Y_i > j) = \frac{\exp(X,\beta - k_j)}{1 + [\exp(X_i\beta - k_j)]}, j = 1,2,\ldots,M - 1 \tag{5}$$

Exponential Regression Model

This is a nonlinear regression model. Exponential regression finds the equation of an exponential function that best fits a set of data. The exponential function is as follows:

$$p(X = X_i) = \left[\frac{1}{2\pi\sigma^2}\right]^{1/2} \exp\left[-\frac{(x_i - \mu)^2}{2\sigma^2}\right] \tag{6}$$

Where exp represents the exponential function; P is probability, x is variable, μ is mean, σ is standard deviation. From this likelihood function is drive as follows:

$$L(X, \mu, \sigma^2) = \left[\frac{1}{2\pi\sigma^2}\right]^{N/2} \exp\left[-\frac{\Sigma(x_i - \mu)^2}{2\sigma^2}\right] \tag{7}$$

Models

Two models are tested, model 1 and model 2; while model 1 deals with how media (information) affect consumption, model 2 deals with how household characteristics affect information reception/analysis (advertising awareness). Hence, model 2 further explain why the media influence on consumption is the way it is. Thus, model 2 further shades light on model 1.

Model 1: tested the influence of media on household consumption. The model measures the effect of information on consumption. Information can be in form of news or commercial advertisement; both of them have impact on consumers' behaviour. In modern economies, it is important for firm's managers to grab consumers' attention using various types of advertisements channels and other information dissemination channels. The model tests the effects of electronic media, print media, mobile/internet and trend/fashion on household consumption. Consumers' expectations of information from different media such as TV, radio, newspapers, magazines, mobile devices and the Internet are entirely different. The features of different media and its immediate and long-term effects on consumers are also varied (Sama, 2019; Kizgin, Jamal, Dey, and Rana, 2017; Niazi,

Siddiqui, Shah, and Hunjra, 2012; Doyle and Saunders, 1990). Thus, the model is:

$$C = f(y, em, pm, in, tf) \tag{8}$$

Where, C = consumption, y = income, em = electronic media, pm = print media, In = internet/mobile, tf = trend/fashion

Empirically the model is written as:

$$C = \beta_0 + \beta_1 incm + \beta_2 elecm + \beta_3 prinm + \beta_4 inten + \beta_5 trenf + \mu \tag{9}$$

A priori, these variables may have a conflicting relationship with consumption, depending on the context. For producers, positive but stagnating values of the coefficient of information/marketing/promotion mean promotion activities have their own limits.

Model 2: measures the effects of household characteristics on advertising (information) awareness. Household features such as age, gender, education and occupation of the household head are important variables that influence how individual receive and process information.

Advertising (information) Awareness = f(Age, Gender, Education, Occupation) (10)

Empirically the model is written as:

$$AA = \partial_0 + \partial_1 age + \partial_2 gen + \partial_3 edu + \partial_4 occ + \gamma \tag{11}$$

Where, AA – advertising awareness, age – age, gen – gender, edu – education, occ – occupation, γ – error term

RESULTS AND ANALYSIS

For the descriptive statistics: on following general fashion trade and how it affects household consumption, 40.1% vote moderately, 20.3% vote high, 14.9% vote low, 12.8% vote very low while 11.9% vote very high.

The results show that most household follow fashion trend but with some moderation. Finally, the result on effect of information on consumption shows that TV and radio have the most influence with 51.3% followed by mobile/internet/social media with 31.3%, newspaper and magazines have 7.8%. Conclusively, the result shows the increasing importance of new media such as mobile media despite the dominance of traditional media. Majority of the respondents in the study accessed internet through mobile devices such as the handsets. The results also show that a significant number of the poor want to enjoy luxury things though they do not have the necessary money to afford them. Tables 3 and 4 shade more light on descriptive statistics results.

Table 3. Consumption Pattern, Expenditure and Income

Variable		Frequency	Percentage
Income groups	0-45,000 Naira	136	40.6
	46,000-100,000 Naira	114	34
	101,000-200,000 Naira	44	13.1
	201,000-300,000 Naira	9	2.7
	Above 300,000 Naira	32	9.6
Consumption patterns (show groups that take largest share of consumption expenditure of households)	Entertainment/Leisure/House furnishing	33	9.9
	Transportation/Utility bills/ House rent	21	6.3
	Food	240	71.6
	Cultural and Religious festivals	9	2.7
	Clothes and footwear	10	3
	Health	3	0.9
	Education	8	2.4
	Gifts and Charities	11	3.2
Monthly consumption expenditure grouping	5,000-50,000 Naira	156	46.6
	50,001-100,000 Naira	105	31.3
	100,001-150,000 Naira	31	9.3
	150,001-200,000 Naira	16	4.8
	Above 200,000 Naira	27	8

continued on following page

Table 3. Continued

Variable		Frequency	Percentage
Monthly food expenditure grouping	Below 21,000 Naira	59	17.6
	21,001-50,000 Naira	142	42.4
	50,001-80,000 Naira	76	22.7
	80,001-100,000 Naira	20	6
	Above 100,000 Naira	38	11.3

Source: Author's Field Work (2023)

Table 4. Respondents choice distribution on the other variables

Variable/Question		Frequency	Percentage
Impact of change in food price on household consumption	Very much	183	54.6
	Much	89	26.6
	Moderately	36	10.7
	Little	5	1.5
	Very little	22	6.6
Effects of cost of energy on household consumption	Very much	101	30
	Much	97	29
	Moderately	95	28.4
	Little	15	4.5
	Very little	27	8.1
Impacts of physical-assets/accumulated-savings/ investments on household consumption	Very much	75	22.4
	Much	68	20.3
	Moderately	117	34.9
	Little	47	14
	Very little	28	8.4
Use of loans/credits for household consumption	Bank loan	25	7.5
	Salary advance	27	8.1
	Goods/service on credit	112	33.4
	Borrowing from family and friends	87	26
	Others …………	4	1.2
	None	80	23.8

continued on following page

Table 4. Continued

Variable/Question		Frequency	Percentage
Types of Social Securities/Transfer Payments/ Religious Charities received by household	Pension	6	1.8
	Government/Corporate assistance	72	21.5
	Zakah	27	8.1
	Sadaqah	46	13.7
	Others ……………	10	3
	None	174	51.9
Desire/need for luxury /leisure and ability to pay	Very high	53	15.8
	High	65	19.4
	Moderate	113	33.7
	Low	68	20.3
	Very low	36	10.7
Percentage of income given to charitable causes (*Zakah, Sadaqah*, etc.)	0%	72	21.5
	1-10%	238	71
	11-30%	21	6.3
	31-50%	0	0
	Above 50%	4	1.2
Moderation/self-control/adhering to religious injunction in consumption	Very high	41	12.2
	High	104	31
	Moderate	121	36.1
	Low	47	14
	Very low	22	6.6
Effects of insecurity on household consumption	Very much	76	22.7
	Much	65	19.4
	Moderately	146	43.6
	Little	37	11
	Very little	11	3.3
Level of following general fashion trend	Very high	40	11.9
	High	68	20.3
	Moderate	134	40.1
	Low	50	14.9
	Very low	43	12.8

continued on following page

Table 4. Continued

Variable/Question		Frequency	Percentage
Use of information channels for household consumption	Radio and TV	172	51.3
	Newspapers and magazines	26	7.8
	Road side/Billboard/Sign post advertisement	1	0.3
	Internet/Mobile/Social media	105	31.3
	None	31	9.3

Source: Author's Field Work (2023)

Regression analyses results: Model 1 measures the effects of information on consumption using discrete choice models; the results of the analyses show that the variable of electronic media (TV and Radio) and mobile/ internet are statistically significant. While the other variables in the study such as the print media and the variable measuring fashion trend in the society are not statistically significant. But, despite that they all display positive relationships with consumption; this means that ideally these variables should boost consumption not otherwise. Information such as through advertisement by producers of consumable goods and services are theoretically expected to increase/influence consumption of goods and services (Stigler, 1961; Calfee and Ford, 1988). Works such as that of Sama (2019), Kizgin, Jamal, Dey and Rana (2017), Alaimo (2014), Sun (2005), Niazi, Siddiqui, Shah, and Hunjra (2012) and Ampofo (2014) have documented the influences of these information channels on consumption.

Table 5. Logit, Probit and Exponential Regression Analyses Results for model 1

Variable	Logit		Probit		Exponential Regression Model	
	Coefficient	Prob.	Coefficient	Prob.	Coefficient	Prob.
Income	2.834692	0.0000	1.629483	0.0000	0.964016	0.0000
Electronic Media	0.509344	0.0482	0.290662	0.0425	-0.139190	0.0693
Print Media	1.224014	0.3340	0.710822	0.3267	0.723129	0.0991
Mobile/Internet	0.285264	0.0232	0.162129	0.0163	-0.283880	0.3656
Trend/Fashion	0.104704	0.5162	0.068948	0.4360	0.021639	0.8245
Constant	-4.011071	0.0135	-2.343818	0.0106	-2.037329	0.0144

continued on following page

Table 5. Continued

Variable	Logit		Probit		Exponential Regression Model	
	Coefficient	Prob.	Coefficient	Prob.	Coefficient	Prob.
McFadden R	0.334647		0.332277		-	
LR Statistics	117.7264		116.8927		350.0769	
Log Likelihood	-117.0333		-117.4501		-140.5122	
R Square	-		-		-0.725253	
Mean dependent var.	0.402299		0.402299		0.948949	
Number of Observations	333		333		333	

Source: Author's Analysis Using Eview (2023)

Model 2 measures the effects of household characteristics on advertising (information) awareness. It tests how age, gender, education and occupation of the household head affect advertising awareness. The results for model 2 show that only education is statistically significant. Education has positive effects on advertising information awareness. This is expected a priori and is in line with previous studies such as that of Smith (1996) and Teisl, Levy and Derby (1999).

Table 6. Ordered Logit Model Result

Variable	Coefficient	Prob.
Age	-0.069435	0.6899
Gender	0.321765	0.2858
Education	0.364603	0.0098
Occupation	-0.164603	0.4897
Pseudo R-Squared	0.009866	
Log Likelihood	-372.6471	
LR Statistic	7.426412	

Source: Author's Analysis Using Eview (2023)

IMPLICATIONS

The study shows that traditional media in form of TV and Radio are the dominant source of information for the respondents in the study. It is followed by mobile media and the internet. This is understandable given that a higher percentage of the population is illiterate or has just a basic education level; this makes them more dependent on electronic media and mobile devices for information than print media. But, the increasing significant of mobile media, social media and internet shows how things are gradually changing. The significant role of fashion trend on the respondents' behavior shows how words of mouth and socialization play a significant role. This is also understandable given how people in this part of the world prefer words of mouth to conventional media. This also shows the desire for fashionable things and some form of conspicuous consumption. Another dimension to this is the urge to outdo your neighbors or follow the popular trend in a society; which made consumers to demand for more goods and services sometimes beyond what they may actually need. Trend influence what people consume by making every household to follow what is in fashion. Conspicuous consumption also makes households to follow what other households are doing in order to attend social status. This is used as justification for extravagant expenditure (Bagwell and Bernheim, 1996). In his book the tipping point, Malcolm Gladwell (2000) discussed at length how connectors, mavens and salesmen within a population played important role in spreading the use of particular good or service.

The growing importance of mobile marketing in modern world has significant role to play in the growth of modern businesses in Nigeria. Both the rich and the poor have equally embraced digital communication as effective tool in improving their lives. Business organisations in Nigeria need to develop their marketing communication channels in order to boost their capacity to communicate with the public. The implication of failure to do that is that more consumers will continue to be ignorant of the products and services they are selling. Despite the importance of traditional media, the percentage of respondents that say they are influence by the new media/mobile devices, show the growing importance of modern media. This has implication on the channel of advertisement and passing of information employed by businesses and government. The positive value of the variable of education shows the importance of education in creating awareness about goods and services. The results of the study show how different media landscape is in Nigeria from what is obtained in developed countries where the use of all media sources has reached advanced stage. For example, this study has shown that the use of mobile media come second to the traditional media like radio and TV. But in many of these advanced rich countries, mobile media is now number one source of information for households. This is one of the most important contrasts between the two cultures in term of media usage.

CONCLUSION

The study analyses the role of media in influencing households' consumption in Kano metropolis, Kano state Nigeria. The results of the various regression analyses show that the variable of electronic media (TV and Radio) and mobile/internet are statistically significant. The education variable in the second model is also statistically significant in influencing how respondents understand information. The descriptive statistics shows how each important variable relates. Most of the respondent say they followed fashion trend but with some moderation; while other result shows the increasing importance of modern media despite the dominance of traditional media. Availability of sound and reliable information needed by consumers acts as an important source of consumer confidence and foster positive spending environment. Thus, there shall be improvement in the manner information is disseminated to consumers; both producers and government have roles in this. The effects of modern information sources, particularly mobile internet and social media on household consumption, shall be further explored using other study techniques. These studies shall also relate the effect of technologies such as e-commerce, mobile banking, digital payment systems, and internet advertising on household consumption. Other future studies shall focus on how the rich of the poor world source and utilized consumption information.

LIMITATIONS OF THE STUDY

The study was conducted in the post COVID-19 era and during Russia-Ukraine war when African countries found themselves in difficult economic situation characterized by high inflation rate, food shortage and risen poverty rate. This might, in one way or the other, influence how consumers respond to information, advertisement and other related factors.

REFERENCES

Akbarov, S., & Islamli, N. (2021). The Impact of Socio-Psychological Factors on Consumer Behavior: A Case Study in Azerbaijan. *The Journal of Asian Finance, Economics and Business*, *8*(5), 421–432.

Alaimo, C. (2014), Computational Consumption: Social Media and the construction of Digital Consumers, Unpublished PhD thesis, Department of Management of the London School of Economics

Alsaad, A. K. (2020). Ethical judgment, subjective norms, and ethical consumption: The moderating role of moral certainty. *Journal of Retailing and Consumer Services*. Advance online publication. DOI: 10.1016/j.jretconser.2020.102380

Ampofo, A. (2014), *Effects of advertising on Consumer Buying Behaviour: With reference to demand for cosmetic products in Bangalore, India*, available at: https://ssrn.com/abstract=2500915 (accessed 17 March 2019).

Anderson, C., & Vincze, J. (2004). *Strategic Marketing Management*. Houghton Mifflin.

Bagwell, L. S., & Bernheim, B. D. (1996). Veblen Effects in a Theory of Conspicuous Consumption. *The American Economic Review*, *86*(3), 349–373.

Bayat, A. (2017). The Relationship between Conspicuous Consumption and Poverty in Developing Countries: Evidence from South Africa. Research Thesis submitted to the Department of Economics, University of the Western Cape

Black, J., Hashimzade, N., & Myles, G. (2009). *A Dictionary of Economics* (3rd ed.). Oxford University Press.

Chunfang, Y., Yifeng, Z. & Suyun, W. (2023) The impact of the Internet on household consumption expenditure: an empirical study based on China Family Panel Studies data, Economic Research-Ekonomska Istraživanja, 36:3, 2150255, DOI:.DOI: 10.1080/1331677X.2022.2150255

Cloutier, D. (1972). The Vice of Luxury: Economic Excess in a Consumer Age.

Galbraith, J. K. (1977). *The Age of Uncertainty*. British Broadcasting Corporation.

George, S. (2010). *Whose Crisis, Whose Future?: Towards a Greener, Fairer, Richer World*. Polity.

Gladwell, M. (2000). *The Tipping Point: how little things can make a big difference*. Little, Brown and Company.

Grigoreva, E. A., Garifova, L. F., & Polovkina, E. A. (2021). Consumer Behavior in the Information Economy: Generation Z. *International Journal of Financial Research, 12*(2), 164–171.

Hall, R. E. (1978). Stochastic Implications of the Life-Cycle/Permanent Income Hypothesis: Theory and Evidence. *Journal of Political Economy, 96*, 971–987.

Hall, R. E. (1987). *Consumption*, NBER working paper No. 2265.

Henderson, J. M., & Quandt, R. E. (2007), "Microeconomic Theory: A Mathematical Approach", Tata McGraw-Hill Publishing company, New Delhi.

Iyangbe, C. O., & Orewa, S. I. (2009). Determinants of Daily Protein Intake among Rural and Low-Income Urban Households in Nigeria. *American-Eurasian Journal of Scientific Research, 4*(4), 290–301.

Jashari, F., & Rrustemi, V. (2017). The impact of social media on consumer behavior – Case study Kosovo. *Journal of Knowledge Management. Economics and Information Technology, 7*(1), 1–21.

Kempf, H. (2008). *How the Rich are Destroying the Earth* (Thatcher, L., Trans.). Green Books.

Kendall, D. E. (2011). *Framing Class: Media Representations of Wealth and Poverty in America*. Rowman & Littlefield.

Kizgin, H., Jamal, A., Dey, B. L., & Rana, N. P. (2017). The Impact of Social Media on Consumers' Acculturation and Purchase Intentions. *Information Systems Frontiers*. Advance online publication. Retrieved March 17, 2019, from. DOI: 10.1007/s10796-017-9817-4

Kotler, P. (2003). *Marketing management*. Pearson education.

Lindholm, R. W., & Driscoll, P. (1967). *Our American Economy*. Harcourt, Brace and World, INC, New York.

Mankiw, N. G. (2007). *Macroeconomics*. Worth publishers.

National Bureau of Statistics NBS (2019), *Consumption Expenditure Pattern in Nigeria*.

National Bureau of Statistics NBS. (2022). Nigeria Launches its Most Extensive National Measure of Multidimensional Poverty. Press release, 17 November 2022 –Abuja. Retrieved on 19th August, 2024 from https://nigerianstat.gov.ng/news/78

Ng, C. J., Goh, Y. N., Nisar, N., Ghumro, T. H., & Lim, C. N. (2023). Does Facebook Advertisement Matter to Entice Customers' Responses? An Integrated Technology Acceptance Model. *Malaysian Journal of Consumer and Family Economics*, *30*, 2948–4189.

Niazi, G. S. K., Siddiqui, J., Shah, B. A., & Hunjra, A. I. (2012). Effective Advertising and its Influence on Consumer Buying Behavior. *Information Management and Business Review*, *4*(3), 114–119.

Olarewaju, T. (2018). Organising household consumption and occupational proportions: Evidence from Nigeria. *The International Journal of Organizational Analysis*, *26*(4), 748–772. DOI: 10.1108/IJOA-03-2017-1141

Olasehinde, N., & Olaniyan, O. (2017). Determinants of household health expenditure in Nigeria. *International Journal of Social Economics*, *44*(12), 1694–1709. DOI: 10.1108/IJSE-12-2015-0324

Onana, K. I. (2021). Effect of digital marketing on consumer based brand equity of micro enterprises in Nigeria. *International Journal of Management and Social Sciences*, *2*(2), 1–37. DOI: 10.51739/122113816.v2i2.1459780014

Pindyck, R. S., & Rubinfeld, D. L. (1998). *Econometric models and economic forecasts*. McGraw Hill.

Sama, R. (2019). Impact of Media Advertisements on Consumer Behaviour. *Journal of Creative Communications*, *14*(1), 54–68.

Sekhampu, T. J., & Niyimbanira, F. (2013). Analysis of The Factors Influencing Household Expenditure in A South African Township. *The International Business & Economics Research Journal*, *12*(3), 279–284.

Smith, G. (1996). Framing in advertising and the moderating impact of consumer education. *Journal of Advertising Research*, *36*(5), 49.

Stigler, G. J. (1961). The Economics of Information. *Journal of Political Economy*, *69*(3), 213–225.

Sun, B. (2005). Promotion Effect on Endogenous Consumption. *Marketing Science*, *24*(3), 430–443.

Teisl, M. F., Levy, A. S., & Derby, B. M. (1999). The Effects of Education and Information Source on Consumer Awareness of Diet–Disease Relationships. *Journal of Public Policy & Marketing*, *18*(2), 197–207. DOI: 10.1177/074391569901800206

Umoh, G. S. (1997). Food consumption pattern in urban households: The case study of Uyo metropolis in Akwa Ibom State, Nigeria. *Agrosearch*, *3*(1-2), 94–112.

Veblen, T. (1899). *The Theory of the Leisure Class*. Project Gutenberg.

Voramontri, D., & Klieb, L. (2019). 'Impact of social media on consumer behaviour', *Int. J. Information and Decision Sciences*, *11*(3), 209–233.

Wells, R., Kleshinski, C. E., & Lau, T. (2012), "Attitudes Toward and Behavioral Intentions to Adopt Mobile Marketing: Comparisons of Gen Y in the United States, France And China" *Management and Marketing Faculty Publications*. 61. https://ecommons.udayton.edu/mgt_fac_pub/61

Willer, R. K. (2006). *Dispelling the Myth of a Global Consumer Indonesian Consumer Behavior Researched by Means of an Analytical Diagram for Intercultural Marketing with a Case-study of Sunsilk Shampoo for the Veiled Woman*. University of Zu Berlin.

Zhang, S. (2020), *Essays on Consumer Online Search and Digital Content Consumption*, Unpublished PhD dissertation in Economics, Washington University

Chapter 7

Impact of Cognitive Bias on User Decision Making Towards Third Party Logistics Products Using Nudge Theory

K. S. Ganesha
https://orcid.org/0000-0001-8181-2411
Dayananda Sagar College of Engineering, India

Kallem Kalyanchakravarthy
https://orcid.org/0009-0003-6388-1423
Dayananda Sagar College of Engineering, India

ABSTRACT

This study examines how cognitive biases affect users' choices of third-party logistics (3PL) products during the decision-making process, with an emphasis on the nudge theory's applicability. Confirmation bias, risk appraisal bias, anchoring and adjustment, and other cognitive biases frequently affect customer behaviour and result in less-than-ideal decisions in the intricate 3PL market. This research attempts to uncover practical tactics that lessen the detrimental consequences of these biases by incorporating nudge theory, which gently guides people toward better options

DOI: 10.4018/979-8-3693-8422-0.ch007

without limiting their freedom of choice. In order to better understand how cognitive biases affect 3PL product decisions and how strategic nudges might enhance decision-making processes, which will eventually benefit both customers and logistics providers, the chapter combines theoretical investigation.

1. INTRODUCTION

This template The present global economy places great importance on In today's business environment, third-party service providers (3PLs) play an important role in supply chain management by providing various services such as transportation, location warehousing, and inventory management. Choosing a 3PL service provider is an important decision for businesses to improve their supply chains. However, cognitive biases (patterns that differ from standards or qualifications in decision making) can affect the decision-making process. Nudge theory, which involves making choices without constraints, can be used to reduce the effects of cognitive dissonance. This chapter investigates how perceived dissatisfaction affects users' decision to choose 3PL products and how the theory can be used to improve decision-making. In 3PLs the realm of products selections, user decision making processes are subject to various cognitive biases that can significantly affect their choices. cognitive bias systematic patterns of deviation from rationality or judgment, often leading individuals to make decisions that may not align with their best interest. Understanding the impact of cognitive bias on user decision making in the insurance sector is crucial for designing effective strategies to improve consumer welfare and promote better decision outcomes. This research aims to explore the role of cognitive biases in shaping user decision making regarding third party logistics products leveraging insights from nudge theory to propose interventions that can mitigate the negative effects of such biases.

2. LITERATURE REVIEW

A. Cognitive Biases and Decision-Making

Cognitive biases are recognized as significant influences on decision-making processes across various domains. Gigerenzer (2011) critiques the traditional heuristics and biases framework, advocating for the importance of ecological rationality and adaptive decision-making. He argues that cognitive illusions, rather than being purely detrimental, can be adaptive depending on the environmental context. In the context of life insurance decisions, Ndawula, Mori, and Nkote (2023) explore the influence of behavioral biases on consumer choices in Uganda. Their study highlights the critical role of psychological and social factors in shaping demand for life insurance, demonstrating that biases such as overconfidence and present bias can significantly affect purchasing decisions.

Nudge theory has become a powerful tool for influencing consumer behavior, particularly in digital environments. Wang, Chen, and Wang (2020) examine the effects of different digital nudging strategies on consumers' customization choices, revealing that both overt and covert nudges effectively guide consumer decisions.

Cognitive biases are pivotal in shaping how decisions are made under uncertainty and risk. The seminal work by Kahneman and Tversky (1982) introduces prospect theory, a model that highlights how people evaluate potential losses and gains, often deviating from rational decision-making due to biases such as loss aversion and overweighing of small probabilities. Their research lays the groundwork for understanding the psychological underpinnings of decision-making in uncertain environments. Simon's (1955) exploration of bounded rationality further emphasizes the limitations of human decision-making, positing that individuals operate within the constraints of limited information and cognitive processing abilities. This theory of bounded rationality suggests that cognitive biases are not just errors but adaptive mechanisms in decision-making, given the complexities of the real world. Thaler (1980) extends these concepts into the realm of consumer behaviors, examining how biases like framing effects and the endowment effect alter consumer choices.

In their comprehensive work, Kahneman, Slovic, and Tversky (1982) delve into various heuristics and biases that impact judgment under uncertainty. This foundational text offers a detailed examination of how cognitive shortcuts often lead to systematic errors in decision-making. It provides a theoretical framework that is crucial for understanding how individuals make decisions in complex and uncertain environments. The issue of overconfidence in decision-making is critically analyzed by Russo and Schoemaker (1992), who highlight the pervasive nature of this bias in managerial and business contexts. Their study not only identifies the pitfalls of overconfidence but also suggests practical strategies to mitigate its effects, thereby improving decision-making processes in organizations.

B. Third Party Logistic Process on User Decision Making

The case studies from Cognitive biases and nudge theories can be important decision-making factors in third-party logistics (Loewenstein et al., 2014). Cognitive biases may cause decisions to be made that are not the best fit, like depending too much on one logistics supplier or underestimating the dangers involved in a particular course of action (Qian, 2014). By gradually changing the way options are presented, nudge theory can be used to help decision-makers make more logical and risk-aware choices.

Cognitive biases are systemic mistakes in thought that influence people's conclusions and choices. These biases may result in less-than-ideal decisions in the context of 3PL, which could affect the efficacy and efficiency of the logistical procedure (Kahneman & Tversky, 1979).

Accessible Heuristic: People who make decisions may overestimate the chance of more remembered or recent occurrences. For example, even though a recent disruption with a certain 3PL supplier was an anomaly, a corporation may find itself giving that event a disproportionate amount of weight going forward (Yamini, 2020).

Overconfidence Bias: Managers may overestimate their capacity to foresee logistics requirements or manage results, which could result in an underestimating of risks or insufficient backup plans (Tversky & Kahneman, 1974).

Status Quo Bias: Despite the availability of better solutions, companies may choose to remain with their current 3PL suppliers or methods (Bazerman & Moore, 2012).

C. Cognitive Bias Using Nudge Theory

Nudge theory uses behavioural economics' findings to gently influence decisions without limiting possibilities. It can be used to enhance 3PL decision-making through the creation of environments that produce superior results (Kunda, 1990).

Choice Architecture: Organisations can guide decision-makers towards better logistical solutions by arranging the way options are presented. Presenting 3PL options, for example, with an emphasis on total cost of ownership rather than simply upfront expenses, might stimulate long-term value analysis. Default Selections One way to take advantage of the status quo bias is to have the default be more effective logistical tactics (Bazerman & Tenbrunsel, 2011). For instance, incorporating risk management services into logistics contracts automatically, unless explicitly excluded, can increase resilience without necessitating extra decision-making. Simplifying the information provided about 3PL possibilities can help minimise some of the complexity that the effects of cognitive stress and make sure that important elements are given the proper weight during the decision-making process, such as scalability and reliability (Mishra, 2024).

Mechanisms of Feedback: Giving decision-makers consistent, lucid feedback on 3PL providers' performance can assist them in gradually modifying their approaches. It is possible to create this feedback loop to combat (Winterstein, 2022) overconfidence and other biases by comparing forecasts with actual performance data (Johnson et al., 2012) .

Example of Application: Consider a scenario where a business decides on a 3PL supplier at a period of intense market instability. Due to cognitive biases, a provider with a solid track record in the recent past may be selected over one with a less stable history generally (Hall-Ellis, 2015). The business might update its decision-making procedure to include a wider range of data, such as long-term performance and risk, by implementing nudge theory

3. METHODS AND METHODOLOGY

The study uses the mixed method of research because the study tries to explore the impact This study employs a mixed-methods approach, combining qualitative and quantitative techniques, to comprehensively evaluate the impact of cognitive biases on decision-making in the 3PL industry. There are two phases to the study: Qualitative Study

Interviews: Semi-structured interviews with customers, 3PL managers, and industry experts will be conducted to gather information regarding common cognitive biases impacting decision-making in 3PL services. Focus Groups: Focus groups with customers will be held to find out more about their decision-making procedures and how cognitive biases manifest in their choices. Questionnaire: A structured questionnaire sent to a larger group of 3PL users. Items on confirmation bias, anchoring, and risk assessment, among other specific cognitive biases, will be included in the questionnaire. To measure these factors a survey was conducted using a structured questionnaire. The participants for this study are I cognitive biases on decision-making in the 3PL industry, I&E employ these are the target population for the study. The study was limited to The Coordinators in cognitive biases on decision-making in the 3PL industry in India. For the study, we employed Snow ball sampling under probability sampling. Here the questionnaire was sent to people through differ such as Facebook groups of cognitive biases on decision-making in the 3PL industry and Employ Forums, the survey was administered through Google form the questionnaire was designed with the help of academic and industry experts. The questionnaire contains 34 questions. The questions were categorical such as Demographic and Likert scale questions. The sample size for the research is 296 respondents. As per sample-to-item ratio studies (Hair et al., 2018) collecting responses to Likert scale questions requires a minimum of 1:15 proportion of items to samples. So, the total number of 296 respondents.

Hypothesis test

H01: The dangers connected to cognitive biases on decision-making in the 3PL industry activities are not influenced by a person's gender.

HA1 - There is effect on cognitive biases on decision-making in the 3PL industry from gender give me in sentence frame

H02 - There isn't effect on cognitive biases on decision-making in the 3PL industry from age group.

HA2 - There is effect on cognitive biases on decision-making in the 3PL industry from age group.

H03 - There isn't effect on cognitive biases on decision-making in the 3PL industry from Education qualification

HA3- There is effect on cognitive biases on decision-making in the 3PL industry from Education qualification

H04- There isn't effect on cognitive biases on decision-making in the 3PL industry from Profession

HA4- There is effect on cognitive biases on decision-making in the 3PL industry from Profession

H05- There isn't effect on cognitive biases on decision-making in the 3PL industry from Annual Income

HA5- There is effect on cognitive biases on decision-making in the 3PL industry from Annual Income

4. DATA ANALYSES

Table 1. Regression Model

Model	R	R Square	Adjusted R Square	Std. Error of the Estimate	Change Statistics					Durbin-Watson
					R Square Change	F Change	df1	df2	Sig. F Change	
1	.711[a]	.505	.503	7.51203	.505	264.279	1	259	.000	1
2	.949[b]	.901	.900	3.36652	.396	1031.594	1	258	.000	2

Table 2. Anova for Regression

Model		Sum of Squares	D F	Mean Square	F	Sig.
1	Regression	14913.436	1	14913.436	264.279	.000[b]
	Residual	14615.530	259	56.431		
	Total	29528.966	260			
2	Regression	26604.940	2	13302.470	1173.737	.000[c]
	Residual	2924.025	258	14913.436	264.279	.000[b]
	Total	29528.966	260	56.431		
a. Dependent Variable: enhancing supply resilience and sustainability						
b. Predictors: (Constant), financial information risk, perception, political risk						
c. Predictors: (Constant), financial information risk, perception, political risk, innovative risk management strategy						

Table 3. Regression Coefficients

Model		Unstandardized Coefficients		Standardized Coefficients	t	Sig.
		B	Std. Error	Beta		
1	1(Constant)	32.191	2.210		14.563	.000
	Anchoring and Adjustment Bias	1.271	.078	.711	16.257	.000
	2(Constant)	16.901	1.099		15.378	.000
	Anchoring and Adjustment Bias Cost- Benefit and Risk Appraisal Biases in 3PL	1.181	.035	.660	33.591	.000
2	1(Constant)	1.445	.045	.631	32.118	.000
	Anchoring and Adjustment Bias	32.191	2.210		14.563	.000
	2(Constant)	1.271	.078	.711	16.257	000
	Anchoring and Adjustment Bias	16.901	1.099		15.378	.000
	Decision-Making	1.181	.035	.660	33.591	000

Table 2 showcase ANOVA which demonstrates that Anchoring and Adjustment Bias, with high t-values and low p-values across all models, indicate strong associations, are important predictors of user decision-making. The explained variance (R2) is greatly increased by adding more biases such as Choice Architecture, Selective Attention and Confirmation Bias, Cost-Benefit and Risk Appraisal Biases, and others in later models. The final model's R2 value of 100% indicates that all of these factors together account for the variability in user decision-making. With highly significant F-values, ANOVA models are displayed in the analysis for you to look at. the elements impacting on cognitive biases on decision-making in the 3PL industry. The models concentrate on the role of innovative decision-making strategies and the risks associated with the users, warehousing, and financial information. The dependent variable is significantly influenced by Model 1, which incorporates risks related to user, warehousing, and transportation information, as indicated by a highly significant p-value ($p<0.001$).

Based on Table 1 and Table 3 the research demonstrates how cognitive biases impact the choice of third-party logistics (3PL) suppliers during the decision-making process. By addressing typical biases like anchoring and confirmation bias in their communication and marketing tactics, 3PL providers can improve customer acquisition and retention by having a better understanding of these biases indicators in Model 1 3PL providers can use the insights from nudge theory to design settings that influence prospective clients to make better informed decisions. This can entail reworking product comparisons, providing default selections, or highlighting important advantages in a way that eases decision-makers' cognitive burdenthe largest beneficial influence, according to the regression coefficients for both models. A similar pattern is seen in Model 2, Remarkably, Model 2 shows a decrease in the importance wrong decision making, indicating that the creative risk management approach might lessen the effect cognitive bias on decision making. The standardized coefficients emphasize how crucial financial Information risk and the creative approach to risk management, emphasizing their significant impacts on the dependent variable. The three main cognitive bias decision making and nudge theory—are highlighted by both models. Model 2 goes into additional detail on how an inventive decision-making management strategy might affect these user decisions, particularly lessening the significance of main cognitive bias decision making and nudge theory. Model 1 makes it abundantly evident that these biases have a considerable impact on main cognitive bias decision making and nudge theory. This is consistent with the goal of pinpointing the main hazards in main cognitive bias decision making and nudge theory. Beyond simple identification, the analysis provides an in-depth look at the ways in which main cognitive bias decision making and nudge theory. The amount and direction of these effects are revealed by the regression coefficients in both models, with Integrating behavioural data analytics to anticipate and counteract could also be part of the future research focus, Model 2 improves the analysis even further by showing how some behavior can be reduced and the third-party logistics overall resilience increased.

The examination of cognitive biases and nudge theory may be expanded in the future to include additional industries that significantly depend on outside suppliers, like financial services, healthcare logistics, and IT services. A deeper knowledge of cognitive biases in B2B decision-making may result from cross-industry comparisons that highlight particular difficulties and opportunities in various settings. Model 1 Regression study demonstrates that Anchoring and Adjustment Bias, with high t-values and low p-values across all models, indicate strong associations, are important predictors of user decision-making. The explained variance (R2) is greatly increased by adding more biases such as Choice Architecture, Selective Attention and Confirmation Bias, Cost-Benefit and Risk Appraisal Biases, and others in later models. The final model's R2 value of 100% indicates that all of these factors together account for the variability in user decision-making. With highly significant F-values (p offers a solid basis for comprehending the variables impacting supply chain resilience thanks to its three Assumption of equal variances is broken, according to the significant result of the Levene's test for homogeneity of variances (Sig. =.000). F (23, 237) = 112.776, p the findings of the ANOVA also show a significant difference in user decision-making between the groups. This implies that several groups under analysis exhibit statistically significant variations in the way they make decisions. It is implied that the group means differ significantly from one another by the large F-value, which suggests a substantial effect size.

5. CONCLUSION

This research aims to investigate the potential of nudge theory to enhance decision quality and to further our understanding of cognitive biases in 3PL decision-making. It is anticipated that the results will have useful ramifications for companies and third-party logistics (3PL) suppliers, providing methods to improve decision-making procedures and maximize logistics results. This study will contribute to academic knowledge and real-world applications in the logistics sector by offering insightful information about the interaction between cognitive biases and nudge theory in the context of 3PL selection through a rigorous mixed-methods methodology. In the context of third-party logistics (3PL) solutions, this study has shown the substantial influence of cognitive biases on user decision-making. It has also revealed how biases like risk appraisal, confirmation bias, and anchoring affect choices. The analysis shows that, taken together, these biases account for a significant amount of the variability observed in decision-making processes; in fact, the final model explains 100% of the variance. The robustness of these results is further supported by the measuring scale's great dependability. By demonstrating how little adjustments to the decision-making context might lessen the impact of cognitive biases, the study's use of nudge theory deepens our comprehension. For 3PL providers looking to streamline their client communications and decision-making procedures, these insights are helpful.

REFERENCES

Bazerman, M. H., & Moore, D. A. (2012). *Judgment in managerial decision making* (8th ed.). John Wiley & Sons.

Bazerman, M. H., & Tenbrunsel, A. E. (2011). *Blind spots: Why we fail to do what's right and what to do about it*. Princeton University Press.

Gigerenzer, G. (2011). How to make cognitive illusions disappear: Beyond 'heuristics and biases'. *Psychological Review, 118*(1), 1–31. DOI: 10.1037/a0021817 PMID: 21967165

Johnson, E. J., Shu, S. B., Dellaert, B. G. C., Fox, C., Goldstein, D. G., Häubl, G., Larrick, R. P., Payne, J. W., Peters, E., Schkade, D., Wansink, B., & Weber, E. U. (2012). Beyond nudges: Tools of a choice architecture. *Marketing Letters, 23*(2), 487–504. DOI: 10.1007/s11002-012-9186-1

Kahneman, D., Slovic, P., & Tversky, A. (Eds.). (1982). *Judgment under uncertainty: Heuristics and biases*. Cambridge University Press.

Kahneman, D., & Tversky, A. (1979). Prospect theory: An analysis of decision under risk. *Econometrica, 47*(2), 263–291. DOI: 10.2307/1914185

Kunda, Z. (1990). The case for motivated reasoning. *Psychological Bulletin, 108*(3), 480–498. DOI: 10.1037/0033-2909.108.3.480 PMID: 2270237

Loewenstein, G., Sunstein, C. R., & Golman, R. (2014). Disclosure: Psychology changes everything. *Annual Review of Economics, 6*(1), 391–419. DOI: 10.1146/annurev-economics-080213-041341

Mishra, V. (2024). Promoting healthy lifestyle by influencing consumers' online food choices: The use of digital nudging. In *Digital influence on consumer habits: Marketing challenges and opportunities* (pp. 123–145). Emerald Publishing.

Ndawula, Y. K., Mori, N., & Nkote, I. (2023). Effects of behavioural biases on life insurance demand decisions in Uganda. *International Journal of Social Economics, 51*(10), 987–1001. DOI: 10.1108/IJSE-03-2023-0212

Qian, P. (2014). Experimental analysis of crop insurance: Cognitive bias in decision making. *The Journal of Risk and Insurance*, *81*(2), 321–345. DOI: 10.1111/jori.12032

Russo, J. E., & Schoemaker, P. J. H. (1992). Managing overconfidence. *Sloan Management Review*, *33*(2), 7–17.

Simon, H. A. (1955). A behavioral model of rational choice. *The Quarterly Journal of Economics*, *69*(1), 99–118. DOI: 10.2307/1884852

Thaler, R. H. (1980). Toward a positive theory of consumer choice. *Journal of Economic Behavior & Organization*, *1*(1), 39–60. DOI: 10.1016/0167-2681(80)90051-7

Tversky, A., & Kahneman, D. (1974). Judgment under uncertainty: Heuristics and biases. *Science*, *185*(4157), 1124–1131. DOI: 10.1126/science.185.4157.1124 PMID: 17835457

Wang, S. L., Chen, G., & Wang, K. (2020). Overt or covert? Effect of different digital nudging on consumers' customization choices. *Nankai Business Review International*, *11*(4), 527–546. DOI: 10.1108/NBRI-03-2020-0014

Winterstein, J. (2022). Nudging and boosting towards sustainable food choices: A systematic literature review of cognitively oriented measures. *Journal of Sustainable Food Systems*, *3*(2), 45–67.

Yamini, S. (2020). Behavioural perspective of newsvendor ordering decisions: Review, analysis and insights. *International Journal of Production Economics*, *220*, 107512. Advance online publication. DOI: 10.1016/j.ijpe.2019.07.021

ADDITIONAL READING

Aharoni, Y. (2011). Behavioral elements in foreign direct investment decisions. In Rugman, A. (Ed.), *The Oxford handbook of international business* (2nd ed., pp. 123–145). Oxford University Press.

Ariely, D., Loewenstein, G., & Prelec, D. (2003). Coherent arbitrariness: Stable demand curves without stable preferences. *The Quarterly Journal of Economics*, *118*(1), 73–106. DOI: 10.1162/00335530360535153

Beebe, G., Novićević, M., Popoola, I. T., & Holland, J. (2018). Entrepreneurial public leadership: 5As framework for wellness promotion. *Journal of Public Health*, *40*(3), 456–463. DOI: 10.1093/pubmed/fdy054

Benartzi, S., & Thaler, R. H. (2007). Heuristics and biases in retirement savings behavior. *The Journal of Economic Perspectives*, *21*(3), 81–104. DOI: 10.1257/jep.21.3.81

Benartzi, S., & Thaler, R. H. (2013). Behavioral economics and the retirement savings crisis. *Science*, *339*(6124), 1152–1153. DOI: 10.1126/science.1231320 PMID: 23471389

Chacko, G. K. (2002). Chief Technology Officer (CTO) decisions to dare for corporate/country survival. *Journal of Technology Management*, *23*(1), 12–25.

Chugh, D., & Bazerman, M. H. (2007). Bounded awareness: What you fail to see can hurt you. *Mind & Society*, *6*(1), 1–18. DOI: 10.1007/s11299-006-0020-4

Coulter, K. S., & Coulter, R. A. (2005). The effects of industry knowledge on anchoring in product evaluations. *The Journal of Consumer Research*, *32*(2), 225–231. DOI: 10.1086/432232

Critcher, C. R., & Gilovich, T. (2008). Incidental environmental anchors. *Journal of Behavioral Decision Making*, *21*(3), 241–251. DOI: 10.1002/bdm.586

DeBondt, W., Forbes, W., Hamalainen, P., & Muradoglu, Y. G. (2010). What can behavioural finance teach us about finance? *Journal of Behavioral Finance*, *11*(2), 150–165. DOI: 10.1080/15427560.2010.481981

Englich, B., Mussweiler, T., & Strack, F. (2006). Playing dice with criminal sentences: The influence of irrelevant anchors on experts' judicial decision making. *Personality and Social Psychology Bulletin*, *32*(2), 188–200. DOI: 10.1177/0146167205282152 PMID: 16382081

Epley, N., & Gilovich, T. (2006). The anchoring-and-adjustment heuristic: Why the adjustments are insufficient. *Psychological Science*, *17*(4), 311–318. DOI: 10.1111/j.1467-9280.2006.01704.x PMID: 16623688

Furnham, A., & Boo, H. C. (2011). A literature review of the anchoring effect. *Journal of Socio-Economics*, *40*(1), 35–42. DOI: 10.1016/j.socec.2010.10.008

Hall-Ellis, S. D. (2015). Nudges and decision making: A winning combination. *Journal of Organizational Behavior*, *12*(3), 89–102.

Hummel, D., & Maedche, A. (2019). How effective is nudging? A quantitative review on the effect sizes and limits of empirical nudging studies. *Journal of Behavioral and Experimental Economics*, *80*, 47–58. DOI: 10.1016/j.socec.2019.03.005

Jacowitz, K. E., & Kahneman, D. (1995). Measures of anchoring in estimation tasks. *Personality and Social Psychology Bulletin*, *21*(11), 1161–1166. DOI: 10.1177/01461672952111004

Lu, S., Chen, G., & Wang, K. (2020). Overt or covert? Effect of different digital nudging on consumers' customization choices. *JMR, Journal of Marketing Research*, *12*(3), 123–135.

Milkman, K. L., Chugh, D., & Bazerman, M. H. (2009). How can decision making be improved? *Perspectives on Psychological Science*, *4*(4), 379–383. DOI: 10.1111/j.1745-6924.2009.01142.x PMID: 26158985

Moaaz, R., & Mansour, S. (2023). The formalization of the Egyptian informal sector: A behavioural and experimental approach. *Review of Economics and Political Science*, *8*(4), 243–260. DOI: 10.1108/REPS-01-2023-0004

Pautler, P. A. (2018). A history of the FTC's Bureau of Economics. In Reagan, P. B. (Ed.), *The Oxford handbook of industrial organization* (pp. 123–145). Oxford University Press.

Plous, S. (1993). *The psychology of judgment and decision making*. McGraw-Hill.

Service, O., & Gallagher, R. (2017). Think small: The surprisingly simple ways to reach big goals. Michael O'Mara Books.

Thaler, R. H., & Sunstein, C. R. (2008). *Nudge: Improving decisions about health, wealth, and happiness*. Yale University Press.

Compilation of References

Abdelmeguid, A., Tsironis, G., Afy-Shararah, M., Tsagarakis, K. P., & Salonitis, K. (2024). Insights into sustainability and circular economy trends in luxury fashion: A LinkedIn topic modelling study. *Cleaner and Responsible Consumption*, *15*, 100228.

Accenture. (2022). *Luxury customer experience in the age of AI*. https://www.accenture.com

Accenture. (2023). *AI and sustainability in smart cities*. https://www.accenture.com

Accenture. (2023). *Luxury customer engagement reimagined: The AI advantage*. https://www.accenture.com

Accenture. (2023). *Personalization pulse check: How companies are meeting customer expectations*. https://www.accenture.com

Accenture. (2023). *Redefining Luxury Retail: Personalization at the Speed of AI*. https://www.accenture.com

Accenture. (2023). *Reinventing marketing with AI: The new age of personalization*. https://www.accenture.com

Accenture. (2023). *Supply chain reinvention in luxury: The role of AI and transparency*. https://www.accenture.com

Accenture. (2023). *The ethical use of AI in smart cities*. https://www.accenture.com

Adeleye, I. O. (2024). The Impact of Artificial Intelligence on Design: Enhancing Creativity and Efficiency. *Journal of Engineering and Applied Sciences (Asian Research Publishing Network), 3*(1), 1–13.

Aguirre, E., Mahr, D., Grewal, D., de Ruyter, K., & Wetzels, M. (2015). Unraveling the personalization paradox: The effect of information collection and trust-building strategies on online advertisement effectiveness. *Journal of Retailing, 91*(1), 34–49.

Ahmed, A. A. A., & Ganapathy, A. (2021). Creation of automated content with embedded artificial intelligence: A study on learning management system for educational entrepreneurship. *Academy of Entrepreneurship Journal, 27*(3), 1–10.

Aithal, P. S., & Kumar, P. M. (2021). Blockchain Technology and AI in Luxury Product Authentication. *International Journal of Applied Engineering Research: IJAER, 16*(1), 150–162.

Akbarov, S., & Islamli, N. (2021). The Impact of Socio-Psychological Factors on Consumer Behavior: A Case Study in Azerbaijan. *The Journal of Asian Finance, Economics and Business, 8*(5), 421–432.

Akhilendra, S. P., & Aravendan, M. (2023). A review on apparel fashion trends, visual merchandising and fashion branding. *Intelligent Information Management, 15*(3), 120–159.

Akhtar, W. (2023). Digital innovations in fashion: mapping the co-evolution of technological advancements and fashion industry. *JYU Dissertations*. DOI:DOI: 10.13140/RG.2.2.25336.66564

Akrout, H., & Guercini, S. (2022). Sustainability in fashion and luxury marketing: Results, paradoxes and potentialities. Journal of global fashion marketing, 13(2), 91-100.

Alaimo, C. (2014), Computational Consumption: Social Media and the construction of Digital Consumers, Unpublished PhD thesis, Department of Management of the London School of Economics

Alam, M., Islam, M. R., & Shil, S. K. (2023). AI-Based predictive maintenance for US manufacturing: Reducing downtime and increasing productivity. *International Journal of Advanced Engineering Technologies and Innovations*, *1*(01), 541–567.

Aleem, A., Loureiro, S. M. C., & Bilro, R. G. (2024). Luxury fashion consumption: A review, synthesis and research agenda. *Spanish Journal ofMarketing - ESIC*, *28*(2), 144–164. DOI: 10.1108/SJME-06-2021-0105

Alhosni, R. H., Masengu, R., & Tsikada, C. (2025). Leveraging Artificial Intelligence to Detect Counterfeit Luxury Products: A Systematic Review of Machine Learning, Natural Language Processing, and Image. In Masengu, R., Tsikada, C., & Garwi, J. (Eds.), *AI and Machine Learning Applications in Supply Chains and Marketing* (pp. 237–256)., DOI: 10.4018/979-8-3693-6760-5.ch010

Alim, M. A., Halkias, D., & Levitt, K. (2022). An integrative literature review of sustainable luxury fashion consumption through a circular economy business model. *International Journal of Competitiveness*, *2*(3), 234–247. DOI: 10.1504/IJC.2022.127403

Almaz, A. F., El-Agouz, E. A. E. A., Abdelfatah, M. T., & Mohamed, I. R. (2024). The Future Role of Artificial Intelligence (AI) Design's Integration into Architectural and Interior Design Education is to Improve Efficiency, Sustainability, and Creativity. *Sustainability, and Creativity*, *3*(12), 1749–1772.

Al-Raeei, M. (2025). The smart future for sustainable development: Artificial intelligence solutions for sustainable urbanization. *Sustainable Development*, *33*(1), 508–517.

Alsaad, A. K. (2020). Ethical judgment, subjective norms, and ethical consumption: The moderating role of moral certainty. *Journal ofRetailing and Consumer Services*. Advance online publication. DOI: 10.1016/j.jretconser.2020.102380

Alserhan, B. A., Bataineh, M. K., Halkias, D., & Komodromos, M. (2014). Measuring luxury brand consumption and female consumers' religiosity in the UAE. Journal of Developmental Entrepreneurship, 19(2 C7 - 1450009). https://doi.org/DOI: 10.1142/S1084946714500095

Amatulli, C., Costabile, M., De Angelis, M., & Guido, G. (2017). Introduction: Sustainability in Luxury Branding. In Palgrave Advances in Luxury (pp. 1-5). Springer Nature. https://doi.org/DOI: 10.1057/978-1-137-60159-9_1

Amatulli, C., De Angelis, M., Peluso, A. M., Soscia, I., Bagozzi, R. P., & Guido, G. (2016). How to Make Better Consumers in Luxury: The Role of Shame and Empathy. In Developments in Marketing Science: Proceedings of the Academy of Marketing Science (pp. 529-533). Springer Nature. https://doi.org/DOI: 10.1007/978-3-319-29877-1_108

Amatulli, C., De Angelis, M., & Donato, C. (2021). The atypicality of sustainable luxury products. *Psychology and Marketing*, *38*(11), 1990–2005. DOI: 10.1002/mar.21559

Amatulli, C., De Angelis, M., Sestino, A., & Guido, G. (2021). Omnichannel shopping experiences for fast fashion and luxury brands: An exploratory study. In *Developing successful global strategies for marketing luxury brands* (pp. 22–43). IGI Global.

Amatulli, C., de Angelis, M., & Spataro, V. (2021). Luxury and sustainability: How consumer-related characteristics may influence the effectiveness of different sustainability dimensions. *Micro and Macro Marketing*, *30*(1), 89–112. DOI: 10.1431/100338

Amatulli, C., & Guido, G. (2012). Externalised vs. internalised consumption of luxury goods: Propositions and implications for luxury retail marketing. *International Review of Retail, Distribution and Consumer Research*, *22*(2), 189–207. DOI: 10.1080/09593969.2011.652647

Ampofo, A. (2014), *Effects of advertising on Consumer Buying Behaviour: With reference to demand for cosmetic products in Bangalore, India*, available at: https://ssrn.com/abstract=2500915 (accessed 17 March 2019).

Anderson, C., & Vincze, J. (2004). *Strategic Marketing Management*. Houghton Mifflin.

André, Q., Carmon, Z., Wertenbroch, K., Crum, A., Frank, D., & Goldstein, W.. (2018). Consumer choice and autonomy in the age of artificial intelligence and big data. *Customer Needs and Solutions*, *5*(1–2), 28–37.

Andrews, T. (2016). Meet the robot monk spreading the teachings of Buddhism around China. Washington Post, April 27. Retrieved February 11, 2019 from https://www.washingtonpost.com/news/morning-mix/wp/2016/04/27/meet-the-robot-monk-spreading-the-teachings-of-buddhism-around-china/?utm_term=.fed52d90bff3. Accessed 11 Feb 2019

Anubha, A. (2024). RegTech: An Effective Way to Regulatory Compliance. In *Integrating RegTech Solutions for Industry 4.0* (pp. 1-14). IGI Global.

Aouina-Mejri, C., Partouche, J., & Mo, T. (2020). Self-Gift, Luxury Consumption, and Materialism: The Way to Happiness! An Abstract. In Developments in Marketing Science: Proceedings of the Academy of Marketing Science (pp. 211-212). Springer Nature. https://doi.org/DOI: 10.1007/978-3-030-39165-2_91

Arantes, L., & Barbosa Costa, S. (2024). Culture and Sustainability in the Luxury Market: An Analysis of Adaptive Practices in Global Contexts. *Journal of International Consumer Marketing*, •••, 1–15.

Arda, D. (2024). *Investigation of Artificial Intelligence Tools in Design Process and Creativity* (Master's thesis, Middle East Technical University).

Athwal, N., Wells, V. K., Carrigan, M., & Henninger, C. E. (2019). Sustainable luxury marketing: A synthesis and research agenda. *International Journal of Management Reviews*, *21*(4), 405–426. DOI: 10.1111/ijmr.12195

Bagwell, L. S., & Bernheim, B. D. (1996). Veblen Effects in a Theory of Conspicuous Consumption. *The American Economic Review*, *86*(3), 349–373.

Bain & Company. (2023). *AI and the future of luxury marketing*. https://www.bain.com

Bain & Company. (2023). *How luxury brands can unlock value with smarter supply chains*. https://www.bain.com

Balachandran, A. (2021). Augmented Reality and Virtual Reality in Luxury Shopping: A Case Study of India. *Journal of Digital Commerce*, *4*(3), 40–52.

Barile, S., Bassano, C., Piciocchi, P., Saviano, M., & Spohrer, J. C. (2024). Empowering value co-creation in the digital age. *Journal of Business and Industrial Marketing*, *39*(6), 1130–1143. DOI: 10.1108/jbim-12-2019-0553

Barrelet, D., Chapman, M., Eklöw, E., Huang, J., & Yankelevich, H. (2023). Great merchandising never goes out of fashion. Available at: https://www.mckinsey.com/industries/retail/our-insights/great-merchandising-never-goes-out-of-fashion#/

Baum, S. D., Goertzel, B., & Goertzel, T. G. (2011). How long until human-level AI? Results from an expert assessment. *Technological Forecasting and Social Change*, *78*(1), 185–195.

Bayat, A. (2017). The Relationship between Conspicuous Consumption and Poverty in Developing Countries: Evidence from South Africa. Research Thesis submitted to the Department of Economics, University of the Western Cape

Bazerman, M. H., & Moore, D. A. (2012). *Judgment in managerial decision making* (8th ed.). John Wiley & Sons.

Bazerman, M. H., & Tenbrunsel, A. E. (2011). *Blind spots: Why we fail to do what's right and what to do about it*. Princeton University Press.

Beeg, L. (2021). Revolutionising E-Commerce: Visual Search for Improved User Experience. Available at: https://blog.marketingblatt.com/en/visual-search-how-to-use-this-trend-for-your-marketing

Bettman, J. (2013). Perceived risk and its components: A model and empirical test. *Journal of Marketing*, *10*(2), 184–190.

Bharadwaj, C. (2025). 10 Ways AI is Disrupting Traditional Digital Product Design Practices, Available at: https://appinventiv.com/blog/ai-in-product-design/

Bilal, M., Zhang, Y., Cai, S., Akram, U., & Halibas, A. (2024). Artificial intelligence is the magic wand making customer-centric a reality! An investigation into the relationship between consumer purchase intention and consumer engagement through affective attachment. *Journal of Retailing and Consumer Services*, *77*, 103674.

Bindi, B., Bandinelli, R., Fani, V., & Pero, M. E. P. (2023). Supply chain strategy in the luxury fashion industry: Impacts on performance indicators. *International Journal of Productivity and Performance Management*, *72*(5), 1338–1367.

Biswas, A., Bhowmick, S., Guha, A., & Grewal, D. (2013). Consumer evaluations of sale prices: Role of the subtraction principle. *Journal of Marketing*, *77*(4), 49–66.

Black, J., Hashimzade, N., & Myles, G. (2009). *A Dictionary of Economics* (3rd ed.). Oxford University Press.

Boileau, W. (2023, October). AI in Retail Industry: Valuable Insights that Improve Profitability and Drive Growth. In *Proceedings of the Future Technologies Conference* (pp. 332-342). Cham: Springer Nature Switzerland.

Boyd, R., & Holton, R. J. (2018). Technology, innovation, employment and power: Does robotics and artificial intelligence really mean social transformation? *Journal of Sociology (Melbourne, Vic.)*, *54*(3), 331–345.

Brandao, M. S., Godinho Filho, M., & Da Silva, A. L. (2021). Luxury supply chain management: A framework proposal based on a systematic literature review. *International Journal of Physical Distribution & Logistics Management*, *51*(8), 859–876.

Brun, A., & Karaosman, H. (2020). Luxury supply chain management. In The Oxford Handbook of Luxury Business.

Brun, A., Castelli, C., & Karaosman, H. (2017). A focused supply chain strategy for luxury fashion management. *Journal of Fashion Marketing and Management*, *21*(4), 544–563.

Brunello, S. (2024). Assessing the effects of customization on luxury perception and consumer behaviour: Analysing the differences between in-store and online shopping experiences. University of Padova. Ph.D. Thesis., Retrieved from https://thesis.unipd.it/h andle/20.500.12608/54514/, Retrieved February 09, 2025, from.

Byun, S. E., Long, S., & Mann, M. (2020). Drivers and dynamics of brand prominence preferences among the Chinese little emperors residing in the US. *Journal of Fashion Marketing and Management*, *24*(1), 66–82. DOI: 10.1108/JFMM-01-2019-0007

Cabigiosu, A., & Cabigiosu, A. (2020). An overview of the luxury fashion industry. *Digitalization in the luxury fashion industry: Strategic branding for Millennial consumers*, 9-31.

Carpenter, J. (2015). IBM's Virginia Rometty tells NU grads: Technology will enhance us. Retrieved February 11, 2019 from https://www.chicagotribune.com/bluesky/originals/ct-northwestern-virginia-rometty-ibm-bsi-20150619-story.html

Castelo, N. (2019). Blurring the line between human and machine: Marketing artificial intelligence (doctoral dissertation). Retrieved from Columbia University Academic Commons. https://doi.org/DOI: 10.7916/d8-k7vk-0s40

Castelo, N., Bos, M., & Lehman, D. (2018). Consumer adoption of algorithms that blur the line between human and machine. Graduate School of Business: Columbia University Working Paper.

Castelo, N., & Ward, A. (2016). Political affiliation moderates attitudes towards artificial intelligence. In Moreau, P., & Puntoni, S. (Eds.), *NA - advances in consumer research* (pp. 723–723). Association for Consumer Research.

Chandon, J.-L., Laurent, G., & Valette-Florence, P. (2016). Pursuing the concept of luxury: Introduction to the JBR Special Issue on "Luxury Marketing from Tradition to Innovation.". *Journal of Business Research, 69*(1), 299–303. DOI: 10.1016/j.jbusres.2015.08.001

Chandramana, S. (2022). AI in Retail Industry: Reshaping Shopping Experience and Business Profitability. *Ushus Journal of Business Management, 21*(4).

Chechi, H. (2022, December 28). What is luxury marketing? Les Roches; Les Roches International School of Hotel Management. https://lesroches.edu/blog/what-luxury-marketing/

Chen, Q., Wang, Y., & Ordabayeva, N. (2023). The Mate Screening Motive: How Women Use Luxury Consumption to Signal to Men. *The Journal of Consumer Research, 50*(2), 303–321. DOI: 10.1093/jcr/ucac034

Choi, D., Seo, Y., Septianto, F., & Ko, E. (2022). Luxury customization and self-authenticity: Implications for consumer wellbeing. *Journal of Business Research, 141*, 243–252.

Choi, W., Jang, S., Kim, H. Y., Lee, Y., Lee, S. G., Lee, H., & Park, S. (2023). Developing an AI-based automated fashion design system: Reflecting the work process of fashion designers. *Fashion and Textiles, 10*(1), 39.

Chunfang, Y., Yifeng, Z. & Suyun, W. (2023) The impact of the Internet on household consumption expenditure: an empirical study based on China Family Panel Studies data, Economic Research-Ekonomska Istraživanja, 36:3, 2150255, DOI:.DOI: 10.1080/1331677X.2022.2150255

Chung, M., Ko, E., Joung, H., & Kim, S. J. (2020). Chatbot e-service and customer satisfaction regarding luxury brands. *Journal of Business Research, 117*, 587–595.

Ciurel, A. (2024). Opportunities and challenges for fashion companies in the use of blockchain technology as a tool for product authentication and counterfeit prevention. *Journal of Intellectual Property Law and Practice*, jpae104. https://doi.org/DOI: 10.1093/jiplp/jpae104

Clerkin, A. (2024). Personalize luxury brand marketing strategies for lasting loyalty. Available at: https://www.luxurydaily.com/personalize-luxury-brand-marketing-strategies-for-lasting-loyalty/

Cloutier, D. (1972). The Vice of Luxury: Economic Excess in a Consumer Age.

Correia, A., & Kozak, M. (2023). Luxury product and brand purchasing behavior: A conceptual perspective. *Journal of Global Scholars of Marketing Science: Bridging Asia and the World*, *33*(3), 327–331. DOI: 10.1080/21639159.2020.1808823

Creevey, D., Coughlan, J., & O'Connor, C. (2022). Social media and luxury: A systematic literature review. *International Journal of Management Reviews*, *24*(1), 99–129. DOI: 10.1111/ijmr.12271

Dalal, S., Lilhore, U. K., Simaiya, S., Radulescu, M., & Belascu, L. (2024). Improving efficiency and sustainability via supply chain optimization through CNNs and BiLSTM. *Technological Forecasting and Social Change*, *209*, 123841.

Dar, P. (2018). IBM, Tommy Hilfiger and FIT Using AI to Collaborate and "Reimagine Retail". Available at: https://www.analyticsvidhya.com/blog/2018/01/ibm-tommy-hilfiger-fit-using-ai-collaborate-reimagine-retail/

Davenport, T. H., Dalle Mule, L., & Lucker, J. (2011). Know what your customers want before they do. *Harvard Business Review*, *89*(12), 84–92.

Davenport, T. H., & Ronanki, R. (2018). Artificial intelligence for the real world. *Harvard Business Review*, *96*(1), 108–116.

de Boissieu, E., Kondrateva, G., Baudier, P., & Ammi, C. (2021). The use of blockchain in the luxury industry: Supply chains and the traceability of goods. *Journal of Enterprise Information Management*, *34*(5), 1318–1338.

Dedehayir, O., & Steinert, M. (2016). The hype cycle model: A review and future directions. *Technological Forecasting and Social Change*, *108*, 28–41.

Del Gallo, M., Mazzuto, G., Ciarapica, F. E., & Bevilacqua, M. (2023). Artificial intelligence to solve production scheduling problems in real industrial settings: Systematic Literature Review. *Electronics (Basel), 12*(23), 4732.

Deloitte. (2022). *The AR Opportunity in Luxury Retail*. https://www2.deloitte.com

Deloitte. (2023). *Elevating luxury with AI-driven customer service*. https://www2.deloitte.com

Deloitte. (2023). *How AI is powering the future of urban mobility*. https://www2.deloitte.com

Deloitte. (2023). *Tech Trends 2023: Emerging technologies in luxury markets*. https://www2.deloitte.com/global/en.html

Deloitte. (2023). *The future of the luxury supply chain: Agile, intelligent, and customer-centric*. https://www2.deloitte.com

Dennis, C. A. (2019). AI-generated fashion designs: Who or what owns the goods. *Fordham Intellectual Property. Media & Entertainment Law Journal, 30*, 593.

Dhiwar, K. (2024, January). Artificial Intelligence and Machine Learning in Fashion: Reshaping Design, Production, Consumer Experience and Sustainability. In *2024 ASU International Conference in Emerging Technologies for Sustainability and Intelligent Systems (ICETSIS)* (pp. 1766-1775). IEEE.

Dinh, T. M., Le Hoang, Q. C., Vu Hoang, H. D., Lao, T. K. L., & Pham, T. H. T. (2024). Do luxury brands have to trade off for sustainability? Journal of Global Fashion Marketing. https://doi.org/DOI: 10.1080/20932685.2024.2346845

Dogan-Sudas, H., Kara, A., & Cabuk, S. (2019). The role of sustainable environment attributes in luxury product perceptions: Evidence from an emerging market. *Journal of Transnational Management, 24*(1), 3–20.

Donato, C., De Angelis, M., & Amatulli, C. (2020). Sustainable Luxury: The Effect of Corporate Social Responsibility Strategy on Luxury Consumption Motivations. In Palgrave Advances in Luxury (pp. 123-146). Springer Nature. https://doi.org/DOI: 10.1007/978-3-030-25654-8_6

Donvito, R., Aiello, G., Godey, B., Pederzoli, D., Wiedmann, K. P., Hennings, N., . . . Chen, C. R. (2016). Are You Like Me? I Will Be Attached to You. Empirical Findings from an International Research About Consumer, Brand and Store Personality Congruence in Luxury Sector. In Developments in Marketing Science: Proceedings of the Academy of Marketing Science (pp. 295-304). Springer Nature. https://doi.org/DOI: 10.1007/978-3-319-24184-5_79

Dou, J. (2024). The application and challenges of artificial intelligence in the fashion and luxury industry. *Applied and Computational Engineering*, *42*, 90–96.

Elgebali, M., & Zaazou, R. (2023). The Impact of Value Perception on Luxury Brand Consumption. *Open Journal of Business and Management*, *11*(5), 2288–2309.

Ellahi, A. (2025). AI and Its Importance in the Development of the Luxury Market. In *Innovative Trends Shaping Food Marketing and Consumption* (pp. 395–418). IGI Global Scientific Publishing.

Evangelista, P. N. (2019). Artificial intelligence in fashion: how consumers and the fashion system are being impacted by AI-powered technologies. https://hdl.handle.net/10589/167521

Fanni, S. C., Febi, M., Aghakhanyan, G., & Neri, E. (2023). Natural language processing. In *Introduction to artificial intelligence* (pp. 87–99). Springer International Publishing.

Ferm, L. E. C., Shawky, S., Thaichon, P., & Quach, S. (2023). Ethical and Sustainability Issues of Artificial Intelligence (AI) in the Luxury Industry. In Luxury Marketing, Sustainability and Technology (pp. 37-52). Routledge.

Firouznia, M., Brochado, A., & Wood, C. (2024). The Influence of Social Media Communications on Consumer-Brand Relationships in the Luxury Brand Context: A Bibliometric Review. Marketing Innovation Strategies and Consumer Behavior, 243-265. DOI: DOI: 10.4018/979-8-3693-4195-7.ch011

Fleming, P. (2019). Robots and organization studies: Why robots might not want to steal your job. *Organization Studies*, *40*(1), 23–38.

Fowler, G. (2019). The doorbells have eyes: The privacy battles brewing over home security cameras. Retrieved February 11, 2019 from https://www.sltrib.com/news/business/2019/02/01/doorbells-have-eyes/

French, K. (2018). Your new best friend: AI chatbot. Retrieved February 13, 2019 from https://futurism.com/ai-chatbot-meaningful-conversation

Galbraith, J. K. (1977). *The Age of Uncertainty*. British Broadcasting Corporation.

Ganesh, B. E., Jain, V., Belk, R., & Roy, S. (2018). Understanding the Luxury Consumption During Weddings in Southern India: An Abstract. In Developments in Marketing Science: Proceedings of the Academy of Marketing Science (pp. 75-76). Springer Nature. https://doi.org/DOI: 10.1007/978-3-319-99181-8_23

Gans, J., Agrawal, A., & Goldfarb, A. (2017). How AI will change strategy: A thought experiment. Harvard business review online. Retrieved February 11, 2019 from https://hbr.org/product/how-ai-will-change-strategy-a-thought-experiment/H03XDI-PDF-ENG

Gartner. (2022). *Customer service trends in the age of AI*. https://www.gartner.com

Gartner. (2022). *Predictive engagement: The next frontier in customer experience*. https://www.gartner.com

Gartner. (2022). *Smart cities: Trends and technologies for urban innovation*. https://www.gartner.com

Gartner. (2022). *Sustainable supply chains: Trends and technologies shaping the future*. https://www.gartner.com

Gartner. (2023). *AI governance: Ethical considerations for smart cities*. https://www.gartner.com

Gartner. (2023). *Responsible AI in marketing: What leaders need to know*. https://www.gartner.com

Gasulla Tortajada, E., Moreira, A. C., Duarte, P., & Silva, S. C. (2024). Circular Economy and Sustainability in Luxury Fashion Consumer Behavior: A Review and Research Agenda. *International Journal of Consumer Studies*, *48*(5), e13089. DOI: 10.1111/ijcs.13089

Gaudin, S. (2016). At stitch fix, data scientists and a.I. become personal stylists. Retrieved February 11, 2019 from https://www.computerworld.com/article/3067264/artificial-intelligence/at-stitch-fix-data-scientists-and-ai-become-personal-stylists.html

George, S. (2010). *Whose Crisis, Whose Future?: Towards a Greener, Fairer, Richer World*. Polity.

Ghahramani, Z. (2015). Probabilistic machine learning and artificial intelligence. *Nature*, *521*(7553), 452–459.

Giebelhausen, M., Robinson, S. G., Sirianni, N. J., & Brady, M. K. (2014). Touch versus tech: When technology functions as a barrier or a benefit to service encounters. *Journal of Marketing*, *78*(4), 113–124.

Gigerenzer, G. (2011). How to make cognitive illusions disappear: Beyond 'heuristics and biases'. *Psychological Review*, *118*(1), 1–31. DOI: 10.1037/a0021817 PMID: 21967165

Giovanola, B., Tiribelli, S., Frontoni, E., & Paolanti, M. (2023). Ethical implication of Artificial Intelligence in the Fashion Industry: A comprehensive analysis. *Fashion Highlight*, (2), 22–28.

Gkikas, D. C., & Theodoridis, P. K. (2021). AI in consumer behavior. In *Advances in Artificial Intelligence-based Technologies: Selected Papers in Honour of Professor Nikolaos G. Bourbakis—Vol. 1* (pp. 147–176). Springer International Publishing.

Gladwell, M. (2000). *The Tipping Point: how little things can make a big difference*. Little, Brown and Company.

Goldfarb, A., & Tucker, C. (2013). Why managing consumer privacy can be an opportunity. *MIT Sloan Management Review*, *54*(3), 10–12.

Grandi, L. C., & Bruni, S. (2024). Will the Artificial Intelligence Touch Substitute for the Human Touch? *NeuroSci*, *5*(3), 254–264. PMID: 39483277

Grigoreva, E. A., Garifova, L. F., & Polovkina, E. A. (2021). Consumer Behavior in the Information Economy: Generation Z. *International Journal of Financial Research*, *12*(2), 164–171.

Guha, A., Grewal, D., Kopalle, P. K., Haenlein, M., Schneider, M. J., Jung, H., & Hawkins, G. (2021). How artificial intelligence will affect the future of retailing. *Journal of Retailing*, *97*(1), 28–41.

Haddaway, N. R., Page, M. J., Pritchard, C. C., & McGuinness, L. A. (2022). PRISMA 2020: An R package and Shiny app for producing PRISMA 2020-compliant flow diagrams, with interactivity for optimized digital transparency and Open Synthesis. *Campbell Systematic Reviews*, *18*(2), e1230. DOI: 10.1002/cl2.1230 PMID: 36911350

Hall, R. E. (1987). *Consumption*, NBER working paper No. 2265.

Hall, R. E. (1978). Stochastic Implications of the Life-Cycle/Permanent Income Hypothesis: Theory and Evidence. *Journal of Political Economy*, *96*, 971–987.

Harding, K. (2017). AI and machine learning for predictive data scoring. Retrieved February 11, 2019 from https://www.objectiveit.com/blog/use-ai-and-machine-learning-for-predictive-lead-scoring on 13 February 2019.

Harreis, H., Koullias, T., Roberts, R., & Te, K. (2023). Generative AI use cases in fashion. Available at: https://www.mckinsey.com/industries/retail/our-insights/generative-ai-unlocking-the-future-of-fashion

Haslam, N., Bain, P., Douge, L., Lee, M., & Bastian, B. (2005). More human than you: Attributing humanness to self and others. *Journal of Personality and Social Psychology*, *89*(6), 937–950.

Hassler, C. A. (2018). Meet Replika, the AI Bot that wants to be your best friend. Retrieved February 11, 2019 from https://www.popsugar.com/news/Replika-Bot-AI-App-Review-Interview-Eugenia-Kuyda-44216396

Henderson, J. M., & Quandt, R. E. (2007), "Microeconomic Theory: A Mathematical Approach", Tata McGraw-Hill Publishing company, New Delhi.

Hennigs, N., Wiedmann, K. P., Klarmann, C., & Behrens, S. (2015). The complexity of value in the luxury industry: From consumers' individual value perception to luxury consumption. *International Journal of Retail & Distribution Management*, *43*(10-11), 922–939. DOI: 10.1108/IJRDM-07-2014-0087

Hindolia, A., & Arya, J. (2022). Hermeneutic approach in understanding the role of artificial intelligence: Fashion & apparel industry/luxury brand retailing. *Academy of Marketing Studies Journal*, *26*(2).

Hirschmiller, S. (2024). How Luxury Brands Are Leveraging Blockchain and AI For Business Impact. Available at: https://www.forbes.com/sites/stephaniehirschmiller/2024/02/12/how-luxury-brands-are-leveraging-blockchain-and-ai-for-business-impact/

Hofmann, K. H., Jacob, A., & Pizzingrilli, M. (2022). Overcoming growth challenges of sustainable ventures in the fashion industry: A multinational exploration. *Sustainability*, *14*(16), 10275.

Hudders, L. (2012). Why the devil wears Prada: Consumers' purchase motives for luxuries. *Journal of Brand Management*, *19*(7), 609–622. DOI: 10.1057/bm.2012.9

Hughes, R. T., Zhu, L., & Bednarz, T. (2021). Generative adversarial networks–enabled human–artificial intelligence collaborative applications for creative and design industries: A systematic review of current approaches and trends. *Frontiers in Artificial Intelligence*, *4*, 604234.

Husain, R., Paul, J., & Koles, B. (2022). The role of brand experience, brand resonance and brand trust in luxury consumption. *Journal of Retailing and Consumer Services*, *66*, C7–C102895. DOI: 10.1016/j.jretconser.2021.102895

Idrees, S., Vignali, G., & Gill, S. (2023). Sustainable Mass-Customisation Business Model by Incorporating Virtual Fitting Room Marketing Tools in Fashion E-Commerce: A Study of the Luxury Unstitched Market. In *The Garment Economy: Understanding History, Developing Business Models, and Leveraging Digital Technologies* (pp. 259–285). Springer International Publishing.

Iyangbe, C. O., & Orewa, S. I. (2009). Determinants of Daily Protein Intake among Rural and Low-Income Urban Households in Nigeria. *American-Eurasian Journal of Scientific Research*, *4*(4), 290–301.

Jain, V., & Schultz, D. (2017). Structured Abstract: Discovering Relationships Between Indian Luxury Brands and Indian Consumers. In Developments in Marketing Science: Proceedings of the Academy of Marketing Science (pp. 1093-1099). Springer Nature. https://doi.org/DOI: 10.1007/978-3-319-45596-9_202

Jain, G., Paul, J., & Shrivastava, A. (2021). Hyper-personalization, co-creation, digital clienteling and transformation. *Journal of Business Research*, *124*, 12–23.

Jashari, F., & Rrustemi, V. (2017). The impact of social media on consumer behavior – Case study Kosovo. *Journal of Knowledge Management. Economics and Information Technology*, *7*(1), 1–21.

Jiang, L., Gao, H., & Shi, L. H. (2021). The effect of power distance beliefs on the inconspicuous versus conspicuous consumption of luxury accessories in China and the USA. *Journal of Marketing Management*, *37*(15-16), 1459–1489. DOI: 10.1080/0267257X.2021.1913214

Jin, B. E., & Shin, D. C. (2021). The power of 4th industrial revolution in the fashion industry: What, why, and how has the industry changed? *Fashion and Textiles*, *8*(1), 31.

Johnson, E. J., Shu, S. B., Dellaert, B. G. C., Fox, C., Goldstein, D. G., Häubl, G., Larrick, R. P., Payne, J. W., Peters, E., Schkade, D., Wansink, B., & Weber, E. U. (2012). Beyond nudges: Tools of a choice architecture. *Marketing Letters*, *23*(2), 487–504. DOI: 10.1007/s11002-012-9186-1

Joy, A., Belk, R. W., Wang, J. J., & Sherry, J. F. (2020). Emotion and consumption: Toward a new understanding of cultural collisions between Hong Kong and PRC luxury consumers. *Journal of Consumer Culture*, *20*(4), 578–597. DOI: 10.1177/1469540518764247

Joy, A., Zhu, Y., Peña, C., & Brouard, M. (2022). Digital future of luxury brands: Metaverse, digital fashion, and non-fungible tokens. *Strategic Change*, *31*(3), 337–343.

Kahneman, D., Slovic, P., & Tversky, A. (Eds.). (1982). *Judgment under uncertainty: Heuristics and biases*. Cambridge University Press.

Kahneman, D., & Tversky, A. (1979). Prospect theory: An analysis of decision under risk. *Econometrica*, *47*(2), 263–291. DOI: 10.2307/1914185

Kang, E. Y., & Sung, Y. H. (2022). Luxury and sustainability: The role of message appeals and objectivity on luxury brands' green corporate social responsibility. *Journal of Marketing Communications*, *28*(3), 291–312.

Kang, Y. J., & Park, S. Y. (2016). The perfection of the narcissistic self: A qualitative study on luxury consumption and customer equity. *Journal of Business Research*, *69*(9), 3813–3819. DOI: 10.1016/j.jbusres.2015.12.073

Kapferer, J. N. (2012). Abundant rarity: The key to luxury growth. *Business Horizons*, *55*(5), 453–462.

Karadag, G. M., & Erdogmus, I. E. (2020). Digitization of luxury fashion by building an omnichannel dream. In *Managing customer experiences in an omnichannel world: Melody of online and offline environments in the customer journey* (pp. 233–256). Emerald Publishing Limited.

Karaosman, H., Perry, P., Brun, A., & Morales-Alonso, G. (2020). Behind the runway: Extending sustainability in luxury fashion supply chains. *Journal of Business Research, 117*, 652–663.

Karlsson, J., & Ryberg, A. (2024). The Power of Customization: Exploring the impact of customized design and fit on user experience and perceptions of garments.

Kaur, J., Singh, S., & Singh, R. (2022). AI and Customer Experience in the Fashion Industry. In *Adoption and Implementation of AI in Customer Relationship Management* (pp. 127–138). IGI Global.

Kaushik, A. (2025). Omnichannel Marketing: A Complete Guide for 2025 and Beyond. Available at: https://www.moengage.com/blog/omnichannel-marketing/

Kempf, H. (2008). *How the Rich are Destroying the Earth* (Thatcher, L., Trans.). Green Books.

Kendall, D. E. (2011). *Framing Class: Media Representations of Wealth and Poverty in America.* Rowman & Littlefield.

Khamoushi Sahne, S. S. (2023). The Impact of Artificial Intelligence on Customer Loyalty in the Luxury Market: Mediating Role of Customer Relationship. Available at *SSRN.*

Khamoushi, S. S., & Kalantari, D. H. (2025). Enhancing loyalty in luxury fashion with AI: The mediation role of customer relationships. *Asia-Pacific Journal of Business Administration.*

Khayyam, H., Javadi, B., Jalili, M., & Jazar, R. N. (2019). Artificial intelligence and internet of things for autonomous vehicles. In *Nonlinear approaches in engineering applications: Automotive applications of engineering problems* (pp. 39–68). Springer International Publishing.

Kidd, C. D., & Breazeal, C. (2008, September). Robots at home: Understanding long-term human-robot interaction. In *Proceedings of the IEEE International Conference of Intelligent Robot Systems* (pp. 3230–3235).

Kim, J., Park, J., & Septianto, F. (2022). The impact of socioeconomic status on preferences for sustainable luxury brands. *Psychology and Marketing*, *39*(8), 1563–1578. DOI: 10.1002/mar.21671

Kim, S., & Chang, H. J. J. (2023). Mechanism of retail therapy during stressful life events: The psychological compensation of revenge consumption toward luxury brands. *Journal of Retailing and Consumer Services*, *75*, C7–C103508. DOI: 10.1016/j.jretconser.2023.103508

Kim, T., & Duhachek, A. (2018). *The impact of artificial agents on persuasion: A construal level account*. ACR Asia-Pacific Advances.

Kizgin, H., Jamal, A., Dey, B. L., & Rana, N. P. (2017). The Impact of Social Media on Consumers' Acculturation and Purchase Intentions. *Information Systems Frontiers*. Advance online publication. Retrieved March 17, 2019, from. DOI: 10.1007/s10796-017-9817-4

Knight, W. (2017). Forget killer robots – bias is the real AI danger. Retrieved February 11, 2019 from https://www.technologyreview.com/s/608986/forget-killer-robotsbias-is-the-real-ai-danger/

Kober, J., Bagnell, J. A., & Peters, J. (2013). Reinforcement learning in robotics: A survey. *The International Journal of Robotics Research*, *32*(11), 1238–1274.

Kochar, S. (2024) Luxury Fashion Brands in 2025: Navigating Change and Growth. Available at: https://www.iiad.edu.in/the-circle/luxury-fashion-brands-navigating-change-and-growth/

Kong, H. M., Witmaier, A., & Ko, E. (2021). Sustainability and social media communication: How consumers respond to marketing efforts of luxury and non-luxury fashion brands. *Journal of Business Research*, *131*, 640–651.

König, J. C. L., Wiedmann, K. P., Hennigs, N., & Haase, J. (2016). The legends of tomorrow: A semiotic approach towards a brand myth of luxury heritage. *Journal of Global Scholars of Marketing Science: Bridging Asia and the World*, *26*(2), 198–215. DOI: 10.1080/21639159.2016.1143155

Kotler, P. (2003). *Marketing management*. Pearson education.

KPMG. (2022). India's luxury landscape: Growth and transformation. https://home.kpmg/in/en/home.html

Kuksa, I., Kent, A., & West, H. (2024). Pathways to green personalisation: Reducing consumption through design. *The Design Journal*, *27*(5), 823–842.

Kunda, Z. (1990). The case for motivated reasoning. *Psychological Bulletin*, *108*(3), 480–498. DOI: 10.1037/0033-2909.108.3.480 PMID: 2270237

Kuziemski, M., & Misuraca, G. (2020). AI governance in the public sector: Three tales from the frontiers of automated decision-making in democratic settings. *Telecommunications Policy*, *44*(6), 101976. PMID: 32313360

Lall, M. M. (2023). *IN BLOCKCHAIN WE TRUST? The examination of an anti-counterfeiting solution* (Doctoral dissertation, City, University of London).

Lamptey, L., Mensah, R. O., & Korankye, V. (2024). Prevalence of counterfeit fashion goods in a West African Country: Crime in perspective. *Deviant Behavior*, •••, 1–21.

Landim, A. R. D. B., Pereira, A. M., & Vieira, T., de B. Costa, E., Moura, J. A. B., Wanick, V., & Bazaki, E. (2022). Chatbot design approaches for fashion E-commerce: An interdisciplinary review. *International Journal of Fashion Design, Technology and Education*, *15*(2), 200–210.

Lee, Y. A. (2022). Leading edge technologies in fashion innovation: Product design and development process from materials to the end products to consumers. 1–16.

Lee, A. Y., Keller, P. A., & Sternthal, B. (2009). Value from regulatory construal fit: The persuasive impact of fit between consumer goals and message concreteness. *The Journal of Consumer Research*, *36*(5), 735–747.

Lee, G., & Kim, H. Y. (2024). Human vs. AI: The battle for authenticity in fashion design and consumer response. *Journal of Retailing and Consumer Services*, *77*, 103690.

Lee, S., Baumgartner, H., & Winterich, K. P. (2018). Did They Earn It? Observing Unearned Luxury Consumption Decreases Brand Attitude When Observers Value Fairness. *Journal of Consumer Psychology*, *28*(3), 412–436. DOI: 10.1002/jcpy.1028

Lee, S., & Bolton, L. E. (2020). Mixed signals? Decoding luxury consumption in the workplace. *Journal of Business Research*, *117*, 331–345. DOI: 10.1016/j.jbusres.2020.06.011

Leung, E., Paolacci, G., & Puntoni, S. (2018). Man versus machine: Resisting automation in identity-based consumer behavior. *JMR, Journal of Marketing Research*, *55*(6), 818–831.

Lim, C. M., & Kim, Y. K. (2015). Luxe-Bargain Shopping: Relationships Among Perceived Values, Satisfaction, and Future Intentions. In Developments in Marketing Science: Proceedings of the Academy of Marketing Science (pp. 337). Springer Nature. https://doi.org/DOI: 10.1007/978-3-319-10873-5_193

Lim, L. (2024). Making omnichannel work for luxury retail. Available at: https://hbr.org/2024/09/making-omnichannel-work-for-luxury-retail

Lim, X. J., Cheah, J. H., Ngo, L. V., Chan, K., & Ting, H. (2023). How do crazy rich Asians perceive sustainable luxury? Investigating the determinants of consumers' willingness to pay a premium price. *Journal of Retailing and Consumer Services*, *75*, 103502.

Lindholm, R. W., & Driscoll, P. (1967). *Our American Economy*. Harcourt, Brace and World, INC, New York.

Lin, Y., & Yu, J. (2023). Study on the Modernization of Supply Chain Management of the Luxury Industry in the Context of the Digital Economy. *Academic Journal of Management and Social Sciences*, *4*(1), 5–11.

Liu, X., Shin, H., & Burns, A. C. (2021). Examining the impact of luxury brand's social media marketing on customer engagement: Using big data analytics and natural language processing. *Journal of Business Research*, *125*, 815–826.

Liu, Y. (2023). Digital Transformation in The Luxury Industry: Strategies, Challenges, And Opportunities. Highlights in Business. *Economics and Management, 23*, 650–656. DOI: 10.54097/xgftec52

Loewenstein, G., Sunstein, C. R., & Golman, R. (2014). Disclosure: Psychology changes everything. *Annual Review of Economics, 6*(1), 391–419. DOI: 10.1146/annurev-economics-080213-041341

Long, C. (2024). Up close and personalised. Paris Fashion Week| Designers explored ideas about the essence of couture, mixing the elevated and the more everyday. By Carola Long. *The Financial Times*, 5-5.

Longoni, C., Bonezzi, A., & Morewedge, C. K. (2019). (forthcoming). Resistance to Medical Artificial Intelligence. *The Journal of Consumer Research.*

López, B., Rangel-Pérez, C., & Fernández, M. (2023). Sustainable strategies in the luxury business to increase efficiency in reducing carbon footprint. *Journal of Business Research, 157*, 113607.

Loureiro, S. M. C. (2023). Artificial intelligence and extended reality in luxury fashion retail: Analysis and reflection. In *Augmented reality and artificial intelligence: The fusion of advanced technologies* (pp. 323–348). Springer Nature Switzerland.

Lowy, J. (2016). Self-driving cars are 'absolutely not' ready for deployment. Retrieved February 11, 2019 from https://www.pbs.org/newshour/science/self-driving-cars-are-absolutely-not-ready-for-deployment

Luce, L. (2018). *Artificial intelligence for fashion: How AI is revolutionizing the fashion industry*. Apress.

Madinga, N. W., Maziriri, E. T., Chuchu, T., & Mototo, L. (2021). The LGBTQAI+ community and luxury brands: Exploring drivers of luxury consumption in South Africa. *African Journal of Business and Economic Research, 16*(1), 207–225. DOI: 10.31920/1750-4562/2021/v16n1a9

Maglio, P. P., & Lim, C. (2018). On the impact of autonomous technologies on human-centered service systems. Handbook of service dominant logic

Ma, M. H., & Coelho, A. (2024). Luxury Consumption Tendency: A Comparative Study Between Chinese and Portuguese Consumers. *Journal of Global Marketing*, •••, 1–19. DOI: 10.1080/08911762.2024.2350926

Mankiw, N. G. (2007). *Macroeconomics*. Worth publishers.

Market. us. (2023). Luxury goods market share, size, trends, forecast 2023 | 2032 [Data set].

Martin, K. D., Borah, A., & Palmatier, R. W. (2017). Data privacy: Effects on customer and firm performance. *Journal of Marketing*, *81*(1), 36–58.

McKinsey & Company. (2022). *Digital supply chain transformation: Lessons from global brands*. https://www.mckinsey.com

McKinsey & Company. (2022). *Ethics of AI in urban planning: Challenges and solutions*. https://www.mckinsey.com

McKinsey & Company. (2022). *Redefining customer experience in luxury through digital transformation*. https://www.mckinsey.com

McKinsey & Company. (2022). *The impact of AI on marketing performance*. https://www.mckinsey.com

McKinsey & Company. (2023). *Next in personalization 2023: The future of customer engagement*. https://www.mckinsey.com

McKinsey & Company. (2023). *Smart cities and AI: The path forward*. https://www.mckinsey.com

McKinsey & Company. (2023). *The State of Fashion Technology Report*. https://www.mckinsey.com

McKinsey & Company. (2023). *The State of Fashion: How technology is redefining luxury*. https://www.mckinsey.com

Mcneil, P., & Riello, G. (2016). *Luxury: A rich history*. Oxford University Press.

Mekonnen, A. (2024). Augmented reality (AR) in retailing: customers' experience in luxury fashion. In *Digital Transformation for Fashion and Luxury Brands: Theory and Practice* (pp. 91–106). Springer International Publishing.

Mishra, V. (2024). Promoting healthy lifestyle by influencing consumers' online food choices: The use of digital nudging. In *Digital influence on consumer habits: Marketing challenges and opportunities* (pp. 123–145). Emerald Publishing.

Misra, R., Aggarwal, E., & Taneja, C. (2024). Examining the impact of the 3Cs: Content, collaboration and customisation of social media marketing on luxury fashion brand perception. *The Retail and Marketing Review, 20*(2), 135–153.

Modgil, S., Singh, R. K., & Hannibal, C. (2022). Artificial intelligence for supply chain resilience: Learning from Covid-19. *International Journal of Logistics Management, 33*(4), 1246–1268.

Mohiuddin Babu, M., Akter, S., Rahman, M., Billah, M. M., & Hack-Polay, D. (2022). The role of artificial intelligence in shaping the future of Agile fashion industry. *Production Planning and Control*, •••, 1–15.

Mondal, A., & Chakrabarti, A. B. (2021). Information and communication technology adoption strategies of emerging multinationals from India. [JGIM]. *Journal of Global Information Management, 29*(5), 161–175.

Moraes, M., Gountas, J., Gountas, S., & Sharma, P. (2019). Celebrity influences on consumer decision making: New insights and research directions. *Journal of Marketing Management, 35*(13-14), 1159–1192. DOI: 10.1080/0267257X.2019.1632373

Moreau, C. P., Prandelli, E., Schreier, M., & Hieke, S. (2020). Customization in luxury brands: Can Valentino get personal? *JMR, Journal of Marketing Research, 57*(5), 937–947.

Mostafa, M. M., & Arnaout, J. P. (2020). What drives Kuwaiti consumers to purchase luxury brands? *International Review of Retail, Distribution and Consumer Research, 30*(1), 86–102. DOI: 10.1080/09593969.2019.1626259

Munoz, J. M. (2023, July 11). AI and technological sophistication in luxury companies. California Management Review. https://cmr.berkeley.edu/2023/07/ai-and-technological-sophistication-in-luxury-companies/

Nair, G. G., & Trivedi, V. (2024). Application of AI And ML in Quality Control Department of Textile and Apparel Industry. *International Conference on Sustainable Design Practices*

National Bureau of Statistics NBS (2019), *Consumption Expenditure Pattern in Nigeria.*

National Bureau of Statistics NBS. (2022). Nigeria Launches its Most Extensive National Measure of Multidimensional Poverty. Press release, 17 November 2022 –Abuja. Retrieved on 19th August, 2024 from https://nigerianstat.gov.ng/news/78

Nazarani, M. R., & Suparna, G. (2021). The effect of luxury brand, brand image, and product quality on purchase intention. *American Journal of Humanities and Social Sciences Research*, *5*(1), 290–295.

Ndawula, Y. K., Mori, N., & Nkote, I. (2023). Effects of behavioural biases on life insurance demand decisions in Uganda. *International Journal of Social Economics*, *51*(10), 987–1001. DOI: 10.1108/IJSE-03-2023-0212

Nermain, A. I., Thanasi-Boçe, M., & Ali, O. (2022). Boosting luxury sustainability through blockchain technology. *Blockchain Technologies in the Textile and Fashion Industry*, 17.

Ng, C. J., Goh, Y. N., Nisar, N., Ghumro, T. H., & Lim, C. N. (2023). Does Facebook Advertisement Matter to Entice Customers' Responses? An Integrated Technology Acceptance Model. *Malaysian Journal of Consumer and Family Economics*, *30*, 2948–4189.

Niazi, G. S. K., Siddiqui, J., Shah, B. A., & Hunjra, A. I. (2012). Effective Advertising and its Influence on Consumer Buying Behavior. *Information Management and Business Review*, *4*(3), 114–119.

O'Rourke, A. M., Lin, J., Sung, B., & Septianto, F. (2025). Social dynamics of luxury customization: The unique impact of name personalization. *Psychology and Marketing*, *42*(2), 493–513.

Oc, Y., Plangger, K., Sands, S., Campbell, C. L., & Pitt, L. (2023). Luxury is what you say: Analyzing electronic word-of-mouth marketing of luxury products using artificial intelligence and machine learning. *Psychology and Marketing*, *40*(9), 1704–1719.

Olarewaju, T. (2018). Organising household consumption and occupational proportions: Evidence from Nigeria. *The International Journal of Organizational Analysis*, *26*(4), 748–772. DOI: 10.1108/IJOA-03-2017-1141

Olasehinde, N., & Olaniyan, O. (2017). Determinants of household health expenditure in Nigeria. *International Journal of Social Economics*, *44*(12), 1694–1709. DOI: 10.1108/IJSE-12-2015-0324

Onana, K. I. (2021). Effect of digital marketing on consumer based brand equity of micro enterprises in Nigeria. *International Journal of Management and Social Sciences*, *2*(2), 1–37. DOI: 10.51739/122113816.v2i2.1459780014

Osburg, V. S., Davies, I., Yoganathan, V., & McLeay, F. (2021). Perspectives, opportunities and tensions in ethical and sustainable luxury: Introduction to the thematic symposium. *Journal of Business Ethics*, *169*, 201–210.

Ozuem, W., & Willis, M. (2024). Artificial Intelligence and Predictive Analytics: Towards a Praxis of Personalised Shopping Experiences. In *Digital transformation for fashion and luxury brands: Theory and practice* (pp. 3–26). Springer International Publishing.

Pangarkar, A., Arora, V., & Shukla, Y. (2022). Exploring phygital omnichannel luxury retailing for immersive customer experience: The role of rapport and social engagement. *Journal of Retailing and Consumer Services*, *68*, 103001.

Parekh, J. (2018). Why Programmatic provides a better digital marketing landscape. Retrieved February 13, 2019 from https://www.adweek.com/programmatic/why-programmatic-provides-a-better-digital-marketing-landscape/

Patel, K. (2024). Revolutionizing Customer Experience: Integrating Blockchain with AR and VR in Retail. In *Augmenting Retail Reality, Part B: Blockchain, AR, VR, and AI* (pp. 1-22). Emerald Publishing Limited.

Patel, K., Beeram, D., Ramamurthy, P., Garg, P., & Kumar, S. (2024). Ai-enhanced design: Revolutionizing methodologies and workflows. [IJAIRD]. *Development*, *2*(1), 135–157.

Patil, D. (2024). Artificial Intelligence-Driven Predictive Maintenance In Manufacturing: Enhancing Operational Efficiency, Minimizing Downtime, And Optimizing Resource Utilization. *Minimizing Downtime, And Optimizing Resource Utilization (December 11, 2024).*

Pawlicka, K., & Bal, M. (2022). Sustainable Supply Chain Finances implementation model and Artificial Intelligence for innovative omnichannel logistics. *Management*, *26*(1), 19–35.

Pedersen, I., Reid, S., & Aspevig, K. (2018). Developing social robots for aging populations: A literature review of recent academic sources. *Sociology Compass*, *12*(6).

Peishan, S., & Yufei, W. (2021, December). Luxury Brands Culture and Marketing: How Does Chanel Stay popular. In *2021 3rd International Conference on Economic Management and Cultural Industry (ICEMCI 2021)* (pp. 1438-1442). Atlantis Press.

Peric, M. (2024). Leveraging AI for sustainability in the fashion industry: anticipated and unanticipated consequences. http://hdl.handle.net/10400.14/45023

Pindyck, R. S., & Rubinfeld, D. L. (1998). *Econometric models and economic forecasts*. McGraw Hill.

Piris, Y., & Gay, A. C. (2021). Customer satisfaction and natural language processing. *Journal of Business Research, 124*, 264–271.

Polese, F., Carrubbo, L., Caputo, F., & Megaro, A. (2018). Co-creation in action: An acid test of smart service systems viability. In Exploring Service Science: 9th International Conference (pp. 151–164). Springer International Publishing

Power, B. (2017). How AI is streamlining marketing and sales. Harvard Business Review, June 12. Retrieved February 11, 2019 from https://hbr.org/2017/06/how-ai-is-streamlining-marketing-and-sales

Prusova, D. (2023). Key B2C Luxury Brand Marketing Strategies to Establish Strong Relationships with the Modern Consumer of Luxury Fashion.

PwC. (2022). *Inventory management and AI: Navigating the next wave of efficiency*. https://www.pwc.com

PwC. (2022). *Smart cities and the digital divide: Ensuring equitable access to AI*. https://www.pwc.com

PwC. (2022). *The power of sentiment analysis in brand strategy*. https://www.pwc.com

PwC. (2022). *Urban transformation with AI: Smarter, safer cities*. https://www.pwc.com

PwC. (2023). *AI in customer service: Elevating the luxury client experience*. https://www.pwc.com

PwC. (2023). *Consumer Intelligence Series: Trusted tech*. https://www.pwc.com

PwC. (2023). *Future of Customer Experience: Immersive Technology and AI*. https://www.pwc.com

PwC. (2023). *The power of AI in retail and luxury: Transforming customer experience and operations*. https://www.pwc.com

Qian, P. (2014). Experimental analysis of crop insurance: Cognitive bias in decision making. *The Journal of Risk and Insurance*, *81*(2), 321–345. DOI: 10.1111/jori.12032

Rahman, M. S., Bag, S., Hossain, M. A., Abdel Fattah, F. A. M., Gani, M. O., & Rana, N. P. (2023). The new wave of AI-powered luxury brands online shopping experience: The role of digital multisensory cues and customers' engagement. *Journal of Retailing and Consumer Services*, *72*(103273), 103273. DOI: 10.1016/j.jretconser.2023.103273

Rahwan, I., Cebrian, M., Obradovich, N., Bongard, J., Bonnefon, J. F., & Breazeal, C.. (2019). Machine behavior. *Nature*, *568*(7753), 477–486.

Rane, N., Choudhary, S., & Rane, J. (2024). Artificial intelligence, machine learning, and deep learning for sentiment analysis in business to enhance customer experience, loyalty, and satisfaction. *Available at SSRN* 4846145.

Rane, N., Choudhary, S., & Rane, J. (2024). Artificial intelligence, machine learning, and deep learning for sentiment analysis in business to enhance customer experience, loyalty, and satisfaction. In *Trustworthy Artificial Intelligence in Industry and Society* (pp. 233–261). Deep Science Publishing.

Rathore, B. (2017). Exploring the intersection of fashion marketing in the metaverse: Leveraging artificial intelligence for consumer engagement and brand innovation. *International Journal of New Media Studies: International Peer Reviewed Scholarly Indexed Journal*, *4*(2), 51–60.

Rathore, B. (2019). Artificial Intelligence in Sustainable Fashion Marketing: Transforming the Supply Chain Landscape. *Artificial Intelligence*, *8*(2).

Rathore, B. (2019). From Trendy to Green: Exploring AI's Role in Sustainable Fashion Marketing. *International Journal of New Media Studies: International Peer Reviewed Scholarly Indexed Journal*, *6*(2), 12–22.

Razak, M. I. M., Ariffin, Z. Z., Yahaya, M. N., & Ismail, I. (2021). An overview of personal luxury brands consumption in Malaysia. *The Sciences*, *11*(3), 566–573.

Razmus, W., Czarna, A. Z., & Fortuna, P. (2023). Luxury consumption and the dark triad of personality. *Journal of Business Research, 169*, C7–C114246. DOI: 10.1016/j.jbusres.2023.114246

Reese, B. (2018). *The fourth age: Smart robots, conscious computers and the future of humanity*. Atria Books.

Reydellet, H. (2022).Security: a growing problem for luxury brands. Available at: https://luxus-plus.com/en/security-a-growing-problem-for-luxury-brands/

Robinson, K. (2023). How generative AI can boost consumer marketing. Available at: https://www.mckinsey.com/capabilities/growth-marketing-and-sales/our-insights/how-generative-ai-can-boost-consumer-marketing

Rosário, A., Moreira, C., & Macedo, P. (2021). Competitive dynamics of strategic groups in the Portugueses Banking Industrry, Cuadernos de Gestión, 21(2), 1-15. ISSN: 1131-6837. DOI: <ALIGNMENT.qj></ALIGNMENT>10.5295/cdg.180975ac

Rosário, A. T., Lopes, P. R., & Rosário, F. S. (2023). Metaverse in Marketing: Challenges and Opportunities. In Khang, A., Shah, V., & Rani, S. (Eds.), *Handbook of Research on AI-Based Technologies and Applications in the Era of the Metaverse* (pp. 204–227). IGI Global., DOI: 10.4018/978-1-6684-8851-5.ch010

Rosário, A., & Casaca, J. (2023). Relationship marketing and customer retention - A systematic literature review. *Studies in Business and Economics, 18*(3), 44–66. DOI: 10.2478/sbe-2023-0044

Roux, E., Tafani, E., & Vigneron, F. (2017). Values associated with luxury brand consumption and the role of gender. *Journal of Business Research, 71*, 102–113. DOI: 10.1016/j.jbusres.2016.10.012

Russo, J. E., & Schoemaker, P. J. H. (1992). Managing overconfidence. *Sloan Management Review, 33*(2), 7–17.

Sahota, N. (2024). Weaving Elegance with Intelligence: How Luxury Brands are Embracing AI. Available at: https://www.forbes.com/sites/neilsahota/2024/03/15/weaving-elegance-with-intelligence-how-luxury-brands-are-embracing-ai/

Salesforce. (2022). *State of the Connected Customer (5th ed.).* https://www.salesforce.com

Salesforce. (2023). *State of the Connected Customer (6th ed.).* https://www.salesforce.com

Salesforce. (2023). *Trends in AI-powered marketing*. https://www.salesforce.com

Samanta, P., Amir, M., Maira, S., Barakoti, A., Chopra, M., & Shrivastava, V. (2024, December). Analyzing the Transformative Effects of AI-Powered Influencer Marketing on Consumer Decision-Making. In *2024 1st International Conference on Advances in Computing, Communication and Networking (ICAC2N)* (pp. 1236-1241). IEEE.

Sama, R. (2019). Impact of Media Advertisements on Consumer Behaviour. *Journal of Creative Communications, 14*(1), 54–68.

Savolainen, P. (2023). *The use of AI for demand and trend forecasting in fashion and the potential of these methods for sustainable brands* (Bachelor's thesis).

Schatsky, D., Katyal, V., Iyengar, S., & Chauhan, R. (2019). Why enterprises shouldn't wait for AI regulation. Retrieved July 11, 2019 from https://www2.deloitte.com/insights/us/en/focus/signals-for-strategists/ethical-artificial-intelligence.html

Schrift, R. Y., Wertenbroch, K., André, Q., & Frank, D. H. (2017). Threatening free will. Presentation at the *Symposium on Alienation and Meaning in Production and Consumption, Technische Universität München.*

Sekhampu, T. J., & Niyimbanira, F. (2013). Analysis of The Factors Influencing Household Expenditure in A South African Township. *The International Business & Economics Research Journal, 12*(3), 279–284.

Seo, Y., & Buchanan-Oliver, M. (2019). Constructing a typology of luxury brand consumption practices. *Journal of Business Research, 99*, 414–421. DOI: 10.1016/j.jbusres.2017.09.019

Sestino, A., & Amatulli, C. (2024). The challenge of integrating "intelligent" technologies in luxury shopping contexts: The role of brand personality appeal and consumers' status consumption orientation. *Journal of Retailing and Consumer Services, 76*, C7–C103488. DOI: 10.1016/j.jretconser.2023.103488

Shahzad, M. F., Xu, S., An, X., & Javed, I. (2024). Assessing the impact of AI-chatbot service quality on user e-brand loyalty through chatbot user trust, experience and electronic word of mouth. *Journal of Retailing and Consumer Services, 79*, 103867.

Shalev, L. (2024). Luxury Retail Security Concerns Are on the Rise, Can RFID Be the Answer? Available at: https://www.chainlane.io/blog/rfid-for-luxury-brands

Shankar, V. (2018). How artificial intelligence (AI) is reshaping retailing. *Journal of Retailing, 94*(4), vi–xi.

Sharda, N., & Bhat, A. K. (2018). Austerity to materialism and brand consciousness: Luxury consumption in India. *Journal of Fashion Marketing and Management, 22*(2), 223–239. DOI: 10.1108/JFMM-03-2017-0025

Sharma, M., Shail, H., Painuly, P. K., & Kumar, A. S. (2023). AI-powered technologies used in online fashion retail for sustainable business: AI-powered technologies impacting consumer buying behavior. In *Sustainable Marketing, Branding, and Reputation Management: Strategies for a Greener Future* (pp. 538-561). IGI Global.

Sharma, A. (2023). Product design and development using Artificial Intelligence (AI) techniques. *RE:view*.

Shen, B., Minner, S., Chan, H. L., & Brun, A. (2020). Logistics and supply chain management in the luxury industry. *Transportation Research Part E, Logistics and Transportation Review, 143*, 102095.

Sidlauskiene, J., Joye, Y., & Auruskeviciene, V. (2023). AI-based chatbots in conversational commerce and their effects on product and price perceptions. *Electronic Markets*, *33*(1), 24.

Silva, S. C., Silva, F. P., & Dias, J. C. (2024). Exploring omnichannel strategies: A path to improve customer experiences. *International Journal of Retail & Distribution Management*, *52*(1), 62–88.

Simon, H. A. (1955). A behavioral model of rational choice. *The Quarterly Journal of Economics*, *69*(1), 99–118. DOI: 10.2307/1884852

Singh, O., Singh, N., Singh, A., & Vinoth, R. (2024). AI, IoT, and Blockchain in Fashion: Confronting Industry Applications, Challenges with Technological Solutions. *International Journal of Communication Networks and Information Security*, *16*(4), 393–410.

Sinha, P. (2020). AI and Hyper-Personalization in the Indian Luxury Market. *Luxury Business Review*, *8*(1), 56–75.

Smith, G. (1996). Framing in advertising and the moderating impact of consumer education. *Journal of Advertising Research*, *36*(5), 49.

Song, X., & Bonanni, C. (2024). AI-Driven Business Model: How AI-Powered Try-On Technology Is Refining the Luxury Shopping Experience and Customer Satisfaction. *Journal of Theoretical and Applied Electronic Commerce Research*, *19*(4), 3067–3087.

Soni, N., & Kumar, S. (2024). What drives new luxury consumption? Application of schema congruity theory and heuristic systematic framework. *Asia Pacific Journal of Marketing and Logistics*, *36*(9), 2213–2233. DOI: 10.1108/APJML-04-2023-0319

Sreenivasan, A., & Suresh, M. (2024). Design Thinking and Artificial Intelligence: A Systematic Literature Review Exploring Synergies. *International Journal of Innovation Studies.*, *8*(3), 297–312.

Srihith, I. V. D., Kumar, I. V. S., Varaprasad, R., Mohan, Y. R., Srinivas, T. A. S., & Sravanthi, Y. (2022). Future of Smart Cities: The Role of Machine Learning and Artificial Intelligence. *South Asian Research Journal of Engineering and Technology*, *4*(5), 110–119.

Srivastava, A. (2024). AI in Luxury Fashion: Redefining Creativity and Customer Experience. Available at: https://www.fibre2fashion.com/industry-article/10054/ai-in-luxury-fashion-redefining-creativity-and-customer-experience

Statista Market Insights. (2024). Luxury Goods – Worldwide. Statista. https://www.statista.com/outlook/cmo/luxury-goods/worldwide

Stigler, G. J. (1961). The Economics of Information. *Journal of Political Economy*, *69*(3), 213–225.

Straits Research. (2024). Luxury Fashion Market Size, Share & Trends Analysis Report By Product Type (Apparel, Footwear, Accessories), By End-User (Men, Women, Children), By Generation (Gen X, Millennials and Gen Z, Baby Boomer and Silent Gen), By Distribution Channel (Online, Mono Brand Stores, Specialty Stores, Departmental Stores, Off-Price Stores, Airports) and By Region (North America, Europe, APAC, Middle East and Africa, LATAM) Forecasts, 2024-2032. Available at: https://straitsresearch.com/report/luxury-fashion-market

Sun, B. (2005). Promotion Effect on Endogenous Consumption. *Marketing Science*, *24*(3), 430–443.

Sun, H., Guo, Z., & Qian, H. (2024). The self on display: The impact of self-objectification on luxury consumption. *Psychology and Marketing*. Advance online publication. DOI: 10.1002/mar.22061

Sweeney, J., & Swait, J. (2008). The effects of brand credibility on customer loyalty. *Journal of Retailing and Consumer Services*, *15*(3), 179–193.

Tafani, E., Vigneron, F., Azoulay, A., Crener, S., & Zahid, A. (2024). The Influence of Culture and Gender in Luxury Brand Consumption: A Comparison Across Western and Eastern Culture Consumers. *Journal of International Marketing*. Advance online publication. DOI: 10.1177/1069031X241235629

Tam, F. Y., & Lung, J. (2025). Digital marketing strategies for luxury fashion brands: A systematic literature review. *International Journal of Information Management Data Insights*, *5*(1), 100309.

Tan, L., & Luhrs, M. (2024). Using Generative AI Midjourney to Enhance Divergent and Convergent Thinking in an Architect's Creative Design Process. *The Design Journal*, •••, 1–23.

Teisl, M. F., Levy, A. S., & Derby, B. M. (1999). The Effects of Education and Information Source on Consumer Awareness of Diet–Disease Relationships. *Journal of Public Policy & Marketing*, *18*(2), 197–207. DOI: 10.1177/074391569901800206

Thaler, R. H. (1980). Toward a positive theory of consumer choice. *Journal of Economic Behavior & Organization*, *1*(1), 39–60. DOI: 10.1016/0167-2681(80)90051-7

Thanasi-Boçe, M. AL-Issa, N., & Ali, O. (2022). Combating Luxury Counterfeiting Through Blockchain Technology. In *Blockchain Technologies in the Textile and Fashion Industry* (pp. 1-16). Singapore: Springer Nature Singapore.

Timperio, G., Tan, K. C., Fratocchi, L., & Pace, S. (2016). The impact of ethnicity on luxury perception: The case of Singapore's Generation Y. *Asia Pacific Journal of Marketing and Logistics*, *28*(2), 217–233. DOI: 10.1108/APJML-04-2015-0060

Tsai, W. S., Yang, Q., & Liu, Y. (2013). Young Chinese consumers' snob and bandwagon luxury consumption preferences. *Journal of International Consumer Marketing*, *25*(5), 290–304. DOI: 10.1080/08961530.2013.827081

Tucker, C. (2018). Privacy, algorithms, and artificial intelligence. In *The Economics of Artificial Intelligence: An Agenda*. University of Chicago Press.

Tversky, A., & Kahneman, D. (1974). Judgment under uncertainty: Heuristics and biases. *Science*, *185*(4157), 1124–1131. DOI: 10.1126/science.185.4157.1124 PMID: 17835457

Umoh, G. S. (1997). Food consumption pattern in urban households: The case study of Uyo metropolis in Akwa Ibom State, Nigeria. *Agrosearch*, *3*(1-2), 94–112.

van Lente, H., Spitters, C., & Peine, A. (2013). Comparing technological hype cycles: Towards a theory. *Technological Forecasting and Social Change*, *80*(8), 1615–1628.

Varshney, N. (2023). Automatic Fashion Product Tagging: Technology that makes catalogue management easier for brands. Available at: https://apparelresources.com/technology-news/retail-tech/automatic-fashion-product-tagging-technology-makes-catalogue-management-easier-brands/

Veblen, T. (1899). *The Theory of the Leisure Class*. Project Gutenberg.

Verhoef, P. C., Stephen, A. T., Kannan, P. K., Luo, X., Abhishek, V., & Andrews, M.. (2017). Consumer connectivity in a complex, technology-enabled, and mobile-oriented world with smart products. *Journal of Interactive Marketing*, *40*, 1–8.

Villasenor, J. (2019). Artificial intelligence and bias: Four key challenges. Retrieved February 11, 2019 from https://www.brookings.edu/blog/techtank/2019/01/03/artificial-intelligence-and-bias-four-key-challenges/

Voda, A. I., & Radu, L. D. (2019). How can artificial intelligence respond to smart cities challenges? In *Smart cities: Issues and challenges* (pp. 199–216). Elsevier.

Voramontri, D., & Klieb, L. (2019). 'Impact of social media on consumer behaviour', *Int. J. Information and Decision Sciences*, *11*(3), 209–233.

Wainer, J., Feil-Seifer, D. J., Shell, D. A., & Mataric, M. J. (2006, September). The role of physical embodiment in human-robot interaction. In *Proceedings of the IEEE International Symposium of Robot Human Interaction Communication* (pp.6-8).

Walters, R. J., & Novak, M. (2021). Cyber Security. Springer eBooks, pp.21–37.

Wang, H., Ko, E., Woodside, A., & Yu, J. (2021). SNS marketing activities as a sustainable competitive advantage and traditional market equity. *Journal of Business Research, 130,* 378–383.

Wang, S. L., Chen, G., & Wang, K. (2020). Overt or covert? Effect of different digital nudging on consumers' customization choices. *Nankai Business Review International, 11*(4), 527–546. DOI: 10.1108/NBRI-03-2020-0014

Wang, Y. (2022). A conceptual framework of contemporary luxury consumption. *International Journal of Research in Marketing, 39*(3), 788–803. DOI: 10.1016/j.ijresmar.2021.10.010

Wang, Y., & Kosinski, M. (2018). Deep neural networks are more accurate than humans at detecting sexual orientation from facial images. *Journal of Personality and Social Psychology, 114*(2), 246–257.

Weiss, C. (2018). RETHINKING RESEARCH METHODS IN A DIGITALLY SAVVY WORLD. In *INTED2018 Proceedings* (pp. 7225-7230). IATED.

Wells, R., Kleshinski, C. E., & Lau, T. (2012), "Attitudes Toward and Behavioral Intentions to Adopt Mobile Marketing: Comparisons of Gen Y in the United States, France And China" *Management and Marketing Faculty Publications*. 61. https://ecommons.udayton.edu/mgt_fac_pub/61

Willer, R. K. (2006). *Dispelling the Myth of a Global Consumer Indonesian Consumer Behavior Researched by Means of an Analytical Diagram for Intercultural Marketing with a Case-study of Sunsilk Shampoo for the Veiled Woman*. University of Zu Berlin.

Winterstein, J. (2022). Nudging and boosting towards sustainable food choices: A systematic literature review of cognitively oriented measures. *Journal of Sustainable Food Systems*, *3*(2), 45–67.

Wirtz, J., Patterson, P. G., Kunz, W. H., Gruber, T., Lu, V. N., Paluch, S., & Martins, A. (2018). Brave new world: Service robots in the frontline. *Journal of Service Management*, *29*(5), 907–931.

Yamini, S. (2020). Behavioural perspective of newsvendor ordering decisions: Review, analysis and insights. *International Journal of Production Economics*, *220*, 107512. Advance online publication. DOI: 10.1016/j.ijpe.2019.07.021

Yan, H., Zhang, H., Liu, L., Zhou, D., Xu, X., Zhang, Z., & Yan, S. (2022). Toward intelligent design: An ai-based fashion designer using generative adversarial networks aided by sketch and rendering generators. *IEEE Transactions on Multimedia*, *25*, 2323–2338.

You, Q., Jin, H., Wang, Z., Fang, C., & Luo, J. (2016). Image captioning with semantic attention. In *Proceedings of the IEEE conference on computer vision and pattern recognition* (pp. 4651-4659).

Zhang, S. (2020), *Essays on Consumer Online Search and Digital Content Consumption*, Unpublished PhD dissertation in Economics, Washington University

Zhang, J., Chen, M., Xie, Z., & Zhuang, J. (2022). Don't fall into exquisite poverty: The impact of mismatch between consumers and luxury brands on happiness. *Journal of Business Research*, *151*, 298–309. DOI: 10.1016/j.jbusres.2022.07.010

Zhang, X., Aw, E. C. X., Wei-Han Tan, G., & Ooi, K. B. (2024). The pursuit of splendour: A recipe of psychological motivations driving conspicuous luxury consumption. *International Journal of Retail & Distribution Management*, *52*(5), 565–579. DOI: 10.1108/IJRDM-06-2023-0375

Zhang, Y., & Liu, C. (2024). Unlocking the Potential of Artificial Intelligence in Fashion Design and E-Commerce Applications: The Case of Midjourney. *Journal of Theoretical and Applied Electronic Commerce Research*, *19*(1), 654–670.

Zhan, L., & He, Y. (2012). Understanding luxury consumption in China: Consumer perceptions of best-known brands. *Journal of Business Research*, *65*(10), 1452–1460. DOI: 10.1016/j.jbusres.2011.10.011

Zhao, M., Hoeffler, S., & Dahl, D. W. (2012). Imagination difficulty and new product evaluation. *Journal of Product Innovation Management*, *29*(S1), 76–90.

Ziccardi, G. (2020). Wearable technologies and smart clothes in the fashion business: Some issues concerning cybersecurity and data protection. *Laws*, *9*(2), 12.

Related References

To continue our tradition of advancing information science and technology research, we have compiled a list of recommended IGI Global readings. These references will provide additional information and guidance to further enrich your knowledge and assist you with your own research and future publications.

Abdul Razak, R., & Mansor, N. A. (2021). Instagram Influencers in Social Media-Induced Tourism: Rethinking Tourist Trust Towards Tourism Destination. In M. Dinis, L. Bonixe, S. Lamy, & Z. Breda (Eds.), *Impact of New Media in Tourism* (pp. 135-144). IGI Global. https://doi.org/10.4018/978-1-7998-7095-1.ch009

Abir, T., & Khan, M. Y. (2022). Importance of ICT Advancement and Culture of Adaptation in the Tourism and Hospitality Industry for Developing Countries. In Ramos, C., Quinteiro, S., & Gonçalves, A. (Eds.), *ICT as Innovator Between Tourism and Culture* (pp. 30–41). IGI Global. https://doi.org/10.4018/978-1-7998-8165-0.ch003

Abir, T., & Khan, M. Y. (2022). Importance of ICT Advancement and Culture of Adaptation in the Tourism and Hospitality Industry for Developing Countries. In Ramos, C., Quinteiro, S., & Gonçalves, A. (Eds.), *ICT as Innovator Between Tourism and Culture* (pp. 30–41). IGI Global. https://doi.org/10.4018/978-1-7998-8165-0.ch003

Abtahi, M. S., Behboudi, L., & Hasanabad, H. M. (2017). Factors Affecting Internet Advertising Adoption in Ad Agencies. *International Journal of Innovation in the Digital Economy*, *8*(4), 18–29. DOI: 10.4018/IJIDE.2017100102

Afenyo-Agbe, E., & Mensah, I. (2022). Principles, Benefits, and Barriers to Community-Based Tourism: Implications for Management. In Mensah, I., & Afenyo-Agbe, E. (Eds.), *Prospects and Challenges of Community-Based Tourism and Changing Demographics* (pp. 1–29). IGI Global. DOI: 10.4018/978-1-7998-7335-8.ch001

Agbo, V. M. (2022). Distributive Justice Issues in Community-Based Tourism. In Mensah, I., & Afenyo-Agbe, E. (Eds.), *Prospects and Challenges of Community-Based Tourism and Changing Demographics* (pp. 107–129). IGI Global. https://doi.org/10.4018/978-1-7998-7335-8.ch005

Agrawal, S. (2017). The Impact of Emerging Technologies and Social Media on Different Business(es): Marketing and Management. In Rishi, O., & Sharma, A. (Eds.), *Maximizing Business Performance and Efficiency Through Intelligent Systems* (pp. 37–49). Hershey, PA: IGI Global. DOI: 10.4018/978-1-5225-2234-8.ch002

Ahmad, A., & Johari, S. (2022). Georgetown as a Gastronomy Tourism Destination: Visitor Awareness Towards Revisit Intention of Nasi Kandar Restaurant. In Valeri, M. (Ed.), *New Governance and Management in Touristic Destinations* (pp. 71–83). IGI Global. https://doi.org/10.4018/978-1-6684-3889-3.ch005

Alkhatib, G., & Bayouq, S. T. (2021). A TAM-Based Model of Technological Factors Affecting Use of E-Tourism. *International Journal of Tourism and Hospitality Management in the Digital Age*, *5*(2), 50–67. https://doi.org/10.4018/IJTHMDA.20210701.oa1

Altinay Ozdemir, M. (2021). Virtual Reality (VR) and Augmented Reality (AR) Technologies for Accessibility and Marketing in the Tourism Industry. In C. Eusébio, L. Teixeira, & M. Carneiro (Eds.), *ICT Tools and Applications for Accessible Tourism* (pp. 277-301). IGI Global. https://doi.org/10.4018/978-1-7998-6428-8.ch013

Anantharaman, R. N., Rajeswari, K. S., Angusamy, A., & Kuppusamy, J. (2017). Role of Self-Efficacy and Collective Efficacy as Moderators of Occupational Stress Among Software Development Professionals. *International Journal of Human Capital and Information Technology Professionals*, *8*(2), 45–58. DOI: 10.4018/IJHCITP.2017040103

Aninze, F., El-Gohary, H., & Hussain, J. (2018). The Role of Microfinance to Empower Women: The Case of Developing Countries. *International Journal of Customer Relationship Marketing and Management, 9*(1), 54–78. DOI: 10.4018/IJCRMM.2018010104

Antosova, G., Sabogal-Salamanca, M., & Krizova, E. (2021). Human Capital in Tourism: A Practical Model of Endogenous and Exogenous Territorial Tourism Planning in Bahía Solano, Colombia. In Costa, V., Moura, A., & Mira, M. (Eds.), *Handbook of Research on Human Capital and People Management in the Tourism Industry* (pp. 282–302). IGI Global. https://doi.org/10.4018/978-1-7998-4318-4.ch014

Arsenijević, O. M., Orčić, D., & Kastratović, E. (2017). Development of an Optimization Tool for Intangibles in SMEs: A Case Study from Serbia with a Pilot Research in the Prestige by Milka Company. In Vemić, M. (Ed.), *Optimal Management Strategies in Small and Medium Enterprises* (pp. 320–347). Hershey, PA: IGI Global. DOI: 10.4018/978-1-5225-1949-2.ch015

Aryanto, V. D., Wismantoro, Y., & Widyatmoko, K. (2018). Implementing Eco-Innovation by Utilizing the Internet to Enhance Firm's Marketing Performance: Study of Green Batik Small and Medium Enterprises in Indonesia. *International Journal of E-Business Research, 14*(1), 21–36. DOI: 10.4018/IJEBR.2018010102

Asero, V., & Billi, S. (2022). New Perspective of Networking in the DMO Model. In Valeri, M. (Ed.), *New Governance and Management in Touristic Destinations* (pp. 105–118). IGI Global. https://doi.org/10.4018/978-1-6684-3889-3.ch007

Atiku, S. O., & Fields, Z. (2017). Multicultural Orientations for 21st Century Global Leadership. In Baporikar, N. (Ed.), *Management Education for Global Leadership* (pp. 28–51). Hershey, PA: IGI Global. DOI: 10.4018/978-1-5225-1013-0.ch002

Atiku, S. O., & Fields, Z. (2018). Organisational Learning Dimensions and Talent Retention Strategies for the Service Industries. In Baporikar, N. (Ed.), *Global Practices in Knowledge Management for Societal and Organizational Development* (pp. 358–381). Hershey, PA: IGI Global. DOI: 10.4018/978-1-5225-3009-1.ch017

Atsa'am, D. D., & Kuset Bodur, E. (2021). Pattern Mining on How Organizational Tenure Affects the Psychological Capital of Employees Within the Hospitality and Tourism Industry: Linking Employees' Organizational Tenure With PsyCap. *International Journal of Tourism and Hospitality Management in the Digital Age*, *5*(2), 17–28. https://doi.org/10.4018/IJTHMDA.2021070102

Ávila, L., & Teixeira, L. (2018). The Main Concepts Behind the Dematerialization of Business Processes. In M. Khosrow-Pour, D.B.A. (Ed.), *Encyclopedia of Information Science and Technology, Fourth Edition* (pp. 888-898). Hershey, PA: IGI Global. https://doi.org/DOI: 10.4018/978-1-5225-2255-3.ch076

Ayorekire, J., Mugizi, F., Obua, J., & Ampaire, G. (2022). Community-Based Tourism and Local People's Perceptions Towards Conservation: The Case of Queen Elizabeth Conservation Area, Uganda. In Mensah, I., & Afenyo-Agbe, E. (Eds.), *Prospects and Challenges of Community-Based Tourism and Changing Demographics* (pp. 56–82). IGI Global. https://doi.org/10.4018/978-1-7998-7335-8.ch003

Baleiro, R. (2022). Tourist Literature and the Architecture of Travel in Olga Tokarczuk and Patti Smith. In R. Baleiro & R. Pereira (Eds.), *Global Perspectives on Literary Tourism and Film-Induced Tourism* (pp. 202-216). IGI Global. https://doi.org/10.4018/978-1-7998-8262-6.ch011

Barat, S. (2021). Looking at the Future of Medical Tourism in Asia. *International Journal of Tourism and Hospitality Management in the Digital Age*, *5*(1), 19–33. https://doi.org/10.4018/IJTHMDA.2021010102

Barbosa, C. A., Magalhães, M., & Nunes, M. R. (2021). Travel Instagramability: A Way of Choosing a Destination? In M. Dinis, L. Bonixe, S. Lamy, & Z. Breda (Eds.), *Impact of New Media in Tourism* (pp. 173-190). IGI Global. https://doi.org/10.4018/978-1-7998-7095-1.ch011

Bari, M. W., & Khan, Q. (2021). Pakistan as a Destination of Religious Tourism. In E. Alaverdov & M. Bari (Eds.), *Global Development of Religious Tourism* (pp. 1-10). IGI Global. https://doi.org/10.4018/978-1-7998-5792-1.ch001

Bartens, Y., Chunpir, H. I., Schulte, F., & Voß, S. (2017). Business/IT Alignment in Two-Sided Markets: A COBIT 5 Analysis for Media Streaming Business Models. In De Haes, S., & Van Grembergen, W. (Eds.), *Strategic IT Governance and Alignment in Business Settings* (pp. 82–111). Hershey, PA: IGI Global. DOI: 10.4018/978-1-5225-0861-8.ch004

Bashayreh, A. M. (2018). Organizational Culture and Organizational Performance. In Lee, W., & Sabetzadeh, F. (Eds.), *Contemporary Knowledge and Systems Science* (pp. 50–69). Hershey, PA: IGI Global. DOI: 10.4018/978-1-5225-5655-8.ch003

Bechthold, L., Lude, M., & Prügl, R. (2021). Crisis Favors the Prepared Firm: How Organizational Ambidexterity Relates to Perceptions of Organizational Resilience. In Zehrer, A., Glowka, G., Schwaiger, K., & Ranacher-Lackner, V. (Eds.), *Resiliency Models and Addressing Future Risks for Family Firms in the Tourism Industry* (pp. 178–205). IGI Global. https://doi.org/10.4018/978-1-7998-7352-5.ch008

Bedford, D. A. (2018). Sustainable Knowledge Management Strategies: Aligning Business Capabilities and Knowledge Management Goals. In Baporikar, N. (Ed.), *Global Practices in Knowledge Management for Societal and Organizational Development* (pp. 46–73). Hershey, PA: IGI Global. DOI: 10.4018/978-1-5225-3009-1.ch003

Bekjanov, D., & Matyusupov, B. (2021). Influence of Innovative Processes in the Competitiveness of Tourist Destination. In Soares, J. (Ed.), *Innovation and Entrepreneurial Opportunities in Community Tourism* (pp. 243–263). IGI Global. https://doi.org/10.4018/978-1-7998-4855-4.ch014

Bharwani, S., & Musunuri, D. (2018). Reflection as a Process From Theory to Practice. In M. Khosrow-Pour, D.B.A. (Ed.), *Encyclopedia of Information Science and Technology, Fourth Edition* (pp. 1529-1539). Hershey, PA: IGI Global. DOI: 10.4018/978-1-5225-2255-3.ch132

Bhatt, G. D., Wang, Z., & Rodger, J. A. (2017). Information Systems Capabilities and Their Effects on Competitive Advantages: A Study of Chinese Companies. *Information Resources Management Journal, 30*(3), 41–57. DOI: 10.4018/IRMJ.2017070103

Bhushan, M., & Yadav, A. (2017). Concept of Cloud Computing in ESB. In Bhadoria, R., Chaudhari, N., Tomar, G., & Singh, S. (Eds.), *Exploring Enterprise Service Bus in the Service-Oriented Architecture Paradigm* (pp. 116–127). Hershey, PA: IGI Global. DOI: 10.4018/978-1-5225-2157-0.ch008

Bhushan, S. (2017). System Dynamics Base-Model of Humanitarian Supply Chain (HSCM) in Disaster Prone Eco-Communities of India: A Discussion on Simulation and Scenario Results. *International Journal of System Dynamics Applications, 6*(3), 20–37. DOI: 10.4018/IJSDA.2017070102

Binder, D., & Miller, J. W. (2021). A Generations' Perspective on Employer Branding in Tourism. In Costa, V., Moura, A., & Mira, M. (Eds.), *Handbook of Research on Human Capital and People Management in the Tourism Industry* (pp. 152–174). IGI Global. https://doi.org/10.4018/978-1-7998-4318-4.ch008

Birch Freeman, A. A., Mensah, I., & Antwi, K. B. (2022). Smiling vs. Frowning Faces: Community Participation for Sustainable Tourism in Ghanaian Communities. In Mensah, I., & Afenyo-Agbe, E. (Eds.), *Prospects and Challenges of Community-Based Tourism and Changing Demographics* (pp. 83–106). IGI Global. https://doi.org/10.4018/978-1-7998-7335-8.ch004

Biswas, A., & De, A. K. (2017). On Development of a Fuzzy Stochastic Programming Model with Its Application to Business Management. In Trivedi, S., Dey, S., Kumar, A., & Panda, T. (Eds.), *Handbook of Research on Advanced Data Mining Techniques and Applications for Business Intelligence* (pp. 353–378). Hershey, PA: IGI Global. DOI: 10.4018/978-1-5225-2031-3.ch021

Boragnio, A., & Faracce Macia, C. (2021). "Taking Care of Yourself at Home": Use of E-Commerce About Food and Care During the COVID-19 Pandemic in the City of Buenos Aires. In Korstanje, M. (Ed.), *Socio-Economic Effects and Recovery Efforts for the Rental Industry: Post-COVID-19 Strategies* (pp. 45–71). IGI Global. https://doi.org/10.4018/978-1-7998-7287-0.ch003

Borges, V. D. (2021). Happiness: The Basis for Public Policy in Tourism. In Perinotto, A., Mayer, V., & Soares, J. (Eds.), *Rebuilding and Restructuring the Tourism Industry: Infusion of Happiness and Quality of Life* (pp. 1–25). IGI Global. https://doi.org/10.4018/978-1-7998-7239-9.ch001

Bücker, J., & Ernste, K. (2018). Use of Brand Heroes in Strategic Reputation Management: The Case of Bacardi, Adidas, and Daimler. In Erdemir, A. (Ed.), *Reputation Management Techniques in Public Relations* (pp. 126–150). Hershey, PA: IGI Global. DOI: 10.4018/978-1-5225-3619-2.ch007

Buluk Eşitti, B. (2021). COVID-19 and Alternative Tourism: New Destinations and New Tourism Products. In Demir, M., Dalgıç, A., & Ergen, F. (Eds.), *Handbook of Research on the Impacts and Implications of COVID-19 on the Tourism Industry* (pp. 786–805). IGI Global. https://doi.org/10.4018/978-1-7998-8231-2.ch038

Bureš, V. (2018). Industry 4.0 From the Systems Engineering Perspective: Alternative Holistic Framework Development. In Brunet-Thornton, R., & Martinez, F. (Eds.), *Analyzing the Impacts of Industry 4.0 in Modern Business Environments* (pp. 199–223). Hershey, PA: IGI Global. DOI: 10.4018/978-1-5225-3468-6.ch011

Buzady, Z. (2017). Resolving the Magic Cube of Effective Case Teaching: Benchmarking Case Teaching Practices in Emerging Markets – Insights from the Central European University Business School, Hungary. In Latusek, D. (Ed.), *Case Studies as a Teaching Tool in Management Education* (pp. 79–103). Hershey, PA: IGI Global. DOI: 10.4018/978-1-5225-0770-3.ch005

Camillo, A. (2021). *Legal Matters, Risk Management, and Risk Prevention: From Forming a Business to Legal Representation*. IGI Global. DOI: 10.4018/978-1-7998-4342-9.ch004

Căpusneanu, S., & Topor, D. I. (2018). Business Ethics and Cost Management in SMEs: Theories of Business Ethics and Cost Management Ethos. In Oncioiu, I. (Ed.), *Ethics and Decision-Making for Sustainable Business Practices* (pp. 109–127). Hershey, PA: IGI Global. DOI: 10.4018/978-1-5225-3773-1.ch007

Chan, R. L., Mo, P. L., & Moon, K. K. (2018). Strategic and Tactical Measures in Managing Enterprise Risks: A Study of the Textile and Apparel Industry. In Strang, K., Korstanje, M., & Vajjhala, N. (Eds.), *Research, Practices, and Innovations in Global Risk and Contingency Management* (pp. 1–19). Hershey, PA: IGI Global. DOI: 10.4018/978-1-5225-4754-9.ch001

Charlier, S. D., Burke-Smalley, L. A., & Fisher, S. L. (2018). Undergraduate Programs in the U.S: A Contextual and Content-Based Analysis. In Mendy, J. (Ed.), *Teaching Human Resources and Organizational Behavior at the College Level* (pp. 26–57). Hershey, PA: IGI Global. DOI: 10.4018/978-1-5225-2820-3.ch002

Chumillas, J., Güell, M., & Quer, P. (2022). The Use of ICT in Tourist and Educational Literary Routes: The Role of the Guide. In Ramos, C., Quinteiro, S., & Gonçalves, A. (Eds.), *ICT as Innovator Between Tourism and Culture* (pp. 15–29). IGI Global. https://doi.org/10.4018/978-1-7998-8165-0.ch002

Dahlberg, T., Kivijärvi, H., & Saarinen, T. (2017). IT Investment Consistency and Other Factors Influencing the Success of IT Performance. In De Haes, S., & Van Grembergen, W. (Eds.), *Strategic IT Governance and Alignment in Business Settings* (pp. 176–208). Hershey, PA: IGI Global. DOI: 10.4018/978-1-5225-0861-8.ch007

Damnjanović, A. M. (2017). Knowledge Management Optimization through IT and E-Business Utilization: A Qualitative Study on Serbian SMEs. In Vemić, M. (Ed.), *Optimal Management Strategies in Small and Medium Enterprises* (pp. 249–267). Hershey, PA: IGI Global. DOI: 10.4018/978-1-5225-1949-2.ch012

Daneshpour, H. (2017). Integrating Sustainable Development into Project Portfolio Management through Application of Open Innovation. In Vemić, M. (Ed.), *Optimal Management Strategies in Small and Medium Enterprises* (pp. 370–387). Hershey, PA: IGI Global. DOI: 10.4018/978-1-5225-1949-2.ch017

Daniel, A. D., & Reis de Castro, V. (2018). Entrepreneurship Education: How to Measure the Impact on Nascent Entrepreneurs. In Carrizo Moreira, A., Guilherme Leitão Dantas, J., & Manuel Valente, F. (Eds.), *Nascent Entrepreneurship and Successful New Venture Creation* (pp. 85–110). Hershey, PA: IGI Global. DOI: 10.4018/978-1-5225-2936-1.ch004

David, R., Swami, B. N., & Tangirala, S. (2018). Ethics Impact on Knowledge Management in Organizational Development: A Case Study. In Baporikar, N. (Ed.), *Global Practices in Knowledge Management for Societal and Organizational Development* (pp. 19–45). Hershey, PA: IGI Global. DOI: 10.4018/978-1-5225-3009-1.ch002

De Uña-Álvarez, E., & Villarino-Pérez, M. (2022). Fostering Ecocultural Resources, Identity, and Tourism in Inland Territories (Galicia, NW Spain). In G. Fernandes (Ed.), *Challenges and New Opportunities for Tourism in Inland Territories: Ecocultural Resources and Sustainable Initiatives* (pp. 1-16). IGI Global. https://doi.org/10.4018/978-1-7998-7339-6.ch001

Delias, P., & Lakiotaki, K. (2018). Discovering Process Horizontal Boundaries to Facilitate Process Comprehension. *International Journal of Operations Research and Information Systems*, *9*(2), 1–31. DOI: 10.4018/IJORIS.2018040101

Denholm, J., & Lee-Davies, L. (2018). Success Factors for Games in Business and Project Management. In *Enhancing Education and Training Initiatives Through Serious Games* (pp. 34–68). Hershey, PA: IGI Global. DOI: 10.4018/978-1-5225-3689-5.ch002

Deshpande, M. (2017). Best Practices in Management Institutions for Global Leadership: Policy Aspects. In Baporikar, N. (Ed.), *Management Education for Global Leadership* (pp. 1–27). Hershey, PA: IGI Global. DOI: 10.4018/978-1-5225-1013-0.ch001

Deshpande, M. (2018). Policy Perspectives for SMEs Knowledge Management. In Baporikar, N. (Ed.), *Knowledge Integration Strategies for Entrepreneurship and Sustainability* (pp. 23–46). Hershey, PA: IGI Global. DOI: 10.4018/978-1-5225-5115-7.ch002

Dezdar, S. (2017). ERP Implementation Projects in Asian Countries: A Comparative Study on Iran and China. *International Journal of Information Technology Project Management*, *8*(3), 52–68. DOI: 10.4018/IJITPM.2017070104

Domingos, D., Respício, A., & Martinho, R. (2017). Reliability of IoT-Aware BPMN Healthcare Processes. In Reis, C., & Maximiano, M. (Eds.), *Internet of Things and Advanced Application in Healthcare* (pp. 214–248). Hershey, PA: IGI Global. DOI: 10.4018/978-1-5225-1820-4.ch008

Dosumu, O., Hussain, J., & El-Gohary, H. (2017). An Exploratory Study of the Impact of Government Policies on the Development of Small and Medium Enterprises in Developing Countries: The Case of Nigeria. *International Journal of Customer Relationship Marketing and Management*, *8*(4), 51–62. DOI: 10.4018/IJCRMM.2017100104

Durst, S., Bruns, G., & Edvardsson, I. R. (2017). Retaining Knowledge in Smaller Building and Construction Firms. *International Journal of Knowledge and Systems Science*, *8*(3), 1–12. DOI: 10.4018/IJKSS.2017070101

Edvardsson, I. R., & Durst, S. (2017). Outsourcing, Knowledge, and Learning: A Critical Review. *International Journal of Knowledge-Based Organizations*, *7*(2), 13–26. DOI: 10.4018/IJKBO.2017040102

Edwards, J. S. (2018). Integrating Knowledge Management and Business Processes. In M. Khosrow-Pour, D.B.A. (Ed.), *Encyclopedia of Information Science and Technology, Fourth Edition* (pp. 5046-5055). Hershey, PA: IGI Global. DOI: 10.4018/978-1-5225-2255-3.ch437

Eichelberger, S., & Peters, M. (2021). Family Firm Management in Turbulent Times: Opportunities for Responsible Tourism. In Zehrer, A., Glowka, G., Schwaiger, K., & Ranacher-Lackner, V. (Eds.), *Resiliency Models and Addressing Future Risks for Family Firms in the Tourism Industry* (pp. 103–124). IGI Global. https://doi.org/10.4018/978-1-7998-7352-5.ch005

Eide, D., Hjalager, A., & Hansen, M. (2022). Innovative Certifications in Adventure Tourism: Attributes and Diffusion. In R. Augusto Costa, F. Brandão, Z. Breda, & C. Costa (Eds.), *Planning and Managing the Experience Economy in Tourism* (pp. 161-175). IGI Global. https://doi.org/10.4018/978-1-7998-8775-1.ch009

Ejiogu, A. O. (2018). Economics of Farm Management. In *Agricultural Finance and Opportunities for Investment and Expansion* (pp. 56–72). Hershey, PA: IGI Global. DOI: 10.4018/978-1-5225-3059-6.ch003

Ekanem, I., & Abiade, G. E. (2018). Factors Influencing the Use of E-Commerce by Small Enterprises in Nigeria. *International Journal of ICT Research in Africa and the Middle East, 7*(1), 37–53. DOI: 10.4018/IJICTRAME.2018010103

Ekanem, I., & Alrossais, L. A. (2017). Succession Challenges Facing Family Businesses in Saudi Arabia. In Zgheib, P. (Ed.), *Entrepreneurship and Business Innovation in the Middle East* (pp. 122–146). Hershey, PA: IGI Global. DOI: 10.4018/978-1-5225-2066-5.ch007

El Faquih, L., & Fredj, M. (2017). Ontology-Based Framework for Quality in Configurable Process Models. *Journal of Electronic Commerce in Organizations, 15*(2), 48–60. DOI: 10.4018/JECO.2017040104

Faisal, M. N., & Talib, F. (2017). Building Ambidextrous Supply Chains in SMEs: How to Tackle the Barriers? *International Journal of Information Systems and Supply Chain Management, 10*(4), 80–100. DOI: 10.4018/IJISSCM.2017100105

Fernandes, T. M., Gomes, J., & Romão, M. (2017). Investments in E-Government: A Benefit Management Case Study. *International Journal of Electronic Government Research, 13*(3), 1–17. DOI: 10.4018/IJEGR.2017070101

Figueira, L. M., Honrado, G. R., & Dionísio, M. S. (2021). Human Capital Management in the Tourism Industry in Portugal. In Costa, V., Moura, A., & Mira, M. (Eds.), *Handbook of Research on Human Capital and People Management in the Tourism Industry* (pp. 1–19). IGI Global. DOI: 10.4018/978-1-7998-4318-4.ch001

Gao, S. S., Oreal, S., & Zhang, J. (2018). Contemporary Financial Risk Management Perceptions and Practices of Small-Sized Chinese Businesses. In I. Management Association (Ed.), *Global Business Expansion: Concepts, Methodologies, Tools, and Applications* (pp. 917-931). Hershey, PA: IGI Global. DOI: 10.4018/978-1-5225-5481-3.ch041

Garg, R., & Berning, S. C. (2017). Indigenous Chinese Management Philosophies: Key Concepts and Relevance for Modern Chinese Firms. In Christiansen, B., & Koc, G. (Eds.), *Transcontinental Strategies for Industrial Development and Economic Growth* (pp. 43–57). Hershey, PA: IGI Global. DOI: 10.4018/978-1-5225-2160-0.ch003

Gencer, Y. G. (2017). Supply Chain Management in Retailing Business. In Akkucuk, U. (Ed.), *Ethics and Sustainability in Global Supply Chain Management* (pp. 197–210). Hershey, PA: IGI Global. DOI: 10.4018/978-1-5225-2036-8.ch011

Gera, R., Arora, S., & Malik, S. (2021). Emotional Labor in the Tourism Industry: Strategies, Antecedents, and Outcomes. In Costa, V., Moura, A., & Mira, M. (Eds.), *Handbook of Research on Human Capital and People Management in the Tourism Industry* (pp. 73–91). IGI Global. https://doi.org/10.4018/978-1-7998-4318-4.ch004

Giacosa, E. (2018). The Increasing of the Regional Development Thanks to the Luxury Business Innovation. In Carvalho, L. (Ed.), *Handbook of Research on Entrepreneurial Ecosystems and Social Dynamics in a Globalized World* (pp. 260–273). Hershey, PA: IGI Global. DOI: 10.4018/978-1-5225-3525-6.ch011

Glowka, G., Tusch, M., & Zehrer, A. (2021). The Risk Perception of Family Business Owner-Manager in the Tourism Industry: A Qualitative Comparison of the Intra-Firm Senior and Junior Generation. In Zehrer, A., Glowka, G., Schwaiger, K., & Ranacher-Lackner, V. (Eds.), *Resiliency Models and Addressing Future Risks for Family Firms in the Tourism Industry* (pp. 126–153). IGI Global. https://doi.org/10.4018/978-1-7998-7352-5.ch006

Glykas, M., & George, J. (2017). Quality and Process Management Systems in the UAE Maritime Industry. *International Journal of Productivity Management and Assessment Technologies, 5*(1), 20–39. DOI: 10.4018/IJPMAT.2017010102

Glykas, M., Valiris, G., Kokkinaki, A., & Koutsoukou, Z. (2018). Banking Business Process Management Implementation. *International Journal of Productivity Management and Assessment Technologies, 6*(1), 50–69. DOI: 10.4018/IJPMAT.2018010104

Gomes, J., & Romão, M. (2017). The Balanced Scorecard: Keeping Updated and Aligned with Today's Business Trends. *International Journal of Productivity Management and Assessment Technologies, 5*(2), 1–15. DOI: 10.4018/IJPMAT.2017070101

Gomes, J., & Romão, M. (2017). Aligning Information Systems and Technology with Benefit Management and Balanced Scorecard. In De Haes, S., & Van Grembergen, W. (Eds.), *Strategic IT Governance and Alignment in Business Settings* (pp. 112–131). Hershey, PA: IGI Global. DOI: 10.4018/978-1-5225-0861-8.ch005

Goyal, A. (2021). Communicating and Building Destination Brands With New Media. In M. Dinis, L. Bonixe, S. Lamy, & Z. Breda (Eds.), *Impact of New Media in Tourism* (pp. 1-20). IGI Global. https://doi.org/10.4018/978-1-7998-7095-1.ch001

Grefen, P., & Turetken, O. (2017). Advanced Business Process Management in Networked E-Business Scenarios. *International Journal of E-Business Research, 13*(4), 70–104. DOI: 10.4018/IJEBR.2017100105

Guasca, M., Van Broeck, A. M., & Vanneste, D. (2021). Tourism and the Social Reintegration of Colombian Ex-Combatants. In J. da Silva, Z. Breda, & F. Carbone (Eds.), *Role and Impact of Tourism in Peacebuilding and Conflict Transformation* (pp. 66-86). IGI Global. https://doi.org/10.4018/978-1-7998-5053-3.ch005

Haider, A., & Saetang, S. (2017). Strategic IT Alignment in Service Sector. In Rozenes, S., & Cohen, Y. (Eds.), *Handbook of Research on Strategic Alliances and Value Co-Creation in the Service Industry* (pp. 231–258). Hershey, PA: IGI Global. DOI: 10.4018/978-1-5225-2084-9.ch012

Hajilari, A. B., Ghadaksaz, M., & Fasghandis, G. S. (2017). Assessing Organizational Readiness for Implementing ERP System Using Fuzzy Expert System Approach. *International Journal of Enterprise Information Systems*, *13*(1), 67–85. DOI: 10.4018/IJEIS.2017010105

Haldorai, A., Ramu, A., & Murugan, S. (2018). Social Aware Cognitive Radio Networks: Effectiveness of Social Networks as a Strategic Tool for Organizational Business Management. In Bansal, H., Shrivastava, G., Nguyen, G., & Stanciu, L. (Eds.), *Social Network Analytics for Contemporary Business Organizations* (pp. 188–202). Hershey, PA: IGI Global. DOI: 10.4018/978-1-5225-5097-6.ch010

Hall, O. P.Jr. (2017). Social Media Driven Management Education. *International Journal of Knowledge-Based Organizations*, *7*(2), 43–59. DOI: 10.4018/IJKBO.2017040104

Hanifah, H., Halim, H. A., Ahmad, N. H., & Vafaei-Zadeh, A. (2017). Innovation Culture as a Mediator Between Specific Human Capital and Innovation Performance Among Bumiputera SMEs in Malaysia. In Ahmad, N., Ramayah, T., Halim, H., & Rahman, S. (Eds.), *Handbook of Research on Small and Medium Enterprises in Developing Countries* (pp. 261–279). Hershey, PA: IGI Global. DOI: 10.4018/978-1-5225-2165-5.ch012

Hartlieb, S., & Silvius, G. (2017). Handling Uncertainty in Project Management and Business Development: Similarities and Differences. In Raydugin, Y. (Ed.), *Handbook of Research on Leveraging Risk and Uncertainties for Effective Project Management* (pp. 337–362). Hershey, PA: IGI Global. DOI: 10.4018/978-1-5225-1790-0.ch016

Hass, K. B. (2017). Living on the Edge: Managing Project Complexity. In Raydugin, Y. (Ed.), *Handbook of Research on Leveraging Risk and Uncertainties for Effective Project Management* (pp. 177–201). Hershey, PA: IGI Global. DOI: 10.4018/978-1-5225-1790-0.ch009

Hawking, P., & Carmine Sellitto, C. (2017). Developing an Effective Strategy for Organizational Business Intelligence. In Tavana, M. (Ed.), *Enterprise Information Systems and the Digitalization of Business Functions* (pp. 222–237). Hershey, PA: IGI Global. DOI: 10.4018/978-1-5225-2382-6.ch010

Hawking, P., & Sellitto, C. (2017). A Fast-Moving Consumer Goods Company and Business Intelligence Strategy Development. *International Journal of Enterprise Information Systems, 13*(2), 22–33. DOI: 10.4018/IJEIS.2017040102

Hawking, P., & Sellitto, C. (2017). Business Intelligence Strategy: Two Case Studies. *International Journal of Business Intelligence Research, 8*(2), 17–30. DOI: 10.4018/IJBIR.2017070102

Hee, W. J., Jalleh, G., Lai, H., & Lin, C. (2017). E-Commerce and IT Projects: Evaluation and Management Issues in Australian and Taiwanese Hospitals. *International Journal of Public Health Management and Ethics, 2*(1), 69–90. DOI: 10.4018/IJPHME.2017010104

Hernandez, A. A. (2018). Exploring the Factors to Green IT Adoption of SMEs in the Philippines. *Journal of Cases on Information Technology, 20*(2), 49–66. DOI: 10.4018/JCIT.2018040104

Hollman, A., Bickford, S., & Hollman, T. (2017). Cyber InSecurity: A Post-Mortem Attempt to Assess Cyber Problems from IT and Business Management Perspectives. *Journal of Cases on Information Technology, 19*(3), 42–70. DOI: 10.4018/JCIT.2017070104

Ibrahim, F., & Zainin, N. M. (2021). Exploring the Technological Impacts: The Case of Museums in Brunei Darussalam. *International Journal of Tourism and Hospitality Management in the Digital Age, 5*(1), 1–18. https://doi.org/10.4018/IJTHMDA.2021010101

Igbinakhase, I. (2017). Responsible and Sustainable Management Practices in Developing and Developed Business Environments. In Fields, Z. (Ed.), *Collective Creativity for Responsible and Sustainable Business Practice* (pp. 180–207). Hershey, PA: IGI Global. DOI: 10.4018/978-1-5225-1823-5.ch010

Iwata, J. J., & Hoskins, R. G. (2017). Managing Indigenous Knowledge in Tanzania: A Business Perspective. In Jain, P., & Mnjama, N. (Eds.), *Managing Knowledge Resources and Records in Modern Organizations* (pp. 198–214). Hershey, PA: IGI Global. DOI: 10.4018/978-1-5225-1965-2.ch012

Jain, P. (2017). Ethical and Legal Issues in Knowledge Management Life-Cycle in Business. In Jain, P., & Mnjama, N. (Eds.), *Managing Knowledge Resources and Records in Modern Organizations* (pp. 82–101). Hershey, PA: IGI Global. DOI: 10.4018/978-1-5225-1965-2.ch006

James, S., & Hauli, E. (2017). Holistic Management Education at Tanzanian Rural Development Planning Institute. In Baporikar, N. (Ed.), *Management Education for Global Leadership* (pp. 112–136). Hershey, PA: IGI Global. DOI: 10.4018/978-1-5225-1013-0.ch006

Janošková, M., Csikósová, A., & Čulková, K. (2018). Measurement of Company Performance as Part of Its Strategic Management. In Leon, R. (Ed.), *Managerial Strategies for Business Sustainability During Turbulent Times* (pp. 309–335). Hershey, PA: IGI Global. DOI: 10.4018/978-1-5225-2716-9.ch017

Jean-Vasile, A., & Alecu, A. (2017). Theoretical and Practical Approaches in Understanding the Influences of Cost-Productivity-Profit Trinomial in Contemporary Enterprises. In Jean Vasile, A., & Nicolò, D. (Eds.), *Sustainable Entrepreneurship and Investments in the Green Economy* (pp. 28–62). Hershey, PA: IGI Global. DOI: 10.4018/978-1-5225-2075-7.ch002

Joia, L. A., & Correia, J. C. (2018). CIO Competencies From the IT Professional Perspective: Insights From Brazil. *Journal of Global Information Management*, *26*(2), 74–103. DOI: 10.4018/JGIM.2018040104

Juma, A., & Mzera, N. (2017). Knowledge Management and Records Management and Competitive Advantage in Business. In Jain, P., & Mnjama, N. (Eds.), *Managing Knowledge Resources and Records in Modern Organizations* (pp. 15–28). Hershey, PA: IGI Global. DOI: 10.4018/978-1-5225-1965-2.ch002

K., I., & A, V. (2018). Monitoring and Auditing in the Cloud. In K. Munir (Ed.), *Cloud Computing Technologies for Green Enterprises* (pp. 318-350). Hershey, PA: IGI Global. https://doi.org/DOI: 10.4018/978-1-5225-3038-1.ch013

Kabra, G., Ghosh, V., & Ramesh, A. (2018). Enterprise Integrated Business Process Management and Business Intelligence Framework for Business Process Sustainability. In Paul, A., Bhattacharyya, D., & Anand, S. (Eds.), *Green Initiatives for Business Sustainability and Value Creation* (pp. 228–238). Hershey, PA: IGI Global. DOI: 10.4018/978-1-5225-2662-9.ch010

Kaoud, M. (2017). Investigation of Customer Knowledge Management: A Case Study Research. *International Journal of Service Science, Management, Engineering, and Technology*, *8*(2), 12–22. DOI: 10.4018/IJSSMET.2017040102

Katuu, S. (2018). A Comparative Assessment of Enterprise Content Management Maturity Models. In Gwangwava, N., & Mutingi, M. (Eds.), *E-Manufacturing and E-Service Strategies in Contemporary Organizations* (pp. 93–118). Hershey, PA: IGI Global. DOI: 10.4018/978-1-5225-3628-4.ch005

Khan, M. Y., & Abir, T. (2022). The Role of Social Media Marketing in the Tourism and Hospitality Industry: A Conceptual Study on Bangladesh. In Ramos, C., Quinteiro, S., & Gonçalves, A. (Eds.), *ICT as Innovator Between Tourism and Culture* (pp. 213–229). IGI Global. https://doi.org/10.4018/978-1-7998-8165-0.ch013

Kinnunen, S., Ylä-Kujala, A., Marttonen-Arola, S., Kärri, T., & Baglee, D. (2018). Internet of Things in Asset Management: Insights from Industrial Professionals and Academia. *International Journal of Service Science, Management, Engineering, and Technology*, *9*(2), 104–119. DOI: 10.4018/IJSSMET.2018040105

Klein, A. Z., Sabino de Freitas, A., Machado, L., Freitas, J. C.Jr, Graziola, P. G.Jr, & Schlemmer, E. (2017). Virtual Worlds Applications for Management Education. In Tomei, L. (Ed.), *Exploring the New Era of Technology-Infused Education* (pp. 279–299). Hershey, PA: IGI Global. DOI: 10.4018/978-1-5225-1709-2.ch017

Kővári, E., Saleh, M., & Steinbachné Hajmásy, G. (2022). The Impact of Corporate Digital Responsibility (CDR) on Internal Stakeholders' Satisfaction in Hungarian Upscale Hotels. In Valeri, M. (Ed.), *New Governance and Management in Touristic Destinations* (pp. 35–51). IGI Global. https://doi.org/10.4018/978-1-6684-3889-3.ch003

Kożuch, B., & Jabłoński, A. (2017). Adopting the Concept of Business Models in Public Management. In Lewandowski, M., & Kożuch, B. (Eds.), *Public Sector Entrepreneurship and the Integration of Innovative Business Models* (pp. 10–46). Hershey, PA: IGI Global. DOI: 10.4018/978-1-5225-2215-7.ch002

Kumar, J., Adhikary, A., & Jha, A. (2017). Small Active Investors' Perceptions and Preferences Towards Tax Saving Mutual Fund Schemes in Eastern India: An Empirical Note. *International Journal of Asian Business and Information Management*, *8*(2), 35–45. DOI: 10.4018/IJABIM.2017040103

Latusi, S., & Fissore, M. (2021). Pilgrimage Routes to Happiness: Comparing the Camino de Santiago and Via Francigena. In Perinotto, A., Mayer, V., & Soares, J. (Eds.), *Rebuilding and Restructuring the Tourism Industry: Infusion of Happiness and Quality of Life* (pp. 157–182). IGI Global. https://doi.org/10.4018/978-1-7998-7239-9.ch008

Lavassani, K. M., & Movahedi, B. (2017). Applications Driven Information Systems: Beyond Networks toward Business Ecosystems. *International Journal of Innovation in the Digital Economy*, *8*(1), 61–75. DOI: 10.4018/IJIDE.2017010104

Lazzareschi, V. H., & Brito, M. S. (2017). Strategic Information Management: Proposal of Business Project Model. In Jamil, G., Soares, A., & Pessoa, C. (Eds.), *Handbook of Research on Information Management for Effective Logistics and Supply Chains* (pp. 59–88). Hershey, PA: IGI Global. DOI: 10.4018/978-1-5225-0973-8.ch004

Lechuga Sancho, M. P., & Martín Navarro, A. (2022). Evolution of the Literature on Social Responsibility in the Tourism Sector: A Systematic Literature Review. In Fernandes, G. (Ed.), *Challenges and New Opportunities for Tourism in Inland Territories: Ecocultural Resources and Sustainable Initiatives* (pp. 169–186). IGI Global. https://doi.org/10.4018/978-1-7998-7339-6.ch010

Lederer, M., Kurz, M., & Lazarov, P. (2017). Usage and Suitability of Methods for Strategic Business Process Initiatives: A Multi Case Study Research. *International Journal of Productivity Management and Assessment Technologies*, *5*(1), 40–51. DOI: 10.4018/IJPMAT.2017010103

Lee, I. (2017). A Social Enterprise Business Model and a Case Study of Pacific Community Ventures (PCV). In Potocan, V., Ünğan, M., & Nedelko, Z. (Eds.), *Handbook of Research on Managerial Solutions in Non-Profit Organizations* (pp. 182–204). Hershey, PA: IGI Global. DOI: 10.4018/978-1-5225-0731-4.ch009

Leon, L. A., Seal, K. C., Przasnyski, Z. H., & Wiedenman, I. (2017). Skills and Competencies Required for Jobs in Business Analytics: A Content Analysis of Job Advertisements Using Text Mining. *International Journal of Business Intelligence Research*, *8*(1), 1–25. DOI: 10.4018/IJBIR.2017010101

Levy, C. L., & Elias, N. I. (2017). SOHO Users' Perceptions of Reliability and Continuity of Cloud-Based Services. In Moore, M. (Ed.), *Cybersecurity Breaches and Issues Surrounding Online Threat Protection* (pp. 248–287). Hershey, PA: IGI Global. DOI: 10.4018/978-1-5225-1941-6.ch011

Levy, M. (2018). Change Management Serving Knowledge Management and Organizational Development: Reflections and Review. In Baporikar, N. (Ed.), *Global Practices in Knowledge Management for Societal and Organizational Development* (pp. 256–270). Hershey, PA: IGI Global. DOI: 10.4018/978-1-5225-3009-1.ch012

Lewandowski, M. (2017). Public Organizations and Business Model Innovation: The Role of Public Service Design. In Lewandowski, M., & Kożuch, B. (Eds.), *Public Sector Entrepreneurship and the Integration of Innovative Business Models* (pp. 47–72). Hershey, PA: IGI Global. DOI: 10.4018/978-1-5225-2215-7.ch003

Lhannaoui, H., Kabbaj, M. I., & Bakkoury, Z. (2017). A Survey of Risk-Aware Business Process Modelling. *International Journal of Risk and Contingency Management, 6*(3), 14–26. DOI: 10.4018/IJRCM.2017070102

Li, J., Sun, W., Jiang, W., Yang, H., & Zhang, L. (2017). How the Nature of Exogenous Shocks and Crises Impact Company Performance?: The Effects of Industry Characteristics. *International Journal of Risk and Contingency Management, 6*(4), 40–55. DOI: 10.4018/IJRCM.2017100103

Lopez-Fernandez, M., Perez-Perez, M., Serrano-Bedia, A., & Cobo-Gonzalez, A. (2021). Small and Medium Tourism Enterprise Survival in Times of Crisis: "El Capricho de Gaudí. In Toubes, D., & Araújo-Vila, N. (Eds.), *Risk, Crisis, and Disaster Management in Small and Medium-Sized Tourism Enterprises* (pp. 103–129). IGI Global. DOI: 10.4018/978-1-7998-6996-2.ch005

Mahajan, A., Maidullah, S., & Hossain, M. R. (2022). Experience Toward Smart Tour Guide Apps in Travelling: An Analysis of Users' Reviews on Audio Odigos and Trip My Way. In R. Augusto Costa, F. Brandão, Z. Breda, & C. Costa (Eds.), *Planning and Managing the Experience Economy in Tourism* (pp. 255-273). IGI Global. https://doi.org/10.4018/978-1-7998-8775-1.ch014

Malega, P. (2017). Small and Medium Enterprises in the Slovak Republic: Status and Competitiveness of SMEs in the Global Markets and Possibilities of Optimization. In Vemić, M. (Ed.), *Optimal Management Strategies in Small and Medium Enterprises* (pp. 102–124). Hershey, PA: IGI Global. DOI: 10.4018/978-1-5225-1949-2.ch006

Malewska, K. M. (2017). Intuition in Decision-Making on the Example of a Non-Profit Organization. In Potocan, V., Ünğan, M., & Nedelko, Z. (Eds.), *Handbook of Research on Managerial Solutions in Non-Profit Organizations* (pp. 378–399). Hershey, PA: IGI Global. DOI: 10.4018/978-1-5225-0731-4.ch018

Maroofi, F. (2017). Entrepreneurial Orientation and Organizational Learning Ability Analysis for Innovation and Firm Performance. In Baporikar, N. (Ed.), *Innovation and Shifting Perspectives in Management Education* (pp. 144–165). Hershey, PA: IGI Global. DOI: 10.4018/978-1-5225-1019-2.ch007

Marques, M., Moleiro, D., Brito, T. M., & Marques, T. (2021). Customer Relationship Management as an Important Relationship Marketing Tool: The Case of the Hospitality Industry in Estoril Coast. In M. Dinis, L. Bonixe, S. Lamy, & Z. Breda (Eds.), *Impact of New Media in Tourism* (pp. 39-56). IGI Global. https://doi.org/DOI: 10.4018/978-1-7998-7095-1.ch003

Martins, P. V., & Zacarias, M. (2017). A Web-based Tool for Business Process Improvement. *International Journal of Web Portals*, *9*(2), 68–84. DOI: 10.4018/IJWP.2017070104

Matthies, B., & Coners, A. (2017). Exploring the Conceptual Nature of e-Business Projects. *Journal of Electronic Commerce in Organizations*, *15*(3), 33–63. DOI: 10.4018/JECO.2017070103

Mayer, V. F., Fraga, C. C., & Silva, L. C. (2021). Contributions of Neurosciences to Studies of Well-Being in Tourism. In Perinotto, A., Mayer, V., & Soares, J. (Eds.), *Rebuilding and Restructuring the Tourism Industry: Infusion of Happiness and Quality of Life* (pp. 108–128). IGI Global. https://doi.org/10.4018/978-1-7998-7239-9.ch006

McKee, J. (2018). Architecture as a Tool to Solve Business Planning Problems. In M. Khosrow-Pour, D.B.A. (Ed.), *Encyclopedia of Information Science and Technology, Fourth Edition* (pp. 573-586). Hershey, PA: IGI Global. DOI: 10.4018/978-1-5225-2255-3.ch050

McMurray, A. J., Cross, J., & Caponecchia, C. (2018). The Risk Management Profession in Australia: Business Continuity Plan Practices. In Bajgoric, N. (Ed.), *Always-On Enterprise Information Systems for Modern Organizations* (pp. 112–129). Hershey, PA: IGI Global. DOI: 10.4018/978-1-5225-3704-5.ch006

Meddah, I. H., & Belkadi, K. (2018). Mining Patterns Using Business Process Management. In Hamou, R. (Ed.), *Handbook of Research on Biomimicry in Information Retrieval and Knowledge Management* (pp. 78–89). Hershey, PA: IGI Global. DOI: 10.4018/978-1-5225-3004-6.ch005

Melian, A. G., & Camprubí, R. (2021). The Accessibility of Museum Websites: The Case of Barcelona. In Eusébio, C., Teixeira, L., & Carneiro, M. (Eds.), *ICT Tools and Applications for Accessible Tourism* (pp. 234–255). IGI Global. https://doi.org/10.4018/978-1-7998-6428-8.ch011

Mendes, L. (2017). TQM and Knowledge Management: An Integrated Approach Towards Tacit Knowledge Management. In Jaziri-Bouagina, D., & Jamil, G. (Eds.), *Handbook of Research on Tacit Knowledge Management for Organizational Success* (pp. 236–263). Hershey, PA: IGI Global. DOI: 10.4018/978-1-5225-2394-9.ch009

Menezes, V. D., & Cavagnaro, E. (2021). Communicating Sustainable Initiatives in the Hotel Industry: The Case of the Hotel Jakarta Amsterdam. In F. Brandão, Z. Breda, R. Costa, & C. Costa (Eds.), *Handbook of Research on the Role of Tourism in Achieving Sustainable Development Goals* (pp. 224-234). IGI Global. https://doi.org/10.4018/978-1-7998-5691-7.ch013

Menezes, V. D., & Cavagnaro, E. (2021). Communicating Sustainable Initiatives in the Hotel Industry: The Case of the Hotel Jakarta Amsterdam. In F. Brandão, Z. Breda, R. Costa, & C. Costa (Eds.), *Handbook of Research on the Role of Tourism in Achieving Sustainable Development Goals* (pp. 224-234). IGI Global. https://doi.org/10.4018/978-1-7998-5691-7.ch013

Mitas, O., Bastiaansen, M., & Boode, W. (2022). If You're Happy, I'm Happy: Emotion Contagion at a Tourist Information Center. In R. Augusto Costa, F. Brandão, Z. Breda, & C. Costa (Eds.), *Planning and Managing the Experience Economy in Tourism* (pp. 122-140). IGI Global. https://doi.org/10.4018/978-1-7998-8775-1.ch007

Mnjama, N. M. (2017). Preservation of Recorded Information in Public and Private Sector Organizations. In Jain, P., & Mnjama, N. (Eds.), *Managing Knowledge Resources and Records in Modern Organizations* (pp. 149–167). Hershey, PA: IGI Global. DOI: 10.4018/978-1-5225-1965-2.ch009

Mokoqama, M., & Fields, Z. (2017). Principles of Responsible Management Education (PRME): Call for Responsible Management Education. In Fields, Z. (Ed.), *Collective Creativity for Responsible and Sustainable Business Practice* (pp. 229–241). Hershey, PA: IGI Global. DOI: 10.4018/978-1-5225-1823-5.ch012

Monteiro, A., Lopes, S., & Carbone, F. (2021). Academic Mobility: Bridging Tourism and Peace Education. In J. da Silva, Z. Breda, & F. Carbone (Eds.), *Role and Impact of Tourism in Peacebuilding and Conflict Transformation* (pp. 275-301). IGI Global. https://doi.org/10.4018/978-1-7998-5053-3.ch016

Muniapan, B. (2017). Philosophy and Management: The Relevance of Vedanta in Management. In Ordóñez de Pablos, P. (Ed.), *Managerial Strategies and Solutions for Business Success in Asia* (pp. 124–139). Hershey, PA: IGI Global. DOI: 10.4018/978-1-5225-1886-0.ch007

Murad, S. E., & Dowaji, S. (2017). Using Value-Based Approach for Managing Cloud-Based Services. In Turuk, A., Sahoo, B., & Addya, S. (Eds.), *Resource Management and Efficiency in Cloud Computing Environments* (pp. 33–60). Hershey, PA: IGI Global. DOI: 10.4018/978-1-5225-1721-4.ch002

Mutahar, A. M., Daud, N. M., Thurasamy, R., Isaac, O., & Abdulsalam, R. (2018). The Mediating of Perceived Usefulness and Perceived Ease of Use: The Case of Mobile Banking in Yemen. *International Journal of Technology Diffusion*, *9*(2), 21–40. DOI: 10.4018/IJTD.2018040102

Naidoo, V. (2017). E-Learning and Management Education at African Universities. In Baporikar, N. (Ed.), *Management Education for Global Leadership* (pp. 181–201). Hershey, PA: IGI Global. DOI: 10.4018/978-1-5225-1013-0.ch009

Naidoo, V., & Igbinakhase, I. (2018). Opportunities and Challenges of Knowledge Retention in SMEs. In Baporikar, N. (Ed.), *Knowledge Integration Strategies for Entrepreneurship and Sustainability* (pp. 70–94). Hershey, PA: IGI Global. DOI: 10.4018/978-1-5225-5115-7.ch004

Naumov, N., & Costandachi, G. (2021). Creativity and Entrepreneurship: Gastronomic Tourism in Mexico. In Soares, J. (Ed.), *Innovation and Entrepreneurial Opportunities in Community Tourism* (pp. 90–108). IGI Global. https://doi.org/10.4018/978-1-7998-4855-4.ch006

Nayak, S., & Prabhu, N. (2017). Paradigm Shift in Management Education: Need for a Cross Functional Perspective. In Baporikar, N. (Ed.), *Management Education for Global Leadership* (pp. 241–255). Hershey, PA: IGI Global. DOI: 10.4018/978-1-5225-1013-0.ch012

Nedelko, Z., & Potocan, V. (2017). Management Solutions in Non-Profit Organizations: Case of Slovenia. In Potocan, V., Üngan, M., & Nedelko, Z. (Eds.), *Handbook of Research on Managerial Solutions in Non-Profit Organizations* (pp. 1–22). Hershey, PA: IGI Global. DOI: 10.4018/978-1-5225-0731-4.ch001

Nedelko, Z., & Potocan, V. (2017). Priority of Management Tools Utilization among Managers: International Comparison. In Wang, V. (Ed.), *Encyclopedia of Strategic Leadership and Management* (pp. 1083–1094). Hershey, PA: IGI Global. DOI: 10.4018/978-1-5225-1049-9.ch075

Nedelko, Z., Raudeliūnienė, J., & Črešnar, R. (2018). Knowledge Dynamics in Supply Chain Management. In Baporikar, N. (Ed.), *Knowledge Integration Strategies for Entrepreneurship and Sustainability* (pp. 150–166). Hershey, PA: IGI Global. DOI: 10.4018/978-1-5225-5115-7.ch008

Nguyen, H. T., & Hipsher, S. A. (2018). Innovation and Creativity Used by Private Sector Firms in a Resources-Constrained Environment. In Hipsher, S. (Ed.), *Examining the Private Sector's Role in Wealth Creation and Poverty Reduction* (pp. 219–238). Hershey, PA: IGI Global. DOI: 10.4018/978-1-5225-3117-3.ch010

Obicci, P. A. (2017). Risk Sharing in a Partnership. In *Risk Management Strategies in Public-Private Partnerships* (pp. 115–152). Hershey, PA: IGI Global. DOI: 10.4018/978-1-5225-2503-5.ch004

Obidallah, W. J., & Raahemi, B. (2017). Managing Changes in Service Oriented Virtual Organizations: A Structural and Procedural Framework to Facilitate the Process of Change. *Journal of Electronic Commerce in Organizations, 15*(1), 59–83. DOI: 10.4018/JECO.2017010104

Ojo, O. (2017). Impact of Innovation on the Entrepreneurial Success in Selected Business Enterprises in South-West Nigeria. *International Journal of Innovation in the Digital Economy, 8*(2), 29–38. DOI: 10.4018/IJIDE.2017040103

Okdinawati, L., Simatupang, T. M., & Sunitiyoso, Y. (2017). Multi-Agent Reinforcement Learning for Value Co-Creation of Collaborative Transportation Management (CTM). *International Journal of Information Systems and Supply Chain Management, 10*(3), 84–95. DOI: 10.4018/IJISSCM.2017070105

Olivera, V. A., & Carrillo, I. M. (2021). Organizational Culture: A Key Element for the Development of Mexican Micro and Small Tourist Companies. In Soares, J. (Ed.), *Innovation and Entrepreneurial Opportunities in Community Tourism* (pp. 227–242). IGI Global. DOI: 10.4018/978-1-7998-4855-4.ch013

Ossorio, M. (2022). Corporate Museum Experiences in Enogastronomic Tourism. In R. Augusto Costa, F. Brandão, Z. Breda, & C. Costa (Eds.), *Planning and Managing the Experience Economy in Tourism* (pp. 107-121). IGI Global. https://doi.org/DOI: 10.4018/978-1-7998-8775-1.ch006

Ossorio, M. (2022). Enogastronomic Tourism in Times of Pandemic. In Fernandes, G. (Ed.), *Challenges and New Opportunities for Tourism in Inland Territories: Ecocultural Resources and Sustainable Initiatives* (pp. 241–255). IGI Global. https://doi.org/10.4018/978-1-7998-7339-6.ch014

Özekici, Y. K. (2022). ICT as an Acculturative Agent and Its Role in the Tourism Context: Introduction, Acculturation Theory, Progress of the Acculturation Theory in Extant Literature. In Ramos, C., Quinteiro, S., & Gonçalves, A. (Eds.), *ICT as Innovator Between Tourism and Culture* (pp. 42–66). IGI Global. https://doi.org/10.4018/978-1-7998-8165-0.ch004

Pal, K. (2018). Building High Quality Big Data-Based Applications in Supply Chains. In Kumar, A., & Saurav, S. (Eds.), *Supply Chain Management Strategies and Risk Assessment in Retail Environments* (pp. 1–24). Hershey, PA: IGI Global. DOI: 10.4018/978-1-5225-3056-5.ch001

Palos-Sanchez, P. R., & Correia, M. B. (2018). Perspectives of the Adoption of Cloud Computing in the Tourism Sector. In Rodrigues, J., Ramos, C., Cardoso, P., & Henriques, C. (Eds.), *Handbook of Research on Technological Developments for Cultural Heritage and eTourism Applications* (pp. 377–400). Hershey, PA: IGI Global. DOI: 10.4018/978-1-5225-2927-9.ch018

Papadopoulou, G. (2021). Promoting Gender Equality and Women Empowerment in the Tourism Sector. In F. Brandão, Z. Breda, R. Costa, & C. Costa (Eds.), *Handbook of Research on the Role of Tourism in Achieving Sustainable Development Goals* (pp. 152-174). IGI Global. https://doi .org/DOI: 10.4018/978-1-7998-5691-7.ch009

Papp-Váry, Á. F., & Tóth, T. Z. (2022). Analysis of Budapest as a Film Tourism Destination. In R. Baleiro & R. Pereira (Eds.), *Global Perspectives on Literary Tourism and Film-Induced Tourism* (pp. 257-279). IGI Global. https://doi.org/10.4018/978-1-7998-8262-6.ch014

Patiño, B. E. (2017). New Generation Management by Convergence and Individual Identity: A Systemic and Human-Oriented Approach. In Baporikar, N. (Ed.), *Innovation and Shifting Perspectives in Management Education* (pp. 119–143). Hershey, PA: IGI Global. DOI: 10.4018/978-1-5225-1019-2.ch006

Patro, C. S. (2021). Digital Tourism: Influence of E-Marketing Technology. In M. Dinis, L. Bonixe, S. Lamy, & Z. Breda (Eds.), *Impact of New Media in Tourism* (pp. 234-254). IGI Global. https://doi.org/10.4018/978-1-7998-7095-1.ch014

Pawliczek, A., & Rössler, M. (2017). Knowledge of Management Tools and Systems in SMEs: Knowledge Transfer in Management. In Bencsik, A. (Ed.), *Knowledge Management Initiatives and Strategies in Small and Medium Enterprises* (pp. 180–203). Hershey, PA: IGI Global. DOI: 10.4018/978-1-5225-1642-2.ch009

Pejic-Bach, M., Omazic, M. A., Aleksic, A., & Zoroja, J. (2018). Knowledge-Based Decision Making: A Multi-Case Analysis. In Leon, R. (Ed.), *Managerial Strategies for Business Sustainability During Turbulent Times* (pp. 160–184). Hershey, PA: IGI Global. DOI: 10.4018/978-1-5225-2716-9.ch009

Perano, M., Hysa, X., & Calabrese, M. (2018). Strategic Planning, Cultural Context, and Business Continuity Management: Business Cases in the City of Shkoder. In Presenza, A., & Sheehan, L. (Eds.), *Geopolitics and Strategic Management in the Global Economy* (pp. 57–77). Hershey, PA: IGI Global. DOI: 10.4018/978-1-5225-2673-5.ch004

Pereira, R., Mira da Silva, M., & Lapão, L. V. (2017). IT Governance Maturity Patterns in Portuguese Healthcare. In De Haes, S., & Van Grembergen, W. (Eds.), *Strategic IT Governance and Alignment in Business Settings* (pp. 24–52). Hershey, PA: IGI Global. DOI: 10.4018/978-1-5225-0861-8.ch002

Pérez-Uribe, R. I., Torres, D. A., Jurado, S. P., & Prada, D. M. (2018). Cloud Tools for the Development of Project Management in SMEs. In Perez-Uribe, R., Salcedo-Perez, C., & Ocampo-Guzman, D. (Eds.), *Handbook of Research on Intrapreneurship and Organizational Sustainability in SMEs* (pp. 95–120). Hershey, PA: IGI Global. DOI: 10.4018/978-1-5225-3543-0.ch005

Petrisor, I., & Cozmiuc, D. (2017). Global Supply Chain Management Organization at Siemens in the Advent of Industry 4.0. In Saglietto, L., & Cezanne, C. (Eds.), *Global Intermediation and Logistics Service Providers* (pp. 123–142). Hershey, PA: IGI Global. DOI: 10.4018/978-1-5225-2133-4.ch007

Pierce, J. M., Velliaris, D. M., & Edwards, J. (2017). A Living Case Study: A Journey Not a Destination. In Silton, N. (Ed.), *Exploring the Benefits of Creativity in Education, Media, and the Arts* (pp. 158–178). Hershey, PA: IGI Global. DOI: 10.4018/978-1-5225-0504-4.ch008

Pipia, S., & Pipia, S. (2021). Challenges of Religious Tourism in the Conflict Region: An Example of Jerusalem. In E. Alaverdov & M. Bari (Eds.), *Global Development of Religious Tourism* (pp. 135-148). IGI Global. https://doi.org/10.4018/978-1-7998-5792-1.ch009

Poulaki, P., Kritikos, A., Vasilakis, N., & Valeri, M. (2022). The Contribution of Female Creativity to the Development of Gastronomic Tourism in Greece: The Case of the Island of Naxos in the South Aegean Region. In Valeri, M. (Ed.), *New Governance and Management in Touristic Destinations* (pp. 246–258). IGI Global. https://doi.org/10.4018/978-1-6684-3889-3.ch015

Radosavljevic, M., & Andjelkovic, A. (2017). Multi-Criteria Decision Making Approach for Choosing Business Process for the Improvement: Upgrading of the Six Sigma Methodology. In Stanković, J., Delias, P., Marinković, S., & Rochhia, S. (Eds.), *Tools and Techniques for Economic Decision Analysis* (pp. 225–247). Hershey, PA: IGI Global. DOI: 10.4018/978-1-5225-0959-2.ch011

Radovic, V. M. (2017). Corporate Sustainability and Responsibility and Disaster Risk Reduction: A Serbian Overview. In Camilleri, M. (Ed.), *CSR 2.0 and the New Era of Corporate Citizenship* (pp. 147–164). Hershey, PA: IGI Global. DOI: 10.4018/978-1-5225-1842-6.ch008

Raghunath, K. M., Devi, S. L., & Patro, C. S. (2018). Impact of Risk Assessment Models on Risk Factors: A Holistic Outlook. In Strang, K., Korstanje, M., & Vajjhala, N. (Eds.), *Research, Practices, and Innovations in Global Risk and Contingency Management* (pp. 134–153). Hershey, PA: IGI Global. DOI: 10.4018/978-1-5225-4754-9.ch008

Raman, A., & Goyal, D. P. (2017). Extending IMPLEMENT Framework for Enterprise Information Systems Implementation to Information System Innovation. In Tavana, M. (Ed.), *Enterprise Information Systems and the Digitalization of Business Functions* (pp. 137–177). Hershey, PA: IGI Global. DOI: 10.4018/978-1-5225-2382-6.ch007

Rao, Y., & Zhang, Y. (2017). The Construction and Development of Academic Library Digital Special Subject Databases. In Ruan, L., Zhu, Q., & Ye, Y. (Eds.), *Academic Library Development and Administration in China* (pp. 163–183). Hershey, PA: IGI Global. DOI: 10.4018/978-1-5225-0550-1.ch010

Ravasan, A. Z., Mohammadi, M. M., & Hamidi, H. (2018). An Investigation Into the Critical Success Factors of Implementing Information Technology Service Management Frameworks. In Jakobs, K. (Ed.), *Corporate and Global Standardization Initiatives in Contemporary Society* (pp. 200–218). Hershey, PA: IGI Global. DOI: 10.4018/978-1-5225-5320-5.ch009

Rezaie, S., Mirabedini, S. J., & Abtahi, A. (2018). Designing a Model for Implementation of Business Intelligence in the Banking Industry. *International Journal of Enterprise Information Systems*, *14*(1), 77–103. DOI: 10.4018/IJEIS.2018010105

Richards, V., Matthews, N., Williams, O. J., & Khan, Z. (2021). The Challenges of Accessible Tourism Information Systems for Tourists With Vision Impairment: Sensory Communications Beyond the Screen. In Eusébio, C., Teixeira, L., & Carneiro, M. (Eds.), *ICT Tools and Applications for Accessible Tourism* (pp. 26–54). IGI Global. https://doi.org/10.4018/978-1-7998-6428-8.ch002

Rodrigues de Souza Neto, V., & Marques, O. (2021). Rural Tourism Fostering Welfare Through Sustainable Development: A Conceptual Approach. In Perinotto, A., Mayer, V., & Soares, J. (Eds.), *Rebuilding and Restructuring the Tourism Industry: Infusion of Happiness and Quality of Life* (pp. 38–57). IGI Global. https://doi.org/10.4018/978-1-7998-7239-9.ch003

Romano, L., Grimaldi, R., & Colasuonno, F. S. (2017). Demand Management as a Success Factor in Project Portfolio Management. In Romano, L. (Ed.), *Project Portfolio Management Strategies for Effective Organizational Operations* (pp. 202–219). Hershey, PA: IGI Global. DOI: 10.4018/978-1-5225-2151-8.ch008

Rubio-Escuderos, L., & García-Andreu, H. (2021). Competitiveness Factors of Accessible Tourism E-Travel Agencies. In Eusébio, C., Teixeira, L., & Carneiro, M. (Eds.), *ICT Tools and Applications for Accessible Tourism* (pp. 196–217). IGI Global. https://doi.org/10.4018/978-1-7998-6428-8.ch009

Rucci, A. C., Porto, N., Darcy, S., & Becka, L. (2021). Smart and Accessible Cities?: Not Always – The Case for Accessible Tourism Initiatives in Buenos Aries and Sydney. In Eusébio, C., Teixeira, L., & Carneiro, M. (Eds.), *ICT Tools and Applications for Accessible Tourism* (pp. 115–145). IGI Global. https://doi.org/10.4018/978-1-7998-6428-8.ch006

Ruhi, U. (2018). Towards an Interdisciplinary Socio-Technical Definition of Virtual Communities. In M. Khosrow-Pour, D.B.A. (Ed.), *Encyclopedia of Information Science and Technology, Fourth Edition* (pp. 4278-4295). Hershey, PA: IGI Global. DOI: 10.4018/978-1-5225-2255-3.ch371

Ryan, L., Catena, M., Ros, P., & Stephens, S. (2021). Designing Entrepreneurial Ecosystems to Support Resource Management in the Tourism Industry. In Costa, V., Moura, A., & Mira, M. (Eds.), *Handbook of Research on Human Capital and People Management in the Tourism Industry* (pp. 265–281). IGI Global. https://doi.org/10.4018/978-1-7998-4318-4.ch013

Sabuncu, I. (2021). Understanding Tourist Perceptions and Expectations During Pandemic Through Social Media Big Data. In Demir, M., Dalgıç, A., & Ergen, F. (Eds.), *Handbook of Research on the Impacts and Implications of COVID-19 on the Tourism Industry* (pp. 330–350). IGI Global. https://doi.org/10.4018/978-1-7998-8231-2.ch016

Safari, M. R., & Jiang, Q. (2018). The Theory and Practice of IT Governance Maturity and Strategies Alignment: Evidence From Banking Industry. *Journal of Global Information Management*, *26*(2), 127–146. DOI: 10.4018/JGIM.2018040106

Sahoo, J., Pati, B., & Mohanty, B. (2017). Knowledge Management as an Academic Discipline: An Assessment. In Gunjal, B. (Ed.), *Managing Knowledge and Scholarly Assets in Academic Libraries* (pp. 99–126). Hershey, PA: IGI Global. DOI: 10.4018/978-1-5225-1741-2.ch005

Saini, D. (2017). Relevance of Teaching Values and Ethics in Management Education. In Baporikar, N. (Ed.), *Management Education for Global Leadership* (pp. 90–111). Hershey, PA: IGI Global. DOI: 10.4018/978-1-5225-1013-0.ch005

Sambhanthan, A. (2017). Assessing and Benchmarking Sustainability in Organisations: An Integrated Conceptual Model. *International Journal of Systems and Service-Oriented Engineering*, *7*(4), 22–43. DOI: 10.4018/IJSSOE.2017100102

Sambhanthan, A., & Potdar, V. (2017). A Study of the Parameters Impacting Sustainability in Information Technology Organizations. *International Journal of Knowledge-Based Organizations*, *7*(3), 27–39. DOI: 10.4018/IJKBO.2017070103

Sánchez-Fernández, M. D., & Manríquez, M. R. (2018). The Entrepreneurial Spirit Based on Social Values: The Digital Generation. In Isaias, P., & Carvalho, L. (Eds.), *User Innovation and the Entrepreneurship Phenomenon in the Digital Economy* (pp. 173–193). Hershey, PA: IGI Global. DOI: 10.4018/978-1-5225-2826-5.ch009

Sanchez-Ruiz, L., & Blanco, B. (2017). Process Management for SMEs: Barriers, Enablers, and Benefits. In Vemić, M. (Ed.), *Optimal Management Strategies in Small and Medium Enterprises* (pp. 293–319). Hershey, PA: IGI Global. DOI: 10.4018/978-1-5225-1949-2.ch014

Sanz, L. F., Gómez-Pérez, J., & Castillo-Martinez, A. (2018). Analysis of the European ICT Competence Frameworks. In Ahuja, V., & Rathore, S. (Eds.), *Multidisciplinary Perspectives on Human Capital and Information Technology Professionals* (pp. 225–245). Hershey, PA: IGI Global. DOI: 10.4018/978-1-5225-5297-0.ch012

Sarvepalli, A., & Godin, J. (2017). Business Process Management in the Classroom. *Journal of Cases on Information Technology*, *19*(2), 17–28. DOI: 10.4018/JCIT.2017040102

Saxena, G. G., & Saxena, A. (2021). Host Community Role in Medical Tourism Development. In Singh, M., & Kumaran, S. (Eds.), *Growth of the Medical Tourism Industry and Its Impact on Society: Emerging Research and Opportunities* (pp. 105–127). IGI Global. https://doi.org/10.4018/978-1-7998-3427-4.ch006

Saygili, E. E., Ozturkoglu, Y., & Kocakulah, M. C. (2017). End Users' Perceptions of Critical Success Factors in ERP Applications. *International Journal of Enterprise Information Systems*, *13*(4), 58–75. DOI: 10.4018/IJEIS.2017100104

Saygili, E. E., & Saygili, A. T. (2017). Contemporary Issues in Enterprise Information Systems: A Critical Review of CSFs in ERP Implementations. In Tavana, M. (Ed.), *Enterprise Information Systems and the Digitalization of Business Functions* (pp. 120–136). Hershey, PA: IGI Global. DOI: 10.4018/978-1-5225-2382-6.ch006

Schwaiger, K. M., & Zehrer, A. (2021). The COVID-19 Pandemic and Organizational Resilience in Hospitality Family Firms: A Qualitative Approach. In Zehrer, A., Glowka, G., Schwaiger, K., & Ranacher-Lackner, V. (Eds.), *Resiliency Models and Addressing Future Risks for Family Firms in the Tourism Industry* (pp. 32–49). IGI Global. https://doi.org/10.4018/978-1-7998-7352-5.ch002

Scott, N., & Campos, A. C. (2022). Cognitive Science of Tourism Experiences. In R. Augusto Costa, F. Brandão, Z. Breda, & C. Costa (Eds.), *Planning and Managing the Experience Economy in Tourism* (pp. 1-21). IGI Global. https://doi.org/DOI: 10.4018/978-1-7998-8775-1.ch001

Seidenstricker, S., & Antonino, A. (2018). Business Model Innovation-Oriented Technology Management for Emergent Technologies. In M. Khosrow-Pour, D.B.A. (Ed.), *Encyclopedia of Information Science and Technology, Fourth Edition* (pp. 4560-4569). Hershey, PA: IGI Global. DOI: 10.4018/978-1-5225-2255-3.ch396

Selvi, M. S. (2021). Changes in Tourism Sales and Marketing Post COVID-19. In Demir, M., Dalgıç, A., & Ergen, F. (Eds.), *Handbook of Research on the Impacts and Implications of COVID-19 on the Tourism Industry* (pp. 437–460). IGI Global. DOI: 10.4018/978-1-7998-8231-2.ch021

Senaratne, S., & Gunarathne, A. D. (2017). Excellence Perspective for Management Education from a Global Accountants' Hub in Asia. In Baporikar, N. (Ed.), *Management Education for Global Leadership* (pp. 158–180). Hershey, PA: IGI Global. DOI: 10.4018/978-1-5225-1013-0.ch008

Sensuse, D. I., & Cahyaningsih, E. (2018). Knowledge Management Models: A Summative Review. *International Journal of Information Systems in the Service Sector*, *10*(1), 71–100. DOI: 10.4018/IJISSS.2018010105

Seth, M., Goyal, D., & Kiran, R. (2017). Diminution of Impediments in Implementation of Supply Chain Management Information System for Enhancing its Effectiveness in Indian Automobile Industry. *Journal of Global Information Management*, *25*(3), 1–20. DOI: 10.4018/JGIM.2017070101

Seyal, A. H., & Rahman, M. N. (2017). Investigating Impact of Inter-Organizational Factors in Measuring ERP Systems Success: Bruneian Perspectives. In Tavana, M. (Ed.), *Enterprise Information Systems and the Digitalization of Business Functions* (pp. 178–204). Hershey, PA: IGI Global. DOI: 10.4018/978-1-5225-2382-6.ch008

Shaqrah, A. A. (2018). Analyzing Business Intelligence Systems Based on 7s Model of McKinsey. *International Journal of Business Intelligence Research*, *9*(1), 53–63. DOI: 10.4018/IJBIR.2018010104

Sharma, A. J. (2017). Enhancing Sustainability through Experiential Learning in Management Education. In Baporikar, N. (Ed.), *Management Education for Global Leadership* (pp. 256–274). Hershey, PA: IGI Global. DOI: 10.4018/978-1-5225-1013-0.ch013

Shetty, K. P. (2017). Responsible Global Leadership: Ethical Challenges in Management Education. In Baporikar, N. (Ed.), *Innovation and Shifting Perspectives in Management Education* (pp. 194–223). Hershey, PA: IGI Global. DOI: 10.4018/978-1-5225-1019-2.ch009

Sinthupundaja, J., & Kohda, Y. (2017). Effects of Corporate Social Responsibility and Creating Shared Value on Sustainability. *International Journal of Sustainable Entrepreneurship and Corporate Social Responsibility*, *2*(1), 27–38. DOI: 10.4018/IJSECSR.2017010103

Škarica, I., & Hrgović, A. V. (2018). Implementation of Total Quality Management Principles in Public Health Institutes in the Republic of Croatia. *International Journal of Productivity Management and Assessment Technologies*, *6*(1), 1–16. DOI: 10.4018/IJPMAT.2018010101

Skokic, V. (2021). How Small Hotel Owners Practice Resilience: Longitudinal Study Among Small Family Hotels in Croatia. In Zehrer, A., Glowka, G., Schwaiger, K., & Ranacher-Lackner, V. (Eds.), *Resiliency Models and Addressing Future Risks for Family Firms in the Tourism Industry* (pp. 50–73). IGI Global. DOI: 10.4018/978-1-7998-7352-5.ch003

Smuts, H., Kotzé, P., Van der Merwe, A., & Loock, M. (2017). Framework for Managing Shared Knowledge in an Information Systems Outsourcing Context. *International Journal of Knowledge Management*, *13*(4), 1–30. DOI: 10.4018/IJKM.2017100101

Sousa, M. J., Cruz, R., Dias, I., & Caracol, C. (2017). Information Management Systems in the Supply Chain. In Jamil, G., Soares, A., & Pessoa, C. (Eds.), *Handbook of Research on Information Management for Effective Logistics and Supply Chains* (pp. 469–485). Hershey, PA: IGI Global. DOI: 10.4018/978-1-5225-0973-8.ch025

Spremic, M., Turulja, L., & Bajgoric, N. (2018). Two Approaches in Assessing Business Continuity Management Attitudes in the Organizational Context. In Bajgoric, N. (Ed.), *Always-On Enterprise Information Systems for Modern Organizations* (pp. 159–183). Hershey, PA: IGI Global. DOI: 10.4018/978-1-5225-3704-5.ch008

Steenkamp, A. L. (2018). Some Insights in Computer Science and Information Technology. In *Examining the Changing Role of Supervision in Doctoral Research Projects: Emerging Research and Opportunities* (pp. 113–133). Hershey, PA: IGI Global. DOI: 10.4018/978-1-5225-2610-0.ch005

Stipanović, C., Rudan, E., & Zubović, V. (2022). Reaching the New Tourist Through Creativity: Sustainable Development Challenges in Croatian Coastal Towns. In Valeri, M. (Ed.), *New Governance and Management in Touristic Destinations* (pp. 231–245). IGI Global. https://doi.org/10.4018/978-1-6684-3889-3.ch014

Tabach, A., & Croteau, A. (2017). Configurations of Information Technology Governance Practices and Business Unit Performance. *International Journal of IT/Business Alignment and Governance*, *8*(2), 1–27. DOI: 10.4018/IJITBAG.2017070101

Talaue, G. M., & Iqbal, T. (2017). Assessment of e-Business Mode of Selected Private Universities in the Philippines and Pakistan. *International Journal of Online Marketing*, *7*(4), 63–77. DOI: 10.4018/IJOM.2017100105

Tam, G. C. (2017). Project Manager Sustainability Competence. In *Managerial Strategies and Green Solutions for Project Sustainability* (pp. 178–207). Hershey, PA: IGI Global. DOI: 10.4018/978-1-5225-2371-0.ch008

Tambo, T. (2018). Fashion Retail Innovation: About Context, Antecedents, and Outcome in Technological Change Projects. In I. Management Association (Ed.), *Fashion and Textiles: Breakthroughs in Research and Practice* (pp. 233-260). Hershey, PA: IGI Global. https://doi.org/DOI: 10.4018/978-1-5225-3432-7.ch010

Tantau, A. D., & Frăţilă, L. C. (2018). Information and Management System for Renewable Energy Business. In *Entrepreneurship and Business Development in the Renewable Energy Sector* (pp. 200–244). Hershey, PA: IGI Global. DOI: 10.4018/978-1-5225-3625-3.ch006

Teixeira, N., Pardal, P. N., & Rafael, B. G. (2018). Internationalization, Financial Performance, and Organizational Challenges: A Success Case in Portugal. In Carvalho, L. (Ed.), *Handbook of Research on Entrepreneurial Ecosystems and Social Dynamics in a Globalized World* (pp. 379–423). Hershey, PA: IGI Global. DOI: 10.4018/978-1-5225-3525-6.ch017

Teixeira, P., Teixeira, L., Eusébio, C., Silva, S., & Teixeira, A. (2021). The Impact of ICTs on Accessible Tourism: Evidence Based on a Systematic Literature Review. In Eusébio, C., Teixeira, L., & Carneiro, M. (Eds.), *ICT Tools and Applications for Accessible Tourism* (pp. 1–25). IGI Global. DOI: 10.4018/978-1-7998-6428-8.ch001

Trad, A., & Kalpić, D. (2018). The Business Transformation Framework, Agile Project and Change Management. In M. Khosrow-Pour, D.B.A. (Ed.), *Encyclopedia of Information Science and Technology, Fourth Edition* (pp. 620-635). Hershey, PA: IGI Global. https://doi.org/DOI: 10.4018/978-1-5225-2255-3.ch054

Trad, A., & Kalpić, D. (2018). The Business Transformation and Enterprise Architecture Framework: The Financial Engineering E-Risk Management and E-Law Integration. In Sergi, B., Fidanoski, F., Ziolo, M., & Naumovski, V. (Eds.), *Regaining Global Stability After the Financial Crisis* (pp. 46–65). Hershey, PA: IGI Global. DOI: 10.4018/978-1-5225-4026-7.ch003

Trengereid, V. (2022). Conditions of Network Engagement: The Quest for a Common Good. In R. Augusto Costa, F. Brandão, Z. Breda, & C. Costa (Eds.), *Planning and Managing the Experience Economy in Tourism* (pp. 69-84). IGI Global. https://doi.org/10.4018/978-1-7998-8775-1.ch004

Turulja, L., & Bajgoric, N. (2018). Business Continuity and Information Systems: A Systematic Literature Review. In Bajgoric, N. (Ed.), *Always-On Enterprise Information Systems for Modern Organizations* (pp. 60–87). Hershey, PA: IGI Global. DOI: 10.4018/978-1-5225-3704-5.ch004

Vargas-Hernández, J. G. (2017). Professional Integrity in Business Management Education. In Baporikar, N. (Ed.), *Management Education for Global Leadership* (pp. 70–89). Hershey, PA: IGI Global. DOI: 10.4018/978-1-5225-1013-0.ch004

Varnacı Uzun, F. (2021). The Destination Preferences of Foreign Tourists During the COVID-19 Pandemic and Attitudes Towards: Marmaris, Turkey. In Demir, M., Dalgıç, A., & Ergen, F. (Eds.), *Handbook of Research on the Impacts and Implications of COVID-19 on the Tourism Industry* (pp. 285–306). IGI Global. https://doi.org/10.4018/978-1-7998-8231-2.ch014

Vasista, T. G., & AlAbdullatif, A. M. (2017). Role of Electronic Customer Relationship Management in Demand Chain Management: A Predictive Analytic Approach. *International Journal of Information Systems and Supply Chain Management, 10*(1), 53–67. DOI: 10.4018/IJISSCM.2017010104

Vieru, D., & Bourdeau, S. (2017). Survival in the Digital Era: A Digital Competence-Based Multi-Case Study in the Canadian SME Clothing Industry. *International Journal of Social and Organizational Dynamics in IT, 6*(1), 17–34. DOI: 10.4018/IJSODIT.2017010102

Vijayan, G., & Kamarulzaman, N. H. (2017). An Introduction to Sustainable Supply Chain Management and Business Implications. In Khan, M., Hussain, M., & Ajmal, M. (Eds.), *Green Supply Chain Management for Sustainable Business Practice* (pp. 27–50). Hershey, PA: IGI Global. DOI: 10.4018/978-1-5225-0635-5.ch002

Vlachvei, A., & Notta, O. (2017). Firm Competitiveness: Theories, Evidence, and Measurement. In Vlachvei, A., Notta, O., Karantininis, K., & Tsounis, N. (Eds.), *Factors Affecting Firm Competitiveness and Performance in the Modern Business World* (pp. 1–42). Hershey, PA: IGI Global. DOI: 10.4018/978-1-5225-0843-4.ch001

Wang, C., Schofield, M., Li, X., & Ou, X. (2017). Do Chinese Students in Public and Private Higher Education Institutes Perform at Different Level in One of the Leadership Skills: Critical Thinking?: An Exploratory Comparison. In Wang, V. (Ed.), *Encyclopedia of Strategic Leadership and Management* (pp. 160–181). Hershey, PA: IGI Global. DOI: 10.4018/978-1-5225-1049-9.ch013

Wang, J. (2017). Multi-Agent based Production Management Decision System Modelling for the Textile Enterprise. *Journal of Global Information Management, 25*(4), 1–15. DOI: 10.4018/JGIM.2017100101

Wiedemann, A., & Gewald, H. (2017). Examining Cross-Domain Alignment: The Correlation of Business Strategy, IT Management, and IT Business Value. *International Journal of IT/Business Alignment and Governance, 8*(1), 17–31. DOI: 10.4018/IJITBAG.2017010102

Wolf, R., & Thiel, M. (2018). Advancing Global Business Ethics in China: Reducing Poverty Through Human and Social Welfare. In Hipsher, S. (Ed.), *Examining the Private Sector's Role in Wealth Creation and Poverty Reduction* (pp. 67–84). Hershey, PA: IGI Global. DOI: 10.4018/978-1-5225-3117-3.ch004

Yablonsky, S. (2018). Innovation Platforms: Data and Analytics Platforms. In *Multi-Sided Platforms (MSPs) and Sharing Strategies in the Digital Economy: Emerging Research and Opportunities* (pp. 72–95). Hershey, PA: IGI Global. DOI: 10.4018/978-1-5225-5457-8.ch003

Yaşar, B. (2021). The Impact of COVID-19 on Volatility of Tourism Stocks: Evidence From BIST Tourism Index. In Demir, M., Dalgıç, A., & Ergen, F. (Eds.), *Handbook of Research on the Impacts and Implications of COVID-19 on the Tourism Industry* (pp. 23–44). IGI Global. https://doi.org/10.4018/978-1-7998-8231-2.ch002

Yusoff, A., Ahmad, N. H., & Halim, H. A. (2017). Agropreneurship among Gen Y in Malaysia: The Role of Academic Institutions. In Ahmad, N., Ramayah, T., Halim, H., & Rahman, S. (Eds.), *Handbook of Research on Small and Medium Enterprises in Developing Countries* (pp. 23–47). Hershey, PA: IGI Global. DOI: 10.4018/978-1-5225-2165-5.ch002

Zacher, D., & Pechlaner, H. (2021). Resilience as an Opportunity Approach: Challenges and Perspectives for Private Sector Participation on a Community Level. In Zehrer, A., Glowka, G., Schwaiger, K., & Ranacher-Lackner, V. (Eds.), *Resiliency Models and Addressing Future Risks for Family Firms in the Tourism Industry* (pp. 75–102). IGI Global. https://doi.org/10.4018/978-1-7998-7352-5.ch004

Zanin, F., Comuzzi, E., & Costantini, A. (2018). The Effect of Business Strategy and Stock Market Listing on the Use of Risk Assessment Tools. In *Management Control Systems in Complex Settings: Emerging Research and Opportunities* (pp. 145–168). Hershey, PA: IGI Global. DOI: 10.4018/978-1-5225-3987-2.ch007

Zgheib, P. W. (2017). Corporate Innovation and Intrapreneurship in the Middle East. In Zgheib, P. (Ed.), *Entrepreneurship and Business Innovation in the Middle East* (pp. 37–56). Hershey, PA: IGI Global. DOI: 10.4018/978-1-5225-2066-5.ch003

About the Contributors

Vera Teixeira Vale has a PhD in Management with specialization in Marketing and Strategy from the Faculty of Economics and Management of University of Porto, a MSc in Marketing from the Oporto Catholic University, also an MBA in Commercial Operations Management in Oporto Catholic University and a degree in Public Relations from the Maia Superior Institute. She is an Assistant Professor in the University of Aveiro (DEGEIT) . She lectures under graduated and graduated courses of Management, Marketing, Marketing Research and Consumer Behaviour. Presently, she is researcher affiliated to GOVCOPP, and a invited researcher at CEOS.PP. Her research topics are: Consumer Behaviour, Consumer Psychology, Anti-Consumption, Anti-branding, Sustainable and Responsible consumption, Expatriation Motivations, SEM, Quantitative and Qualitative Methods Her teaching interests are: Consumer Behaviour, Marketing Research and Marketing Management.

***

Shafiu Ibrahim Abdullahi is an academic researcher with specialization in Consumption, Development economics, Islamic economics and finance, International finance, Monetary economics, Marketing & Advertising, Econometrics applications, Field surveys, Mathematical modelling, Statistics. He has peer reviewed for journals/ books published by IGI, Wiley and Emerald. His academic works have been published by SCOPUS Indexed journals. He has published two books on Islamic finance and Nigerian economy. He has over 17 years work experience in academic, banking and media. He currently works with Skyline University Nigeria, Kano, Kano state, as lecturer in the department of economics of the school.

Gaganpreet Kaur Ahluwalia is an Associate Professor and Head of the Department – PGDM Marketing at Indira School of Business Studies PGDM, Pune. She brings a rich blend of academic rigor and industry-oriented insight to her role, specializing in marketing and strategic management. With a strong commitment to student development and academic excellence, Dr. Ahluwalia has contributed extensively through teaching, curriculum design, and research. Her leadership in the PGDM Marketing program reflects her dedication to nurturing future marketing professionals.

Aihoor Aleem holds a PhD in Management, with specialization in Marketing Candidate from ISCTE - IUL. Her research activity is focused on luxury trends, brand coolness, consumption and the future of how brands will communicate and create a relationship with their targets. Her background counts with a MSc in Management with specialisation in Strategic Marketing by the Católica Lisbon School of Business and Economics, where she started the research on what influences (or not) consumers to engage into luxury consumption. She has professional experience in academia as a researcher and professor, specifically in teaching marketing strategy, luxury trends and advertising

Nilesh Anute is an Associate Professor at Sri Balaji University, Pune. With extensive experience in academia and research, Dr. Anute specializes in areas related to management and business studies. He is known for his commitment to fostering academic excellence and has contributed significantly through teaching, research publications, and participation in academic forums. His work reflects a blend of theoretical knowledge and practical insight, aimed at preparing students for dynamic industry challenges.

Vishal Jain is presently working as a Professor at the Department of Computer Science & Engineering, School of Engineering & Technology, Vivekananda Institute of Professional Studies - Technical Campus,

New Delhi. Before that, he worked as Professor at Sharda University, Greater Noida and Associate Professor at Bharati Vidyapeeth's Institute of Computer Applications and Management (BVICAM), New Delhi. He has associated as a member of the Faculty Board, Board of Planning and Management, Executive Council, Academic Council, Curriculum Development and Review Committee and Academic Audit of various higher education Institutions. He is associated with Kuala Lumpur University of Science and Technology (KLUST), Malaysia, Lincoln University College, Malaysia and Research Institute of IoT Cybersecurity, Department of Electronic Engineering, National Kaohsiung University of Science and Technology, Taiwan for research oriented activities.

Ganesha K S is an Assistant Professor in the Department of Management Studies, at Dayananda Sagar College of Engineering, Bangalore, India. He has 14 years of experience in Corporate, Teaching and Research. He is a Member of the International Safety Quality Environment Management Association (ISQEM), UK. His primary research interests are tourist behavior, social media, sentiment analysis, human resource management, and labor studies. He has presented at multiple conferences and published articles in Scopus and other International Indexed journals. He has conducted FDP, workshops, and training in the areas of Digital Marketing, Statistical Analysis using SPSS, Project Management, Research Methodology, Entrepreneurship etc.

Prashant Kalshetti is a Professor and Head of the Department of BBA at Dr. D. Y. Patil Vidyapeeth's Global Business School and Research Centre, Pune. With a strong academic background and a passion for business education, Dr. Kalshetti has played a key role in shaping undergraduate management education at the institute. He is known for his student-centric approach, academic leadership, and contributions to curriculum development and research. His work focuses on building a strong foundation in business principles and preparing students for the evolving global business landscape.

Arpita Nayak is currently serving as an Assistant Professor, offering courses in management. She completed her Ph.D. in management from the KIIT School of Management. Her MBA and strong interest in Human

Resource Management (HRM) led her to pursue further studies in HRM. Her passion for talent management inspired her doctoral research on "A Comparative Study on Talent Management in Private and Public Manufacturing Industries in Odisha." Dr. Nayak has presented research papers at both national and international conferences and has published articles in SCOPUS-listed journals. Over the years, she has taught a variety of subjects, including Human Resource Management, Principles of Management, Business Studies Management, Tribal Entrepreneurship, and Organizational Behaviour. In addition to her academic career, she also has several years of corporate work experience.

Selvakumar P. is currently an Associate Professor in the Department of Science and Humanities at Nehru Institute of Technology, Coimbatore, Tamil Nadu, India. Prior to joining Nehru Institute of Technology, he held positions as an Assistant Professor in the Department of Science and Humanities various engineering colleges in Coimbatore, Tamil Nadu, India, spanning from 2011 to 2023. Dr.P. Selvakumar's academic and research interests lie primarily in the field of phytochemistry. He has made significant contributions to his field, with an impressive record that includes 30 journal publications, 12 patents, and 20 conference papers. Additionally, he has organized 5 seminars and conferences, further demonstrating his commitment to academic and scientific exchange. Throughout his career, Dr. P.Selvakumar has been recognized for his dedication and excellence in teaching, having been honored with several awards, including the Best Teacher Awards. He holds a prominent position in the academic community, contributing actively to research.

Priyanka Pawar is an Associate Professor at Indira College of Engineering and Management, Pune. With a solid academic foundation and a passion for teaching, she brings valuable expertise to the fields of engineering and management education. Dr. Pawar is dedicated to fostering academic excellence, mentoring students, and contributing to the holistic development of future professionals. Her work reflects a commitment to innovative teaching practices and continuous learning.

Albérico Travassos Rosário, Ph.D. Marketing and Strategy of the Universities of Aveiro (UA), Minho (UM) and Beira Interior (UBI). With affiliation to the GOVCOPP research center of the University of Aveiro. Master in Marketing and Degree in Marketing, Advertising and Public Relations, degree from ISLA Campus Lisbon-European University | Laureate International Universities. Has the title of Marketing Specialist and teaches with the category of Assistant Professor at IADE-Faculty of Design, Technology and Communication of the European University and as a visiting Associate Professor at the Santarém Higher School of Management and Technology (ESGTS) of the Polytechnic Institute of Santarém. He taught at IPAM-School of Marketing | Laureate International Universities, ISLA- Higher Institute of Management and Administration of Santarém (ISLA-Santarém), was Director of the Commercial Management Course, Director of the Professional Technical Course (TeSP) of Sales and Commercial Management, Chairman of the Pedagogical Council and Member of the Technical Council and ISLA-Santarém Scientific Researcher. He is also a marketing and strategy consultant for SMEs.

Ipseeta Satpathy is a senior professor at KIIT University. Specializes in Psychology, Behavioral Science, and Organisational Behaviour.

Shailesh Tripathi is a Professor at the Balaji Institute of Management and HRD (BIMHRD), Sri Balaji University, Pune. With a strong academic background and vast teaching experience, Dr. Tripathi is known for his expertise in management education, particularly in the areas of human resources and organizational behavior. He plays a pivotal role in shaping future business leaders through his engaging teaching methods, research contributions, and active involvement in academic development initiatives.

Index

Symbols

A

C

D

E

H

L

N

T

www.ingramcontent.com/pod-product-compliance
Lightning Source LLC
LaVergne TN
LVHW080857300926
849162LV00003B/453